AF251366

INDIA CHANGES COURSE

INDIA CHANGES COURSE
Golden Jubilee to Millennium

Paul R. Dettman

Westport, Connecticut
London

Library of Congress Cataloging-in-Publication Data

Dettman, Paul R., 1922–
      India changes course : golden jubilee to millennium / by Paul R. Dettman.
          p.   cm.
      Includes bibliographical references and index.
      ISBN 0–275–97308–5 (alk. paper)
      1. India—Politics and government—1977–   2. Bharatiya Janata Party.   I. Title.
      DS480.853.D394   2001
      954.05′2—dc21   00–069291

British Library Cataloguing in Publication Data is available.

Library of Congress Catalog Card Number: 00–069291
ISBN: 0–275–97308–5

First published in 2001

Praeger Publishers, 88 Post Road West, Wesport, CT 06881
An imprint of Greenwood Publishing Group, Inc.
www.praeger.com

Printed in the United States of America

The paper used in this book complies with the
Permanent Paper Standard issued by the National
Information Standards Organization (Z39.48–1984).

10 9 8 7 6 5 4 3 2 1

Copyright Acknowledgment

The author and publisher gratefully acknowledge permission for use of the following material:

Excerpts from *The Bhagavad Gita* by Franklin Edgerton. Used by permission of HarperCollins
Publishers Ltd.

To Jean, without whose questions, suggestions,
and computer skills this book would not be;
to our children—Paul, Carl, Cynthia, Joanna, Kurt, and Sarah,
who helped each step of the way; and
to our good friend Suzanne, whose persistence and
technical expertise were invaluable.

Contents

Photo Essay to Follow Page 74

The Indian Union and Its Neighbors

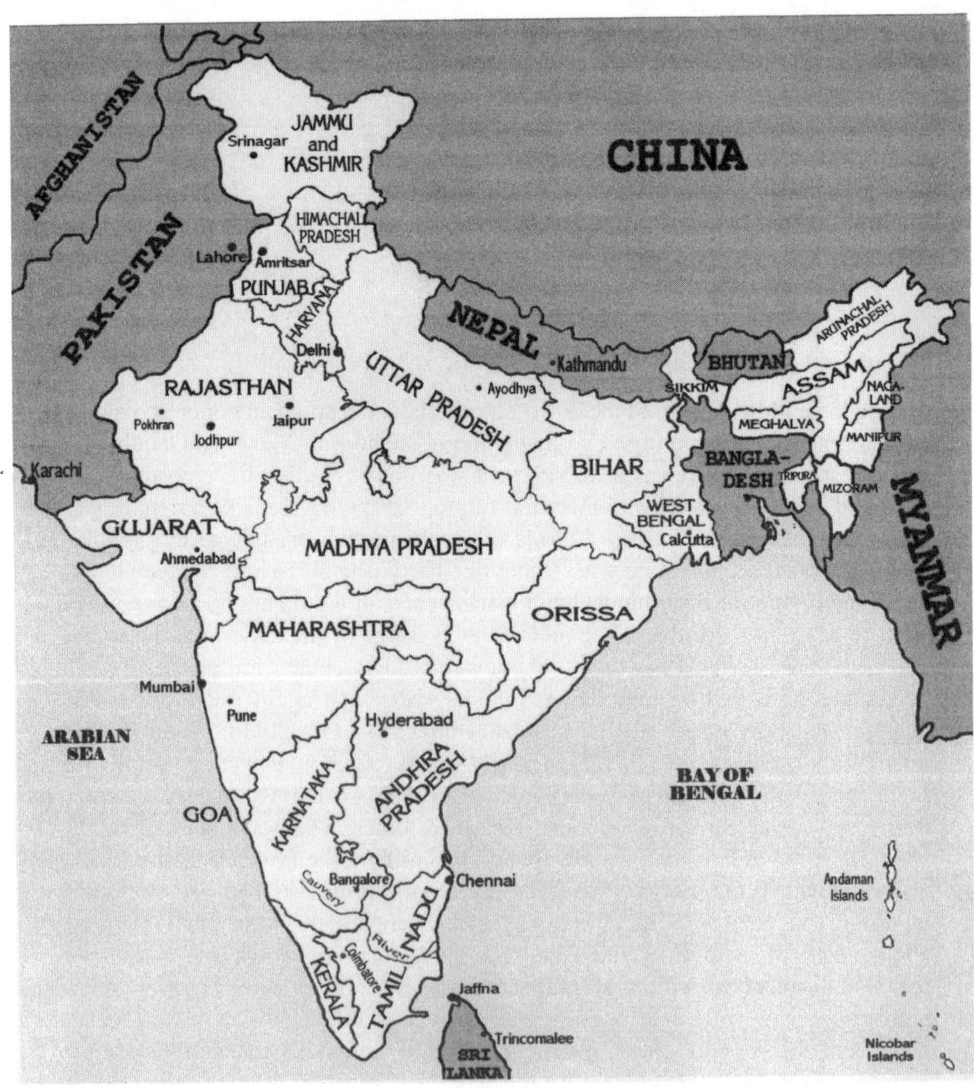

Preface

During the middle decade of the 20th century, India occupied an honored place in the international community. Led by the living memory of Mahatma Gandhi and the statesmanship of Jawaharlal Nehru, it was not only one of the postcolonial countries with a promising democratic future, but the keystone of a nonaligned movement that sought to play the role of a constructive third force in a bipolar world. It was a secular state with stable one-party rule and a socialist economy, dedicated to nuclear disarmament and world peace. It would not be an overstatement to say that the India of the mid-1900s was one of the nations of the world that might have helped over time to guide mankind to a better future.

As the third millennium dawned, India was once again receiving world attention but now as a potential problem rather than as a guiding light for the international community. Its religious and social foundations were basically the same, but, on the political and economic surface of its life, it was a very different India. It was nuclear weapons state. Its armed forces, which numbered 250,000 when it gained Independence, now totaled 1.3 million, the fourth largest military establishment in the world. While its democratic processes had become more vigorous, the secular political culture that had prevailed during the 1950s and 1960s, the golden age of the Congress Party, had given way to a divisive communalism led by the Bharatiya Janata Party (BJP) but practiced by all parties. Stable one-party rule had been replaced by unstable coalition governments dependent for support on a growing number of regional parties. The Nehru dynasty, which had ruled the nation for over three decades, was still alive but in the person of a foreign-born member by marriage.

India's South Asian neighborhood was also very different from what it had been on August 15, 1947. The two principal powers in the region were now armed with nuclear weapons. Conflict between India and Pakistan over Kashmir, which had begun as early as Partition days, was being pursued with renewed bitterness as a result of fighting along the Line of Control and Pakistan's support for a Kashmiri insurgent movement that sought to end India's control over two-thirds of the state. A twenty year old insurrection in Sri Lanka had refused to die because it was supported by Indian as well as Sri Lankan Tamils. India was treating Bangladesh, which had been a part of Pakistan until 1971, as a client state, and, having absorbed Sikkim into the Indian union, was dominating Nepal and Bhutan although they were still, legally speaking, sovereign states.

Beginning its independent life as a political force promoting peace and stability, India had developed by the late 1990s the potential to become a threat to the peace and stability of South Asia and the world. The United States and other world powers, which had taken little or no interest in what had been happening in India during the 1980s and early 1990s, had awakened to the need to take India seriously and to begin negotiations that would promote nuclear nonproliferation and seek a peaceful resolution of the Indo-Pakistani conflict that could escalate into conventional and possibly nuclear war. If this renewed diplomatic engagement was to produce positive results, those who took part needed to have a realistic picture of the India with which they were dealing as they participated in the dialogue.

So far as the United States was concerned, conveying this realistic picture was not an easy task. Only a small number of Americans who took an interest in world affairs paid attention to India, and the impression of India held by many of those who did was that of India during the days of Mahatma Gandhi and Jawaharlal Nehru. If they attempt to engage in dialogue with India with that impression in their minds, they will be thinking about and talking to an India that no longer exists. Confusion and frustration rather than productive discussion will be the result. *India Changes Course: Golden Jubilee to Millennium* was written as an attempt to convey to those who read it a realistic picture of the India that approached the dawn of the 21st century. The book focuses on the last two and a half years of free India's history—the period from August 1997 to January 2000—because the events that took place during that short time span played a decisive role in making India the nation that it is in today's world. But it is the writer's hope that a description and analysis of the highlights of the events of that thirty month period will whet the reader's appetite to take a longer view and delve into what had been going on in India during the more than fifty years that had passed since Jawaharlal Nehru made his famous "Tryst with Destiny" speech from the ramparts of the Red Fort in Delhi. Viewing India from the perspective of the first half century of its existence as a free nation would give the reader a sense of the longer-term significance of the events that transpired during India's Golden Jubilee Year and brought the country to the threshold of the third millennium.

1

Fall of the Gujral Government

So far as its Delhi component was concerned, the August 15, 1997, observance of free India's 50th Anniversary followed the scenario written by the Central Government's Implementation Committee. A special midnight gathering of Parliament was convened, at which a recording of Jawaharlal Nehru's "Tryst with Destiny" speech was played. President Narayanan and Prime Minister I. J. Gujral addressed the members of Parliament, the foreign dignitaries, and the crowd which had gathered for the occasion. Their speeches were followed by a fireworks display and the flood-lighting of public buildings. Even in the nation's capital, the mood was relatively subdued. Preparations had been made to handle an outpouring of 300,000 people, but no more than a third of that number took to the streets. Similar observances, albeit on a smaller scale, did take place in other cities, but the Implementation Committee's directive that the 50th Anniversary should be appropriately observed in every district, city, and town throughout the land was carried out only sporadically. The Indian people had made it plain that their reading of the state of the nation on August 15, 1997, did not give them much cause for celebration.

That message was repeated during the special four day session of Parliament which was called by the speaker of the Lok Sabha (Lower House) to follow the August 15 observance. There was to be only one item on the agenda and that was to discuss the country's current state and to formulate proposals for dealing with its problems. Only a small number of MPs attended, and they agreed that much was wrong. When it came to identifying the actions that Parliament needed to take to set things right, there were almost as many different proposals as there were MPs present. Lessening the possibility that any concrete decisions on ameliorative legislation might emerge from the special session was the fact that those who took part did so as individuals and not as spokespersons for their political parties. The result was that none of the parties represented was committed to voting for the improvements and reforms that their MPs suggested. By the end of the special session, it had become clear that the only consensus that could be arrived at was that the year following August 15, 1997, should be a time of sober stocktaking rather than a time of celebration.

The special session's failure to produce any guidance for legislative action was also a reflection of the virtual paralysis that characterized the coalition Central Government under Prime Minister Gujral during the weeks that ushered in India's Golden Jubilee Year. The "no holds barred" battle that had gone on between Laloo Prasad Yadav and Sharad Yadav for the presidentship of the Janata Dal party had shaken the foundation of the party, which was not only one of the pillars of the United Front's coalition government, but also the party to which the prime minister belonged. Sharad Yadav had emerged victorious, but the price paid was a split that occurred in the party when the defeated Laloo Prasad Yadav and his followers formed the Rashtriya Janata Dal (RJD). Three members of the RJD held ministerial posts in the Gujral government, and the Communist members of the United Front coalition demanded that the prime minister dismiss the three on the ground that they were no longer members of the Janata Dal. Following his usual practice of taking no action where action was required, Gujral refused to demand their resignations even though it was against his own party that they had revolted. The final result of the battle between the Janata Dal's Yadavs was a more fragmented political system, an additional instance of a "do nothing" prime minister's failing to act, and more conflict between the parties that made up his governmental coalition.

The inability of the Central Government to play its vital role in dealing with the country's problems was replicated in one of India's states before August had come to a close. Laloo Prasad Yadav had been charged, along with 55 other Bihari politicians, in the $158 million misappropriation of state funds which had become known as the "fodder" scandal because they had drawn the money to feed cattle and pursue other rural development schemes that did not exist. Despite having to face this charge, he had continued to hold the chief minister's post because his cohorts in the Rashtriya Janata Dal had remained solidly behind him and because Prime Minister Gujral had refused to pressure him to resign. Yadav's political applecart was finally upset when the Patna High Court remanded him to jail pending his trial. Faced now with the prospect of going behind bars, he resigned as Bihar's chief minister and arranged for his followers in the RJD who controlled the state legislature to elect Rabri Devi, his wife and the mother of his nine children, as his successor. With Rabri Devi acting as the conduit through which he conveyed his instructions to members of the Legislative Assembly and state government officials, Laloo Prasad Yadav was able to direct the affairs of Bihar from jail, much as Mayor James Michael Curley had directed the affairs of Boston from jail during 1946.

As the observance of the Golden Jubilee Year that was to follow free India's 50th Anniversary got under way, knowledgeable political observers were certain that the Gujral government's days were numbered, but they did not think that its end would come within four months. Nor were they given any hint regarding the course of political events that would culminate in its downfall. Six years had gone by since the Jain Commission had been appointed to investigate the persons and events involved in Rajiv Gandhi's 1991 assassination, but its report had not yet been presented to Parliament. On November 8, 1997, portions of the commission's report were leaked and published in an Indian periodical. The finding that was highlighted in the leaked portion was that Tamil Nadu's Dravida Munnetra Kazagham (DMK) government had been guilty of "encouraging and assisting" the Tigers of Tamil Eelam (Tamil Tigers), who had been fighting since the early 1980s for Tamil independence in Sri Lanka, and giving them the support and protection that they needed to carry out their plot to assassinate Rajiv Gandhi on Tamil Nadu's soil. The leaked portion did concede that Central Governments under both Indira and Rajiv Gandhi had also backed the Tamil Tiger insurgency during its first decade but found that Delhi's policy had changed from one of support to one of suppression when the 1987 Indian–Sri Lankan agreement had sent the Indian Army into Sri Lanka's Jaffna and Trincomalee areas.

The Jain Commission report revealed that, in spite of this reversal of central government policy, the Tamil Tigers had continued to get "supplies, including arms, ammunition, explosives, and essential items for war against the Indian Peace Keeping Force from Tamil Nadu. That too with the support of the Tamil Nadu [DMK] government and the connivance of law enforcement authorities." The "connivance of law enforcement authorities" took the form of the DMK government's requesting the Tamil Tigers to provide a list of the locations of their hideouts in Tamil Nadu and then instructing the state police to leave them undisturbed. Even more flagrant "connivance" occurred when a Tamil Tiger hit squad in Madras (now known as Chennai) gunned down sixteen members of a rival Sri Lankan Tamil militant group in June 1990, and the state government made no serious effort to apprehend and prosecute the gunmen. According to the commission report, some members of this Tamil hit squad also played a role in the assassination of Rajiv Gandhi, which took place only forty miles from Chennai and only eleven months later.

The names and faces of this shadowy and deadly contingent of Sri Lankan and Indian Tamil conspirators did not become known until seven years later when the Chennai Trial Court sentenced twenty-six men and women to death for planning and carrying out Rajiv Gandhi's assassination and causing the deaths of the nine policemen and six bystanders who were also killed when the sari-hidden bomb exploded. Sixteen of the condemned were Sri Lankan Tamils and ten were Indian Tamils. The Indian police had originally identified forty-one persons as having been involved in the assassination plot. Its three leaders, including the head of the Tamil Tigers, Velupillai Prabakharan, were still at large in Sri Lanka's eastern jungles, and twelve others had been killed when the bomb went off, had committed suicide to avoid capture by the Indian police, or had died during the course of its investigation.

It was Velupillai Prabakharan who had set in motion sometime during September 1990 the plan to eliminate Rajiv Gandhi because he feared that Gandhi's becoming prime minister again as a result of the upcoming general election would lead to a second Indian invasion of the Tamil areas of Sri Lanka. The group of Sri Lankan Tamil Tigers assigned to prepare the way for carrying out the plot slipped into Tamil Nadu disguised as refugees from the fighting in Jaffna and were taken into the "safe houses" that had been set up by their Indian Tamil coconspirators. They were followed in February 1991 by the team of assassins. Three months of traveling and carrying messages between "safe houses" followed, during which the detailed *modus operandi* was worked out for killing Rajiv Gandhi. The lethal device was to be a bomb that would be hidden beneath the sari of a Tamil Tiger woman "martyr" named Dhanu and would be set off when she offered a garland to Rajiv Gandhi on the occasion of his coming to Sriperumbudur on May 21, 1991, to speak at a campaign rally. Since most of the twenty-six men and women condemned to death by the Chennai Court had taken part in the assassination plot only in peripheral ways as messengers or "safe house" operators, it was considered likely that a number of the sentences would be commuted to life imprisonment when they were reviewed by the higher courts.

Since the Jain Commission's investigation had turned up the faces of Congress Indira Party leaders as well as those of the DMK among the Tamil Tigers' supporters, most political observers expected that the president of the Congress Indira Party, Sitaram Kesri, would not make an issue of the findings that had been leaked. Much to their surprise and despite the pledge that he had given to the Congress Indira Party would support the Gujral government for at least two years and his positive personal rapport with Gujral, Kesri used the occasion of a November 12 political rally to announce that, unless the Jain Commission report was laid on Parliament's table on the opening day of its winter session, his party would be forced to reconsider its support of the United Front government.

This move came as no surprise to those who were aware of the intraparty political forces at work behind the scenes. An anti-Kesri faction was bringing pressure to bear on the party president to persuade Sonia Gandhi to become actively involved in party affairs. She had given the first hint that she might enter the political arena in May 1997 when she had become a primary Congress Indira Party member. The Jain Commission's finding that part of the blame for her husband's assassination lay at the foot of the DMK could motivate her to become involved in an effort to punish a party that was a member of the Gujral coalition. Activating the surviving member of the Nehru dynasty could spark a party resurgence that would enhance the Congress Indira Party's prospects of returning to power in Delhi. The party leaders who endorsed this strategy prevailed upon Kesri to make the DMK's connivance with the Tamil Tigers a "do or die" bone of contention with the Gujral government, even though the findings also reflected badly on their own party.

The Gujral government gave in to the Congress Indira Party's threat by presenting the Jain Commission's report to Parliament a week later. Since one of the commission's findings was that Tamil Nadu's DMK government had given moral and political support to the Tamil Tigers, not only during the time when this was also the policy of Indira and Rajiv Gandhi's Central Governments, but also after 1987 when the Rajiv Gandhi government had allied itself with the Sri Lankan government in an effort to stamp out the Tamil insurgency, the Congress Indira Party took only one day to throw down the gauntlet by demanding that the DMK members of Prime Minister Gujral's Council of Ministers be dismissed "forthwith." Failure to meet this demand would result in the Congress Indira Party MPs' withdrawing their support and the end of Gujral's United Front government. As surprising to political observers as was the Congress Indira Party's move to turn the Jain Commission's findings into a "do or die issue" was the United Front's response. Given the high degree of conflict that had been generated within the Front's keystone party by Laloo Prasad Yadav's bitter struggle with Sharad Yadav for the Janata Dal party president's post, it seemed unlikely that the Front's unity would be able to stand up to the additional stress produced by the Congress Indira Party's threat to withdraw its support. To most observers' surprise, the United Front stood firmly behind the decision of its core committee and refused to dismiss the DMK ministers in its government. The Congress Indira Party's reply was to inform President Narayanan that its MPs would no longer support the Gujral government. After a fortnight of political maneuvering, during which the president explored to no avail various ways of avoiding the collapse of the second United Front government, which had survived for an even shorter time then its predecessor, he issued a proclamation on December 5 that dissolved the sitting Lok Sabha and ordered the holding of a general election that would put a new government in power by mid-March 1998.

2

Sonia Gandhi Steals the Spotlight

On December 29, 1997, Sonia Gandhi announced her decision to campaign actively on behalf of the Congress Indira Party. Making it clear from the outset that she did not seek public office, she announced that she would address numerous party rallies in all parts of the country, with three purposes in mind:

- Rehabilitate the reputations of the members of the Nehru dynasty, particularly the reputation of Rajiv Gandhi;
- Help to win parliamentary seats for Congress Indira Party candidates;
- Prevent the BJP from taking control of the Central Government.

Although her effectiveness as a campaigner and her celebrity appeal would become apparent only after she had taken to the hustings, the emergence from political seclusion of the Italian widow of the last member of the Nehru dynasty to hold the prime minister's office was, in itself, enough to set Sonia Gandhi on the way to becoming one of the leading "stars" of the 1998 General Election campaign. So far as its impact on the Congress Indira Party's organization was concerned, her entrance upon the political stage meant that Sitaram Kesri, who would otherwise have led the party into the fray, was destined to take a back seat. But Kesri's was not the most demeaning fate to be suffered by one of the party's organizational stalwarts. The party's former president, Narasimha Rao, was not even allowed to run as one of the party's candidates, ostensibly because he had not used his authority as prime minister to prevent the demolition of the mosque that had been built by the Mogul Emperor Aurangzeb on the traditional site of Rama's birth at Ayodhya and to head off the bloody riots that had followed. Rumor had it that a further reason for refusing to give him the party's ticket was Sonia Gandhi's reluctance to support a former Congress Indira Party prime minister who had ended his political career facing criminal charges.

The first phase of the 1998 General Election campaign got under way on January 11 when Sonia Gandhi, accompanied by her daughter, addressed a Congress Indira Party rally at Sriperumbudur in Tamil Nadu, the town where her husband had been assassinated seven years earlier. It ended on February 14, the day that more than ten bombs were set off by Muslim extremists in Coimbatore in the same state, killing more than 50 people, injuring more than 200 others, and forcing the cancellation of a BJP rally which was to have been addressed by its president, L. K. Advani. The campaign shaped up in ways that were expected in some respects and unexpected in others. As expected, it was waged in ways and by means that reflected the schizophrenic character of late 1990s India—Western on the surface and Indian underneath. On the surface, it was a campaign run with the latest transportation and communication technology—jet aircraft and helicopters as well as television sets and computers. But the messages spread by means of these modern media and represented by its two leading "stars," Sonia Gandhi and A. B. Vajpayee, were ancient ones—dynastic rule, conveyed by the former, and the Hindu way of life, conveyed by the latter.

To a degree that was not expected when it became apparent that India would have to go to the polls less than two years after its last round of national voting, issues took a back seat to personalities. Each of the three political forces that were to play the leading roles in the campaign—the Congress Indira Party, the BJP, and the United Front—began by putting forth detailed manifestos that purported to tell India's voters what programs and policies each would implement if voted into office in Delhi. But, as the campaign unfolded, the issues raised in these party manifestos were eclipsed by the personalities of the principal campaigners. In the case of the Congress Indira Party, this unexpected development, which, in the parliamentary system, would be considered a reversal of priorities, went so far that, when Sitaram Kesri was questioned about the content of his party's manifesto, he replied that it was "whatever Soniaji [an honorific term for Sonia Gandhi] said." Although the BJP's manifesto made it clear that the party continued to stand squarely behind its Hindu fundamentalist program, its campaign focused attention on its choice of A. B. Vajpayee as the prime minister whom it would put into office to give India a strong and stable government.

The only political corruption issue that was highlighted during the campaign was the Bofors guns scandal. Here it was not the issue itself that attracted the spotlight but the campaigner who was personally involved in it. As soon as Sonia Gandhi entered the campaign, everyone knew that questions regarding who had received the Bofors payoff would be asked loudly and clearly, not only because her husband Rajiv Gandhi was the chief protagonist in the scandal, but because the Swiss bank account of the Gandhis' Italian friends, the Quattrochis, had received part of the payoffs made to "so-called" Bofors "agents" who had helped negotiate the deal. What was not expected was that Sonia Gandhi herself would take the initiative to raise this issue by pointing out during the course of one of her earliest speeches that six Central Governments had not produced evidence that she and her husband had received Bofors money and challenging Prime Minister Gujral to reveal the full story of where the money had gone. Gujral's response was that he could not meet her demand because the Swiss government had made it clear that it would not supply additional information if the facts that had been released already were made public before the investigation was completed.

If one were ranking the unexpected aspects of the campaign according to their newsworthiness, the prize would have to be awarded to Sonia Gandhi's emergence as one of its two political "stars." She represented nothing less than the Nehru dynasty's return to life in Italian Roman Catholic form. As such, she introduced a strange phenomenon into Indian politics that surprised observers by the degree to which it received a positive response. Equally surprising was the "about-face" she had performed on December 29 when she announced her decision to campaign for the Congress Indira Party. She had tried her best in 1980 to dissuade Rajiv Gandhi from entering the Indian political arena following his brother Sanjay's death. When the Congress Indira Party asked her immediately after his assassination to replace him as its president, she had declined. For the next six years she had lived in political seclusion, conferring with political leaders, but as a private person rather than as a political leader. She had taken a first step in the direction of becoming politically active in May 1997 when she had become a primary Congress Indira Party member, but, when the party president had pleaded with her at an all-India convention held three months later to become its leader, she had turned a deaf ear.

By the time the president's December 5 proclamation had dissolved the 11th Lok Sabha, the fortunes of the Congress Indira Party had reached their nadir, and it looked as though the party would have to fight for its very survival in the coming election. A fortnight after the election proclamation had been issued, Sitaram Kesri conveyed to Sonia Gandhi a request from the Congress Indira Party's Working Committee that she campaign for the party "at this difficult moment." Twelve days after receiving this plaintive request, she announced that she would accede to it and become an active party campaigner. Even though her participation in the campaign would inevitably place him in a secondary role despite his holding the party president's post, Kesri responded with words that expressed his relief: "My tension is over."

Sonia Gandhi's December 29 statement did not explain why she had decided to end her long-standing seclusion from Indian politics to take on the role of the Congress Indira Party's leading campaigner. Her first explanation, couched in personal terms, was given a fortnight later as part of her first campaign speech: "In the years since Rajiv Gandhi left us, I had chosen to remain a private person and live a life away from the political arena. My grief and loss have been deeply personal. But a time has come when I feel compelled to put aside my own inclinations and step forward. The tradition of duty before personal considerations has been the deepest conviction of the family to which I belong." She did not go on to define the nature of the "duty" to which she referred, but one had only to look at the state of the Congress Indira Party at the close of 1997 to come up with a plausible explanation of what she had in mind.

The party had become a faction-ridden shell of what it had been during its heyday when it had been led by earlier members of the Nehru dynasty. Sitaram Kesri, who had served as party treasurer for seventeen years before his election to the president's post, was incapable of rallying the dispirited party into the fighting shape that would be required to win an election. His talents were limited to those of a party functionary, and he lacked the dynamic personal qualities needed to lead a campaign that would win the support of millions of Indian voters. Unless the Congress Indira Party could find a new standard-bearer who could make it a formidable player in the coming campaign, there was every reason to believe that, with the United Front also in disarray, the BJP would form the next Central Government and a Hindu state would be on the way.

Even though an Italian Roman Catholic member of the Nehru dynasty cut a strange figure on the Indian political stage and even though her taking over the dynasty's mantle and becoming the unofficial leader of the Congress Indira Party constituted a sudden and unexpected turn of political events, Sonia Gandhi proved to be a vigorous campaigner, a spectacular attraction, and a crowd pleaser. During the campaign's first phase alone, she was the "star" at some thirty rallies held at major cities and towns in many parts of the country. By the time the campaign ended, she had traveled 60,000 kilometers and, during the course of thirty-four days, had spoken in 138 constituencies. Often accompanied by her daughter, she drew crowds that sometimes exceeded 100,000.

Her speeches were short, ranging from ten to twenty minutes in length. She delivered them by reading a romanized phonetic version of Hindi script, which, in non-Hindi-speaking areas, was then translated into the local language. Their main themes were simple and were repeated wherever she spoke:

- Her forbears in the Nehru family—Jawaharlal, Indira, and Rajiv—had provided India with exemplary leadership and had made supreme sacrifices for the country;
- Only the Congress Indira Party had the integrity, experience, and support to give India political stability and good government;
- Communal forces [she did not name the BJP, but her hearers knew the party that she had in mind] would destroy the nation's unity and prosperity if they came to power.

While she appealed to her listeners to vote for the Congress Indira Party candidates, she candidly admitted that the party organization had many weaknesses that had to be rectified. Even more surprising was her willingness to apologize for the party's action in authorizing the 1984 military invasion of the Golden Temple at Amritsar, Sikhdom's most holy place, and its inaction in failing to prevent the 1992 demolition of the mosque that had been built by Mogul Emperor Aurangzeb at Ayodhya. While she went out of her way to claim that these "mistakes" were not the fault of her predecessors in the Nehru dynasty, the historically aware among her listeners knew that her predecessors bore complete or partial responsibility for making all of them.

What was most surprising about her *modus operandi* was the way in which she followed the principle that "the best defense is a good offense" by preempting attacks by Congress Indira Party rivals at her most vulnerable points—her foreign birth and upbringing and her personal involvement in the Bofors guns scandal. Instead of waiting for BJP and United Front campaigners to raise these issues against her, she brought them up herself during the initial phase of her campaign appearances. She told her audiences that she was an Indian citizen who had adopted the Indian style of life from the time of her marriage to Rajiv Gandhi and challenged the government to reveal the truth about the Bofors payoffs because, if it did, she contended, the Indian people would see that she and her husband were innocent of any wrongdoing.

Observers of the Indian political scene were unanimous in lauding Sonia Gandhi for the political skill with which she had handled her foray into the campaign and for the spectacular success that she had achieved in attracting huge crowds and commending herself to the millions who flocked to see her. Because she arrived and departed by chartered jet or helicopter and was kept at a distance from the crowds by tight security arrangements (given the fate suffered by her husband and mother-in-law, she had an understandable fear of assassination), she could not get close to her "fans." Because she had a very limited command of Hindi, she was not able to rouse her audiences to a fever pitch, as her mother-in-law had done in earlier campaigns. Not only was she was able to overcome these handicaps, but she managed to create among her hearers a degree of adulation comparable to that given to a movie "star." The crowds came to see Sonia Gandhi even if they had to view her from afar rather than to listen to what she had to say.

Her foreign roots and foreign-accented speech—the appearance and sound of an Italian woman wearing an Indian sari who spoke simple Hindi with an Italian lilt—turned out to be assets rather than liabilities in attracting and pleasing large crowds. They made her all the more fascinating because, in the eyes of ordinary Indians, she was so unusual, so strange—a political phenomenon that was totally without precedent on the Indian political scene. The result was that her "foreign-ness" did not become an issue that her political opponents could use against her with any effect. BJP leaders, especially L. K. Advani, tried to make the slogan "Rome Raj or Ram Raj" ("Rule by Rome or Rule by Rama") a political stick with which to beat her, but few voters responded to their efforts. Still, it had to be admitted that, while Sonia Gandhi performed in a bright spotlight, the Congress Indira Party itself remained in a deep shadow. Her speeches praised the party's past record, especially the contributions of the members of the Nehru dynasty who had led it for almost all of its post-Independence life, but said little about what the party would do if given control of the next Central Government. Much as members of the crowd might have come away ready to give their all for Sonia, she was not standing for a parliamentary seat and had plainly stated that she did not seek the prime minister's office. Members of the overflowing crowds could not vote for her and, unless they were Congress Indira Party supporters to begin with, most of them had a hard time remembering the name of the parliamentary candidates whom she endorsed at her campaign stops.

What was beyond dispute was the positive effect that her campaign had on the morale of those who belonged to the Congress Indira Party. Although she criticized the party's current performance and eclipsed party organizers like Sitaram Kesri, party members up and down its hierarchy and across the country had been given an infusion of confidence and energy that had turned them from a demoralized cadre waiting to be defeated by the BJP into a formidable political force that would not go down without a fight. While Sonia Gandhi's campaigning did not win the Lok Sabha for the Congress Indira Party and its candidates filled only one more seat than the party had captured in 1996, the fact that the party did no worse was largely attributable to the enthusiasm that she aroused among its members and the higher level of campaign effort that they displayed as a result.

3

The Campaign's Other "Star"

If Sonia Gandhi was the "star" Congress Indira Party campaigner, Atal Behari Vajpayee was the "star" performer for its major opponent. the BJP. He did not become a "star" in the same way, because it was his party rather than his "fans" who focused the spotlight on him. At the very beginning of the campaign, the BJP proclaimed that, if it came to power in Delhi. Vajpayee would be India's next prime minister. Unlike Sonia Gandhi. he did not have sole billing. He was backed up by another BJP luminary, the party's president, L. K. Advani. This division of effort was a carryover into the campaign of the strategy that had been followed since the installation of the United Front coalition governments, by which Vajpayee had acted as the "mask" of Hindu chauvinism, giving it a moderate face, and Advani had been the voice of the hard-line Hindu fundamentalism espoused by the Rashtriya Swayarnsevak Sangh (RSS).

The continuation of this strategy was dictated by the BJP's need, if it was to form or lead the next Central Government, to extend its support beyond its traditional Hindu fundamentalist backers, and, at the same time, to hold on to the allegiance of members of the RSS and other Hindu fundamentalist organizations who constituted the core of its support. Vajpayee's assignment was to accomplish the former task. Advani's assignment was to accomplish the latter task. The decision to make Vajpayee preeminent by designating him rather than Advani as the "Prime Minister-to-be" stemmed from his ability to appeal to a broader spectrum of Indian voters and convince them that he was the only politician who could lead a government that would last long enough and be strong enough to carry out its agenda. India had seen two Central Governments fall within eighteen months and had experienced the negative political and economic consequences of continued government instability. Since BJP strategists had read the national mood as one in which India's people were fed up with "do nothing" governments that lasted only a few months and longed more than anything else for an effective polity, they decided to make the promise of a strong and stable government in Delhi the keystone of the party's platform. A. B. Vajpayee was the leader whom they designated to deliver it. At the same time, the BJP took pains to make it clear to its hard core Hindu fundamentalist constituency that its "Prime Minister-to-be" was dedicated to upholding Hindu fundamentalist beliefs and practices, by arranging for him to deliver his final campaign speech in Pune (Poona), the city that had been the bastion of the Hindu extremists of the 1920s and 1930s and the place where the plot to assassinate Mahatma Gandhi had been hatched.

The BJP's strategy of "working both sides of the ideological street" was the major guideline that gave shape to its campaign manifesto. It appealed to its Hindu fundamentalist backers by stating that, while the party had to engage in coalition politics, it would not forget about its Hindutva agenda—its commitment to build a temple dedicated to Rama at Ayodhya, to enact a uniform civil code, and to terminate Jammu and Kashmir's special constitutional status. To attract moderate voters, it promised that its Hindutva agenda would not be imposed upon the country but would be carried out in a "consensual" way through legislation and constitutional reform. The manifesto appealed for the votes of the segments of the population who were not members of the urban middle class and higher castes and who provided the preponderant number of the party's backers, by assuring minorities that they would be protected by a BJP government and the poor that their problems would be solved within ten years of its coming to power.

The support of Indian businessmen was wooed by the manifesto's assurance that the process of economic liberalization would not only be continued but would be speeded up by a BJP government. Its economic policy would differ from the policy of a government led by the Congress Indira Party or the United Front because it would contain a *swadeshi* ingredient, but BJP *swadeshi* would not be the same as Mahatma Gandhi's *swadeshi*. It would stand not for "self-reliance" but for "India first." "India first" would mean that "India will be built by Indians" and foreign capital would not play a dominant role in the development of its economy. Further liberalization would take place but in such a way that the continued viability of Indian businesses would be protected. Foreign investment would be channeled to segments of the economy where Indian resources were deficient but would be excluded from economic activities that were going well in Indian hands. A BJP government would not move India toward economic isolation but would slow down the process of integrating it with the global economy so that Indian businesses would not be wiped out by multinational corporations.

To win the votes of the ardent Indian nationalists who were to be found among all of India's socioeconomic groups, the BJP manifesto took a hard line on the issue of nuclear weapons and their delivery systems. A BJP government would "exercise the option to induct nuclear weapons" and "expedite the development of the Agni [intermediate range] series of ballistic missiles with a view to increasing their range and accuracy." The party adopted the same hard line with respect to India's relations with Pakistan. As Vajpayee had earlier put it: "Our perception of the Indian states of Jammu and Kashmir includes Pakistan-occupied Kashmir and territories handed over by Pakistan to China." In other words, a BJP government would treat all portions of the pre-1947 territory of Jammu and Kashmir now held by Pakistan or China as *irredenta,* unredeemed Indian soil that was part of the motherland that should be recovered. Vajpayee went on to say, more ominously: "We cannot afford to ignore the nuclear bomb producing capabilities of Pakistan, the stockpiling of nuclear arsenal in China and development of nuclear warheads at the U.S. base in Diego Garcia. We will match this threat by developing our nuclear capabilities and keep our options open as a deterrent to safeguard India security and integrity."

If it was to form or lead the new Central Government, the BJP had to widen its appeal, not only to a broader socioeconomic spectrum but to a broader geographic base. Even if it retained a major share of the votes coming from northern and western India and from the Hindi-speaking region, the party's traditional power base, the BJP could not hope to win the 1998 General Election unless it garnered additional support from residents of eastern and southern India and from non-Hindi speakers. The quickest way to achieve this objective was to enter into agreements with regional parties whose support was concentrated in these non-BJP preserves. Such agreements did not take the form of alliances, because they were temporary arrangements between political groups whose ideologies and programs did not usually agree. They were limited to an understanding that the BJP and the regional parties would divide the parliamentary seats that were being contested within a state on a mutually agreeable basis and consolidate their support behind the candidate of the party that had been given the assignment to contest a particular constituency. It was also agreed that all candidates elected to Parliament would support A. B. Vajpayee as India's next prime minister.

Based on interparty understandings worked out before the campaign, the BJP fielded 378 candidates to contest the 535 Lok Sabha seats and agreed with a number of regional parties that mutual support would be given to an additional 126 candidates. These mutual-support arrangements increased to the following extent the BJP's potential for obtaining the backing of MPs from areas beyond the party's historic power base in Uttar Pradesh, Bihar, Harayana, and Gujarat:

Regional Party	State	Number of Constituencies
Shiv Sena	Maharashtra	16
Samatha Party	Bihar	22
Akali Dal	Punjab	8
Harayana Vikar Party	Harayana	4
Biju Janata Dal	Orissa	12
Lok Sakthi	Karnataka	10
Anna DMK	Tamil Nadu	34
Trinamool Congress	West Bengal	20

In addition to widening the geographical base of BJP support, these mutual-support agreements also helped to diffuse the party's image as the standard bearer of a "communal" ideology that put it at odds with parties that espoused "secularism." The BJP had carried this image since Vajpayee's failure following the 1996 General Election to obtain the support of a single other party for a BJP-led coalition government.   Following that embarrassing episode, the BJP had complained that it had been treated as an "untouchable" party with which other parties refused to do business, all because of its Hindu fundamentalist ideology. The fact that eight regional parties, most of which considered themselves to be "secular," had thrown in their lot with the BJP to fight the 1998 election was clear evidence that the BJP was no longer being treated as "untouchable" and that "communalism" versus "secularism" was no longer the buzzword differentiating political parties that it had been in the 1996 General Election.

Even though they were the principal opponents in the race, the two "stars" did not come into open conflict until the closing days of the campaign's first phase. Before the campaign began, many political observers thought that the "Rome Raj or Ram Raj" issue would define the Sonia Gandhi–Vajpayee conflict from the very outset, but it did not become a bone of contention until the halfway point had been reached. The BJP had decided to begin by soft-pedaling Sonia Gandhi's Italian and Roman Catholic origins, and she did likewise, concentrating attention on her Indian citizenship, her Indian lifestyle, and her membership in India's most illustrious political family. Because she had been so successful in following this strategy, L. K. Advani was finally forced to raise the "Rome Raj or Ram Raj" issue by revealing that, although she made much of her Indian citizenship, Sonia Gandhi still carried her Italian passport and by announcing that the BJP was considering a constitutional amendment that would require that the prime minister be a native-born Indian.

If Advani thought that "throwing the fat into the fire" in this way would engender an outcry against a woman who was a "foreigner" and a Roman Catholic and yet was playing a major role in the election campaign, he was mistaken. But his attack on Sonia Gandhi did have the effect of raising her ire. She counterattacked the very next day, accusing A. B. Vajpayee of "slandering" her husband by spreading "lies" about his involvement in the Bofors guns scandal. According to Sonia Gandhi, these "lies" insulted Rajiv Gandhi's "sacrifices" for his country and caused her to protest vehemently against them. Up to this point in the campaign, she had always used the general term "communal forces" to refer to the BJP. Now she explicitly named the BJP as a threat to Indian unity, maintaining that the country could not be governed by its Hindutva ideology. This mid-campaign verbal clash between Sonia Gandhi and L. K. Advani finally reminded voters of the "Rome Raj versus Ram Raj" slogan, but that dichotomy did not become a campaign issue. It also reminded them of another dichotomy—"Sonia Gandhi versus A. B. Vajpayee"—which did become the campaign's major personality confrontation.

4

Requiem for the United Front

The United Front, which had been the third major player in the 1996 General Election and had produced the two coalition governments that emerged from the last two national polls, proved to be a spent force as the 1998 campaign unfolded. Its record of ineffective and unsustainable governance had led to its being discredited in the eyes of Indian voters, and the cohesiveness that had enabled it to stand firm in the face of the Congress Indira Party's demand that it expel the DMK members of the Gujral cabinet had evaporated quickly after its second government had fallen. To make matters worse, the unity of its keystone party, the Janata Dal, had also become a thing of the past. The Janata Dal had suffered splits in the three states where it had been strongest—Bihar, Karnataka, and Orissa. To add insult to injury, two of the three breakaway groups had joined forces with the BJP.

The sorry state of United Front affairs was dramatically displayed by the difficulty that Prime Minister Gujral faced in obtaining a party ticket for the coming election. He had held a Janata Dal seat in Bihar, but Laloo Prasad Yadav's Rashtriya Janata Dal had broken away from the party that had supported Gujral and now controlled the Bihar political scene. So Gujral had to find another location for his attempt to remain a member of Parliament and, in traditional Indian style, he returned to his "native place," the Punjab, to find a political home. What was surprising was not the location of the constituency which he contested, but the party auspices under which he campaigned. Because he was a Punjabi, the Akali Dal, Sikhdom's nationalist party, offered to support him by refraining from putting up a candidate of its own to oppose him and by directing their followers in the Jalandhar constituency to vote for him. Not only was the Akali Dal a "communal" party, founded upon the Sikh religion and pledged to achieving an autonomous Sikh state, but it had joined forces with the BJP to contest the Punjab's parliamentary seats. To the embarrassment of other leaders of the United

Front, which they had claimed since its founding to be the bastion of "secularism" and the nation's hope for keeping "communal" forces at bay, Gujral accepted the Akali Dal's offer and contested the Jalandhar seat with its support. Quite obviously, his desire to remain a player in the Delhi political scene outweighed his commitment to the principles of "secularism," which he had so often commended during his days as the head of the United Front's second government.

In a desperate effort to convince Indian voters that it continued to exist as a unified political force, the United Front issued a joint manifesto, which tried to sound like the Common Programme that had helped it achieve success in the 1996 election campaign. While all of the member parties presumably subscribed to the Front's manifesto, several of its members, including the Communist Party of India (CPI), the Communist Party (Marxist) (CPM), and the Janata Dal, issued manifestos of their own. While these party manifestos echoed the Front's commitment to fight against the "communalism" represented by the BJP and the corruption represented by the Congress Indira Party, they differed with the Front and with each other in other respects. The individualistic line of action taken by the Front's parties in presenting their programs to the voters provided an early hint of disunity because it showed that its various members had decided that they would fare better campaigning under their own banner rather than as part of the widely discredited United Front.

This was a foretaste of what was to come. That the Front's members would follow a "go it on our own" strategy was loudly and clearly proclaimed by the way they carried on their subsequent campaigns, which took the form of "knockdown, drag out" fights, not so much against the Congress Indira Party and the BJP, as against the Front's own members. In Uttar Pradesh, the Samajwadi Party took on the Janata Dal. The Communist Party of India and the Communist Party Marxist battled the Janata Dal in Bihar, Orissa, and Karnataka, and the DMK and Tamil Maanila Congress in Tamil Nadu. The Samyukta Party joined forces with the Congress Indira Party to oppose the Janata Dal and other former United Front parties contesting seats in Maharashtra. Only in West Bengal, Kerala, and Andhra Pradesh did the United Front parties succeed in working out seat-sharing agreements that enabled them to support rather than attack each other.

Prime Minister Gujral tried to make the best of a bad situation by playing the role of principal spokesman for the United Front. He blamed the Congress Indira Party for bringing down the Gujral government, accusing Sitaram Kesri of having gone back on a promise made to India's president that his party would continue for at least two more years the support that it had given to the previous United Front government. He lauded the solidarity that the United Front had displayed in standing firm when the Congress Indira Party had used the "ruse" of the Jain Commission report to attack the DMK ministers in his cabinet. He downplayed the impact that "curiosity" about Sonia Gandhi would have on the campaign results and characterized the challenge that she had issued to his government to reveal the full story of the Bofors gun scandal as nothing more than an attempt to embarrass its prime minister. By focusing attention on the past and saying almost nothing about what a future United Front government would do for the country, Gujral gave his hearers no basis for believing that a future United Front government would be any stronger or any more effective than its predecessors.

5

Polling for the 12th Lok Sabha

The first round of polling, in which 250 million voters cast their ballots, took place on February 16, 1998. In addition to manifesting an unusually peaceful character, the election produced a significant increase in voter turnout. Whereas 57% of the eligible voters had cast ballots in 1991 and 58% in 1996, the 1998 rate of participation rose to 62%. Given the state of political disillusionment that had followed the speedy fall of the two United Front governments, the explanation for this surge in voting could only be found in the persons of the principal campaigners. The political excitement produced by the clash between Sonia Gandhi and A. B. Vajpayee created a degree of interest that brought to the polls millions of voters who would otherwise have stayed at home. While the infusion of this increased political energy did not have a decisive impact on the election's outcome, it made that outcome a more accurate expression of the will of the Indian people.

Counting of ballots began on March 2, and, within two days, the results for all states except Jammu and Kashmir, where polling did not take place until March 7, were announced. This is how they took shape:

Party (with Allies)	Seats Won 12th Lok Sabha	Seats Won 11th Lok Sabha	Difference
BJP	264	184	+80
Congress Indira	168	141	+27
United Front	101	179	-78
Others/Independents	6	35	-29
	539	539	

The BJP and its allied parties enjoyed a 14% increase in votes won, giving them 34% of the total. The United Front parties suffered a loss of 5% in the number of votes that they received and the Congress Indira Party bloc a loss of 2%, giving the former 21% of the total and the latter 27%. The BJP bloc won the largest number of Lok Sabha seats but fewer than a majority. The BJP was victorious on its own in 178 constituencies. Its supporting parties and independents added another 86 seats, bringing the bloc's total to 264. The breakdown of seats won by the BJP's supporting parties was as follows:

Anna DMK and Allies	27
Samatha Party	12
Biju Janata Dal	9
Akali Dal	8
Shiv Sena	6
Trinamool Congress	7
Harayana Lok Dal	4
Lok Sakthi	3
Others	10

Seats won by the Congress Indira Party bloc totaled 168. Of this total, 141 were accounted for by seats gained by the Congress Indira Party on its own. The remaining 27 seats were picked up by supporting parties. All but 10 of the latter category came from North Bihar, where Laloo Prasad Yadav's breakaway RJD had thrown in its lot with the Congress Indira Party in order to frustrate the BJP, which continued to command the field in the southern part of the state.

A state-by-state breakdown of the voting results showed that the BJP had won most of its seats in its strongholds in the north and west and in the Hindi-speaking belt—Uttar Pradesh, Harayana, Madhya Pradesh, and Bihar. It lost heavily in Rajasthan, where it controlled the state government, and in Maharashtra, where it shared state-level political power with the Shiv Sena. Cooperating with its supporting parties, it was able to score breakthroughs in the east by working with the Biju Janata Dal in Orissa, and in the south by working with the Anna DMK in Tamil Nadu, and with the Lok Sakthi in Karnataka. In addition to the increased number of votes supplied by supporting parties, the BJP benefited from the positive voter response elicited by its campaign promise to provide stable government under a strong prime minister: A. B. Vajpayee. After eighteen months of shaky and ineffective United Front governments in Delhi, India's people were looking for a rock-solid regime under an effective leader who would take decisive action to deal with the country's ills. These two factors worked in the BJP's favor to give it, despite its losses in Rajasthan and Maharashtra, 16 more seats than it had held in the 11th Lok Sabha.

Rather than relying, as did the BJP, upon a simple campaign promise of stable government under a strong political leader who was designated at the outset of the campaign as the "Prime Minister -to-be" and upon the support of allied parties, the Congress Indira Party "put all its eggs in one basket." Sonia Gandhi campaigned for her party's candidates but did not run for office herself and talked about the past greatness of the Congress Party and the Nehru dynasty that had led it but not about what a new Congress Indira Party government would do to deal with India's problems. The polling results showed that this strategy did not achieve its desired objective of creating a surge of votes strong enough to win the additional 135 seats that the Congress Indira Party needed to give it a majority in the new Lok Sabha. Although Sonia Gandhi did bring out huge crowds to see and hear her, estimated to have totaled as many as 12 million people, she did not convince large numbers of those who came to her rallies that they should vote for the candidates whom she endorsed. In states where there was already substantial Congress Indira Party support, such as Kerala and Andhra Pradesh, the number of its candidates who were elected in 1998 was about the same as the number elected in 1996. The only states where substantially more Congress Indira Party candidates won were Assam, Rajasthan, and Maharashtra, and there it was strong anti-incumbency sentiment more than Sonia Gandhi's campaigning that accounted for the change in voting patterns. In some of the constituencies where she "starred" at party rallies, party candidates received fewer votes than they had received in 1996. In the country as a whole, the percentage of votes going to Congress Indira Party candidates fell from 28% in 1996 to 25%, an all-time low. Fewer than fifty candidates were elected from the 139 constituencies that Sonia Gandhi had visited.

The "bottom line" of Sonia Gandhi's campaign "blitzkrieg" was that there would be only one more Congress Indira Party member sitting in the new Lok Sabha than the number that had entered following the 1996 election. The party's unexpected gains in Rajasthan and Maharashtra were offset by its unexpected losses in West Bengal, Orissa, and Karnataka. The Congress Indira Party bloc won 27 more seats than two years earlier, but all but one of these additional seats were won by supporting parties. Since she had commended only Congress Indira Party candidates during the campaign and had not mentioned the names of those standing for supporting parties, Sonia Gandhi could not claim any credit for their victories. While the Congress Indira Party's strategy of pinning its hopes on Sonia Gandhi's participation in the campaign turned out to be a mistake insofar as its goal was to enable the party to take control of the 12th Lok Sabha, it would be wrong to conclude that she did the party no good. Even though she did not lead the party to victory or even to a significant increase in its parliamentary clout, she did succeed in reinvigorating its ranks so that it did no worse overall than it had done in 1996. The Congress Indira Party was almost a shambles when President Narayanan had ordered the election of a new Lok Sabha, and President Sitaram Kesri was certainly not the man to infuse its ranks with the renewed vigor needed if the party was to avoid a disastrous showing. Sonia Gandhi turned out to be the woman who could do that job.

If the Congress Indira Party did little better than to hold its own, the United Front did not achieve even that mediocre level of success. The polling results, when compared with its creditable 1996 performance, were little short of a disaster. The number of MPs elected by United Front parties fell from 179 to 101. To make matters worse, the Front could no longer claim to be a national coalition when 55% of its successful candidates came from just two states. Burdened as it was with the abject failure of its two Central Governments and the factionalism that had caused splits in one of its keystone parties, the Janata Dal, and in not one but three states—Bihar, Karnataka, and Orissa—it was expected that the United Front would not do well.

What was not expected was that it would be saddled with an additional burden in the form of anti-incumbency sentiment. The combined weight of these political burdens broke its political back. Three of the United Front's parties were in control of state governments—the DMK in Tamil Nadu, the Telegu Desam Party in Andhra Pradesh, and the Janata Dal in Karnataka—where voters reacted negatively to their performance. They expressed their wrath by voting against most of the candidates put up by these parties for Lok Sabha seats. Of the fourteen parties that had constituted the United Front, only the Communist Party Marxist (CPM), the Communist Party of India (CPI), and the Samajwadi Party held their own. Laloo Prasad Yadav's Rashtriya Janata Dal had managed to capture the pickings in North Bihar, but his party was now running with the Congress Indira Party pack rather than with the United Front. The CPM and the CPI had held the fort in their traditional bastions of West Bengal and Kerala, and the Samajwadi Party had won seats in Uttar Pradesh by capturing the support of Dalits and Muslims who saw themselves threatened by a BJP victory. The candidates of the other United Front parties were disastrously defeated.

Not only in Tamil Nadu, Andhra Pradesh, and Karnataka but throughout the country, voters sent a message that they would hold their governments responsible for what the governments did and what they did not do and would look to others if incumbent ministries did not address the people's needs. That this anti-incumbency feeling was unusually strong was evidenced by the defeat of more than half of the candidates who had held seats in the 11th Lok Sabha and had stood for reelection. India's voters also made it clear that, in seeking alternatives, they were not so much concerned about a party's ideology as about its willingness and ability to deliver the goods that the people wanted. Millions of Indians voted for BJP candidates, not because they supported the party's Hindutva agenda, but because they felt that it was the only party that would provide a strong and stable government in Delhi. Equally clear was the voters' message that they were not bothered if a politician was guilty of corruption, provided he or she would work to give them a better life. Jayalalitha succeeded in leading the Anna DMK to a smashing victory in Tamil Nadu despite the charge which she faced of embezzling tens of millions of rupees during her tenure as chief minister. Laloo Prasad Yadav held on to the votes of enough Biharis to win seventeen Lok Sabha seats for his RJD even though he had campaigned while free on bail and was scheduled to be tried for his implication in Bihar's multimillion dollar "fodder" scandal, the most egregious case of political corruption since Independence.

If the 1998 election results showed that honesty and ideology were not major determinants of how India voted, they provided continuing evidence that caste and religion were. The BJP's strongholds continued to be the north and the west and the Hindi-speaking belt, where the Hindu way of life was deeply entrenched, where domination by the higher castes was the order of the day, and where anti-Muslim feeling was centuries old. Only with the support of other parties was the

BJP able to make inroads into the east and south, where caste and religious forces were not so much on its side. The major political concern of Dalits, "Other Backward Classes" (OBC), and Muslims continued to be whether or not a party would and could provide protection against upper caste domination and exploitation, not whether or not a party espoused a "secular" ideology. So the bulk of the members of these minority and depressed groups voted for RJD, Samajwadi Party, and Communist candidates rather than for BJP candidates.

Generally speaking, voter support based on caste and religious considerations followed expected patterns, but a postelection poll conducted by the *India Today* news magazine showed that a significant number of members of "Other Backward Classes" and a significant minority of members of "Scheduled Castes and Tribes" had voted for BJP candidates. The RJP's promise of stable government under strong leadership had convinced them that their best hope for protection and political and economic assistance lay with a BJP government, even though the leaders of that party were predominantly members of the upper castes. These unexpected polling results revealed that the Hindu fundamentalist party had succeeded in breaking through socioeconomic barriers to win votes from some of the lower orders of Indian society, just as it had succeeded in breaking through geographic barriers to win votes in the east and south.

6

A BJP-Led Government in Delhi

The 1998 General Election returns had produced no party with a majority of MPs in the new Lok Sabha. The BJP and its supporters held 264 seats, the Congress Indira Party bloc 168 seats, and the United Front 101 seats. Not only was the BJP bloc in the strongest position to form a coalition government, but it dominated the field because neither of its opponents held enough seats to offer a serious challenge. Despite these advantages, it had to go through some rough sailing before it could take advantage of them. Although it was only 10 seats short of a majority, the preelection and postelection alliances between the BJP, which had won 178 seats, and the more than a dozen supporting parties, which, together with independents, had won 86 seats, had to remain intact if the coalition was to take office. Maintaining its solidarity did not prove to be easy.

Realizing this fact of postelection political life, the BJP's leaders took the first step to induce its supporting parties to remain on board by agreeing to produce a "National Agenda" which would consist of policies and programs representing a consensus of all the members of the bloc. They announced at the outset that the goal of the coalition government would be to give India a strong and stable government that would deal effectively with the problems faced by its people, not to push the BJP's Hindutva agenda. Since, as one of the BJP strategists put it, the election had been a "Vajpayee wave, not a Ram wave," the "National Agenda" would say nothing about building a Ram Temple at Ayodhya, introducing a "uniform civil code," or terminating Jammu and Kashmir's special constitutional status.

For the other leaders of the BJP's supporting parties, these concessions were enough, but not for Jayalalitha, the doyenne of the Anna DMK and its Tamil auxiliary parties. Acting on behalf of this Tamil cadre, which held 27 seats, she refused to provide a letter of support for a BJP-led coalition government. Given the existence of what she called the "North-South divide"—the traditional conflict between North Indian Aryanism and South Indian Dravidianism—she insisted that the North Indian–based BJP high command include in the "National Agenda" commitments to meet certain specific Tamil demands:

- Tamil Nadu should receive a "fair share" of Cauvery River waters;
- Tamil should be recognized as an "official" language;
- A good number of Tamilians should be included in the Council of Ministers

Jayalalitha made no bones about her reason for making these demands, saying that, since the Anna DMK and its allies were offering the BJP 27 seats' worth of Lok Sabha support, the coalition government that the BJP would lead should "do something for Tamil Nadu."   She also complained that she had been treated with condescension and contempt by the BJP's leaders and insisted that they would have to show more respect if they wanted to retain the support of the twenty-seven MPs for whom she spoke. Since they realized that without the seats controlled by Jayalalitha they would not be able to convince President Narayanan that a BJP-led coalition government would command a majority in the 12th Lok Sabha, Vajpayee and Advani lost no time in meeting her terms. Calling her refusal to provide a letter of support a "misunderstanding," they gave in on all points, with the result that she not only agreed that her twenty-seven MPs would provide votes for the coalition but that the Tamil bloc parties would become members of the new government rather than provide support from outside it.

Even though this major hurdle standing in the way of the BJP's bloc's being requested by the president to form a government had been overcome and six small-party and independent MPs had been added to its parliamentary total, the 264 seats that it represented were still less than a majority. At this crucial point, the help that was needed came, surprisingly enough, from two of the parties affiliated with the United Front. The Telegu Desam Party (TDP), which held 12 seats in the new Lok Sabha, took the first step when its president declared that, because his party did not wish to identify itself with either the BJP or the Congress Indira Party, its MPs would abstain when the vote of confidence in the new government was taken. A few days later, he went further in the BJP's direction by declaring that the TDP was withdrawing from the United Front and would "cooperate" with the Vajpayee government on an "issue by issue" basis. The same day, the head of Kashmir's National Conference stated that its MPs would do likewise. When it turned out that the votes of the TDP MPs were needed to win the vote of confidence, eleven of them actually voted in the affirmative, with the result that it passed 274 to 261.

Two weeks after the counting of the general election ballots had begun, President Narayanan asked A. B. Vajpayee to form a government and gave him ten days to show that his Council of Ministers commanded majority support. Vajpayee was now in the same position as the one he had occupied less than two years earlier when the BJP had emerged from the 1996 General Election holding the most seats. Although he had ended up at that time serving only thirteen days as prime minister because he could not muster a majority of votes to support the Council of Ministers that he had recruited, his "second chance" proved to be a success. On March 19, 1998, he and his forty-two member Council of Ministers were sworn in to become the new BJP-led coalition government. Ten days later, a majority of the members of the Lok Sabha expressed their support, and the Vajpayee regime was officially in place.

The forty-two members of the Council were equally divided between ministers with cabinet rank and ministers of state. Vajpayee retained the external affairs minister's portfolio, and L. K. Advani was given the home minister's post. Ten of the other cabinet ministers were BJP leaders, and the remainder had been selected from the leadership of its supporting parties. Two of the latter group were from the Anna DMK and two from the Samyukta Party, while the other supporting parties were represented by one cabinet member each. Among the ministers of state, thirteen were from the BJP and eight were from supporting parties. All states except West Bengal, Harayana, and Kerala were represented by a cabinet minister or minister of state, but Tamil Nadu enjoyed a bonanza of four ministers with cabinet rank and three in the second tier of executive authority.

The promised "National Agenda for Governance" was made public at the same time that the new prime minister and his Council of Ministers took the oath of office. It was released at a meeting held at Vajpayee's residence where he sat surrounded by the leaders of the parties who supported his government. The setting symbolized his appeal that all parties "develop a national consensus on all major issues confronting the nation." In line with that appeal, the National Agenda pledged that the Vajpayee government would "try for a consensual mode of governance as far as practicable" because, in its words, the "destructive trend of the politics of negativeness and untouchability" had "distorted our body politic in the last few decades." The new government's first commitment to the Indian people was to give them "a stable, honest, transparent, and efficient government capable of accomplishing all-round development."

So far as economic policy was concerned, the Vajpayee government would continue the reform and liberalization process but give it a new *swadeshi* thrust to ensure that economic growth followed the principle that "India will be built by Indians." "We will reappraise and revitalize reforms through giving primacy to removal of unemployment and to accelerated development of infrastructure, particularly energy and power growth. . . . We will carefully analyze the efforts of globalization, calibrate the process of it by devising a time-table to suit our national condition and requirements so as to not undermine but strengthen the national economy, the indigenous industrial base and the financial and service sectors." These policies would seek, not only to bring the economy's annual rate of growth back to 7%, but to pursue the new government's "main theme," which would be to "eradicate unemployment."

Defense would also be treated as a priority policy area. "The state of preparedness, morale, and combat effectiveness of the Armed Forces shall receive early attention and appropriate remedial action. We will establish a National

Security Council to analyze the military, economic, and political threats to the nation, also to continuously advise the government. This course will undertake India's first ever Strategic Defense Review. To ensure the security, territorial integrity and unity of India we will take all necessary steps to exercise all available options. Toward the end we will re-evaluate the nuclear policy and exercise the option to induct nuclear weapons."

All in all, the National Agenda for Governance was, in the words of Chennai's leading newspaper, "a distilled version of the Bharatiya Janata Party's manifesto minus the issues related to Hindutva." In their place, the National Agenda committed the Vajpayee government to pursuing "genuine secularism," which was defined as "a civilized, humane and just civil order which does not discriminate on grounds of caste, religion, colour or sex" and which is based on "equal respect for all faiths." Pursuing this goal would involve "the economic and educational development of the minorities," reservation of 33% of state and national legislative seats for women, and adequate safeguards for the interests of "Scheduled Castes and Tribes" and "Other Backward Classes."

India's increasingly serious demographic and environmental problems received scant attention. They were barely mentioned and then only in general statements that contained no proposals for specific action. On population: "A suitable and judicious mix of incentives and disincentives for population control shall be presented early so that national commitment on this critical issue is obtained." On the environment: "We will establish an appropriate legal framework for the protection of the environment and unveil a National Environmental Policy to balance between development and ecology." The Tamil Nadu items which Jayalalitha had insisted be included were subsumed under general commitments that applied to all states. Her demand that the Vajpayee government see to it that Tamil Nadu received its fair share of Cauvery River waters was taken care of by the commitment to develop a national water policy. Her demand that Tamil be recognized as a "national" language was met by a commitment to constitute a committee that would study the feasibility of designating all of the languages listed in the Constitution as "national" languages. In order to make it clear that Tamil Nadu was not the only state that would receive special attention, the Agenda assured the leaders of the coalition's member parties that "special packages" of programs addressing the needs of particular states would be developed at a later stage.

Following the release of the National Agenda, Vajpayee answered questions from reporters. The policy area that received most of their attention was defense, and, in particular, the BJP-led government's commitment to "exercise the option to induct nuclear weapons." Vajpayee expanded the wording of this commitment by adding the phrase "only if necessary." Some reporters took this to mean that his government would pursue a more moderate line than the one indicated by the unequivocal statements contained in both the BJP's election manifesto and the Vajpayee government's National Agenda. But, since the BJP was already convinced that Pakistan had developed nuclear weapons and was working on missiles that could deliver them, Vajpayee's qualifying phrase did not qualify his government's nuclear weapons commitment because he and the other BJP leaders had already decided that carrying it out was necessary.

Now that the United Front was, for all practical purposes, no more, the only substantial opposition force with which the Vajpayee government had to contend was the Congress Indira Party, which did not constitute an immediate threat even though it held 141 seats in the Lok Sabha. The party that had emerged from the 1998 election with Sonia Gandhi at its head was not only seriously deficient as an organization but its new and unchallenged leader was a relative political novice. Successful as she had been as an election campaigner, it was unlikely that she would be able to make up for her inexperience in parliamentary politics soon enough to enable her to outmaneuver seasoned political hands like Vajpayee and Advani. In making the attempt, she would be faced with the additional handicap of not being herself a member of Parliament. She would not be able to make her own voice heard in Lok Sabha debates but would have to speak through some other Congress Indira Party leader who was an MP. Forced to play her leadership role behind the scenes rather than on the floor of Parliament, she would find it doubly difficult to lead an immediate onslaught against the Vajpayee regime.

The Congress Indira Party would need a number of months at least for its organization to recover from its pre-1998 General Election malaise and for its new leader to learn the "in's and out's" of the Indian political game. The party's reluctance to face another general election in the near future was reflected in Sonia Gandhi's first major speech to a business organization following her election as the Congress Indira Party's president. Instead of speaking as the voice of an opposition that was anxious to take over the reins of government as soon as possible, she assured the Confederation of Indian Industry that her party would offer the Vajpayee government "constructive cooperation" and would support its program for speeding up economic growth. In addition to wanting some time to elapse before another election so that they could deal with their party's internal needs, Sonia Gandhi's political advisers believed that the best way to terminate the Vajpayee regime was to "give it enough rope to hang itself." They believed that, sooner or later, the inept BJP-led government would be discredited by its poor performance in office and that it was politically wiser to allow enough time for this to happen rather than to look for opportunities to bring the government down as soon as possible.

Prime Minister Vajpayee's political skill helped to keep his regime in office beyond its initial 100 days, but its stability was put to its severest test during the weeks immediately preceding the August 15, 1998, end of the Golden Jubilee Year. Not surprisingly, this most serious threat was spearheaded by Vajpayee's political thorn in the flesh, the Anna DMK's Jayalalitha. Not surprisingly, the issue on which she confronted the Vajpayee regime was the division of Cauvery River water between Karnataka and Tamil Nadu. The Supreme Court had enjoined the Central Government to provide by August 12 an official notification documenting the amount of water that had been allocated to Tamil Nadu by the

Cauvery Water Disputes Tribunal. Instead of carrying out the Supreme Court's order, Prime Minister Vajpayee organized and presided over an August 6–7 meeting of the chief ministers of the two states principally involved in the Cauvery River water issue—Karnataka and Tamil Nadu—and the two states peripherally impacted by the tribunal's June 1991 decision—Kerala and Pondicherry. The participants agreed to the creation of a Cauvery Water Authority made up of the prime minister as chairman and the chief ministers of the four riparian   states. With the assistance of a technical committee, this Water Authority would make ongoing decisions as to how the Cauvery River waters were to be distributed.

The day after she received a report of the meeting's outcome, Jayalalitha announced that the Anna DMK and its allied parties categorically rejected its decision to set aside the Cauvery Water Disputes Tribunal's order and to hand over the power to make water-sharing decisions to a Cauvery Water Authority. She then went on to threaten that her twenty-seven MPs would withdraw their support from the Vajpayee government if the prime minister did not notify the Supreme Court that the tribunal's decision rather than the August 6–7 agreement would become official policy. Two days later, Jayalalitha announced that the Anna DMK and its allied parties would "review" their support of the BJP-led government if the prime minister did not take action to endorse the tribunal's order and call a special meeting of Parliament to ratify it. By the next day, it had become evident that Vajpayee was not going to be badgered by Jayalalitha's threat to destabilize his government and was not going to reverse the position taken by the participants in the August 6–7 meeting. One day in advance of its August 12 deadline, the Supreme Court was informed that a notice of the creation of the Cauvery Water Authority had been placed in the official gazette. The Cauvery River water dispute issue not only had been settled on Vajpayee's terms rather than Jayalalitha's terms, but it had been settled in a manner which showed that the prime minister was no longer willing to coddle his Tamil ally in order to keep her and her MP followers in the government's fold. Much to her dismay, he did not bother to consult her after receiving her August 10 demand and did not inform her of his decision in advance of its official announcement.

Jayalalitha's reaction to this rebuff was to convene a meeting of the leaders of the Anna DMK and its allied parties, to take place one day before the beginning of the celebration of the end of the Golden Jubilee Year. Its agenda would be to discuss whether the Tamil parties represented at the meeting should withdraw their support of the Vajpayee regime or recall their representatives who were serving as members of the Council of Ministers and provide support for the government from outside its ranks. In the event, the participants, instead, authorized Jayalalitha to act on their behalf by taking "appropriate action at the appropriate time." When asked by a newspaper reporter what this decision meant, all the meeting's spokesman would say was that the question of withdrawing the bloc's representatives from the Council of Ministers did not arise, thus avoiding any statement that would place limitations on Jayalalitha's options.

During the days that followed the Anna DMK bloc's meeting, it became apparent that the decision to authorize Jayalalitha to take "appropriate action at the appropriate time" was little more than a face-saving device. A leader of one of the Anna DMK's allied parties, speaking to reporters a few days later, predicted: "You will get good news soon. . . . The support will continue and Ms. Jayalalitha will be announcing it. . . . She will not pull down the government and thereby walk into the trap set by the Congress Indira Party. I firmly believe that there is no threat to the Vajpayee government." His prediction followed public statements from leaders of the other allied Tamil parties that they would continue to support the BJP-led government if the Anna DMK's MPs abandoned it. Even with this nudging from her allies, it took Jayalalitha almost a month to bring herself to admit that her attempt to blackmail Prime Minister Vajpayee on the Cauvery River water issue had failed. When the political squabble that it had generated was no longer front-page news and the nation no longer faced the possibility that Prime Minister Vajpayee, who was to deliver the August 15 Anniversary Day speech, might be speaking as the head of a caretaker government, Jayalalitha was in a position where she had to come clean and say to reporters, "our support continues and there is no threat to the government."

The widespread praise that followed the prime minister's firm and skillful handling of the Cauvery waters issue provided his government with at least one response to its critics when they charged that it had accomplished nothing on the domestic front since its assumption of office. Vajpayee's government also gained strength from the credit given to the prime minister by other coalition party leaders for checking Jayalalitha's "loose cannon" antics by defying her when she threatened him with "disastrous consequences" if he did not give in to her Cauvery River water demands. Most importantly, this put the BJP-led government in a stronger political position because it highlighted for the nation the political fact that the opposition parties were not yet in a position to form an alternative government if the Anna DMK bloc withdrew its support and the Vajpayee regime fell. The pre-Anniversary Day threat to the viability of the Vajpayee regime provided opposition parties with the opportunity to join forces with Jayalalitha in an attempt to bring down the BJP-led government, but none of them seized it. The governing coalition had survived the most serious challenge to its viability that had occurred during the first five months of its existence as much because of the opposition's weakness as because of its own inherent strength.

The Congress Indira Party was the only opposition party strong enough to take the lead in promoting an effort to topple the Vajpayee regime, and that party was not in a position to do so. Sonia Gandhi and the other party leaders were determined at this point to let the BJP-led government take "enough rope to hang itself" rather than to try to precipitate its downfall, because they were doubtful about the leaders of some of the parties that would have to be included in a replacement coalition. The two Communist parties had been bitter political enemies of the Congress Party in its various forms for four decades and were not going to change their political spots overnight. The leaders of the Anna DMK bloc were not among the political leaders whom the Congress Party regarded as trustworthy, and the Congress Party leaders did not give Jayalalitha any word of encouragement during the hours that elapsed after the Anna DMK bloc's August 13 meeting authorized her to keep support for the BJP-led government "under review." But these external political factors were not the only reason why the Congress Indira Party was not in a position to help make Jayalalitha's threat of "disastrous consequences" a reality. The party suffered internally from friction among its leaders over who would be the prime minister if a Congress Indira Party–led coalition government were to be constituted. The genesis of this friction went back to the outcome of the 1998 General Election. While the Congress Indira Party had not fared well at the national level, it had scored a major success in Maharashtra by wresting most of that state's Lok Sabha seats from the Shiv Sena–BJP combine that had been the dominant political power up to that point. The leader of the Congress Indira Party's Maharashtrian wing was Sharad Pawar, who had expected to be rewarded for his outstanding performance with a preeminent position in the postelection party organization.

While he was prepared to join forces with the other leaders who felt that Sonia Gandhi's achievements as a campaigner had qualified her for the party's presidency, Pawar felt that, in turn, she should have supported him for the chairmanship of its Parliamentary Committee, especially when he had been elected as an MP and the party president had not. But she failed to support him and, instead, accepted the chairmanship herself. Because Sonia Gandhi was not a Member of Parliament, Pawar had to act as the party's leader in the Lok Sabha, but his elevation to that post did not satisfy his ambition. He became the leader of a faction within the party that took the position that he, rather than Sonia Gandhi, should be chosen as its candidate for the prime minister's post should India's highest political office become available. The divisive issue of who would become prime minister would inevitably come to the surface if the Congress Indira Party were to organize an alternative coalition government under its leadership.

Since the government had not only survived the August crisis caused by Jayalalitha's threat to withdraw the support of her twenty-seven MPs but had emerged politically stronger as a result, at the end of the Golden Jubilee Year the BJP-led government faced reasonable prospects of lasting somewhat longer than either of its two predecessors. So far as stability was concerned, it appeared likely to do better than either the Deve Gowda or the Gujral governments, not so much because of its own strength but because of the weakness of its opposition. Opposition parties held no more than 168 seats in the 12th Lok Sabha. While the parties making up the BJP-led coalition were vulnerable to a fall from power because they controlled only 6 seats more than the 272 needed to constitute a majority, maintaining that narrow margin would be an easier political task for the coalition than gaining the additional 104 seats needed to take over the Central Government would be for the opposition parties.

The BJP party could claim for the time being that it had delivered by the end of the Golden Jubilee Year on its general election campaign promise to provide

India with a stable government. Where it had thus far failed was in delivering on the campaign promise that A. B. Vajpayee would be the prime minister of a strong government. If a strong national government is defined as one that is in a position to deal effectively with the problems a nation faces, the prospects in August 1998 were that, so far as its domestic agenda was concerned, the BJP-led government would fall short.

7

Crashing the Nuclear Club

In that the BJP-led government had accomplished little on the domestic front during its first few months in office, it was much like the Deve Gowda and Gujral regimes that had preceded it. But on the foreign front, it had a different record in one crucially important respect. By the end of the Golden Jubilee Year, the Vajpayee regime had implemented one of the items in its National Agenda that was not a part of its predecessors' agendas. It had taken the first steps to "induct" nuclear weapons into India's defense arsenal. A new program would go forward during the remainder of its term in office—the building of nuclear bombs and the missiles to deliver them.

On May 11, 1998, Prime Minister Vajpayee had shown himself to be the head of a strong government when he read a brief statement informing the world that three tests of nuclear bombs, one of them thermonuclear, had been conducted at Pokhran in the Rajasthan desert, only sixty miles from Pakistan's border. It was revealed later that he had given the order to carry out these three tests on April 10, twenty-two days after his government's inauguration, and that the technical preparations had been going on during the very weeks when his political enemies were labeling him a political "wimp." For several decades, Vajpayee personally and his BJP party had advocated that India develop nuclear weapons. The BJP's 1998 General Election manifesto had called for India's joining the exclusive "nuclear club," and the same proposal had been incorporated in the National Agenda that was to be implemented by the Vajpayee regime. On May 11, that part of its foreign policy agenda had been initiated.

The decision that nuclear bomb tests needed to be conducted as soon as possible after the Vajpayee government had taken charge in Delhi was a product of the BJP's long-standing concerns about the threat to India's security posed by Pakistan. Those concerns went back to 1947 when Pakistan had been created by splitting British India into its Hindu-dominated and Muslim-dominated components, the aftermath of which was the loss of over a million lives and the displacement of more than 12 million people. The concerns continued throughout the next five decades, exacerbated by military clashes with Pakistan over Kashmir in 1948, the Rann of Kutch in 1965, and Bangladesh in 1971. They had been accentuated as recently as April 6, 1998, when Pakistan had announced that it had successfully test fired a missile with a range of 1,500 kilometers and the capability of carrying a nuclear warhead. That Pakistan had political as well as technical reasons for carrying out the test was made obvious by the fact that the missile carried the name of a Muslim general, Ghauri, who had invaded India in the 12th century and conquered a Hindu king. Convinced that the Pakistan threat had evolved to the point where it had taken nuclear form, the Vajpayee government had come to the conclusion that India had to counter it by developing nuclear weapons of its own.

It was certain that India's resuming nuclear tests after an interval of twenty-four years would be condemned by the United States and other countries that had embarked on a program organized around the Nuclear Non Proliferation Treaty (NPT) and the Comprehensive Nuclear Test Ban Treaty (CTBT) to cut back rather than increase the number of nuclear weapons in the world. The Vajpayee government decided that the best way to counteract this expected negative reaction was to build a case for international consumption that the major threat to India's national security was posed, not by Pakistan, but by China. Since India had at its disposal conventional military forces that were far stronger than those of Pakistan and had defeated Pakistan on the three occasions when they had come to blows, the world was hardly likely to believe that India needed nuclear weapons to provide the protection that it needed to counter the Pakistani threat to its security.

China, on the other hand, with armed forces more than double the size of India's, with many times the number of tanks and military aircraft, and with hundreds of nuclear weapons, was a military power vastly stronger than India. Faced with this preponderance of conventional and nuclear forces, India could plausibly argue that it needed nuclear weapons to create a military situation in which China would be deterred from attacking India as it had thirty-six years earlier when the Indo-Chinese border dispute had flared into fighting. So far as the United States was concerned, China was not only its only rival as a super-power, but an increasingly powerful country that had the potential to dominate the Asian continent and exclude American influence from that part of the world. Unlike China, Pakistan was viewed by Indians as the country that the United States would support if "push came to shove" in a new Indo-Pakistani conflict, just as it had in 1971 when President Nixon had sent an aircraft carrier into the Bay of Bengal and had cut off military assistance to India to show American displeasure at the Indian army's invasion of East Pakistan. For both these reasons, the leaders of the Vajpayee government felt that India's case for conducting tests of its "nuclear devices" as the first step in a program to develop nuclear weapons would sound more convincing to the Clinton administration and other world governments if it was presented, not as a response to the real nuclear threat which they saw coming from Pakistan, but as a response to a fictional nuclear threat from China. This alleged Chinese nuclear threat was later made the centerpiece of Prime Minister Vajpayee's letter to President Clinton explaining why his government had felt it necessary to conduct the May 11 and May 13 nuclear bomb tests.

By blaming China for putting India in a position where it had to test its nuclear weapons, India had abruptly reversed the campaign that had been carried on by previous governments since 1988 to improve relations with China. The Sino-Indian "era of good feeling" of the 1950s had been rekindled when Prime Minister Rajiv Gandhi had paid his respects to the Communist leaders in Beijing and had been fueled when Prime Minister Narasimha Rao followed him five years later. The 1993 visit had resulted in an agreement to honor the Line of Actual Control that had marked the positions that the Chinese and Indian forces had occupied when the border war ended in 1962. Henceforth, neither side would use military force to acquire more territory, and both sides would use diplomacy to settle the border dispute. In 1996, Prime Minister Deve Gowda had accepted the proposal that had been put forward almost thirty-five years earlier by China's Prime Minister Chou En-lai that Chinese and Indian troops withdraw twenty kilometers from the Line of Actual Control in order to avoid future clashes. As an additional contribution on India's part toward sustaining the "era of good feeling," he agreed to put on hold the research and development program that had been set in motion to produce a missile capable of reaching several of China's major cities.

Within weeks of assuming office, the Vajpayee regime made a 180 degree turn away from the direction that Sino-Indian relations had taken during the previous decade. Although, as a member of the Samatha Party, Defense Minister George Fernandes was not privy to the decision that had been taken by the top BJP leaders to conduct nuclear bomb tests, he laid the groundwork for basing this decision on the security threat supposedly posed by China. He began a series of speeches which hammered away on the theme that "China is the potential threat Number One" and castigated past political leaders for their "reluctance to face the reality that China's intentions need to be questioned." He cited as evidence that those intentions threatened India's security the fact that China had given technical assistance to Pakistan in developing its nuclear weapons and its 1,500 kilometer "Ghauri" missile and the steps that China had allegedly taken to set up a network of operational and surveillance bases around India, including nuclear missile launchers located in Tibet. Several days before the nuclear tests were conducted, in commenting on the Chinese threat, Fernandes remarked: "There is no soft option in matters of security. If we have to stand up, we have to take the hard option. . . . We have said that if our perception makes us believe that we need to go for the nuclear bomb, we will go for it."

Speaking out of the other side of the government's mouth, some of the other ministers in the Vajpayee regime criticized his attacks on China and admonished him to tone down his rhetoric. But the letter which Prime Minister Vajpayee wrote to President Clinton to explain the Pokhran nuclear bomb tests was based upon Fernandes' contention that China was India's "Number One enemy." Acting in his traditional role as the BJP's "mask," he focused on the Chinese threat as the reason behind his decision to conduct the nuclear tests and brought Pakistan into the picture only as China's ally against India.   As in the past, the BJP's "face" was revealed by Home Minister Advani. Five days after the testing cycle was completed, during a visit to Kashmir, he stated in so many words that India's nuclear weapons program was directed, not toward China, but toward Pakistan. In his words: "India's nuclear weapons capability showed the country's resolve to deal firmly and strongly with Pakistan's hostile designs and activities in Kashmir."

Two days later, he repeated his threat, this time with gloating overtones: "The technical skill displayed at Pokhran was as much a shock to Pakistan as our military prowess in 1971. India has now moved far beyond the previous obsession with our western neighbour. When I spoke of geo-strategic changes the other day, this is precisely what I had in mind." When asked a question regarding the possibility that India's tests might prompt Pakistan to test its "nuclear device," he replied: "In fact, it is Pakistan's clandestine preparations that forced us to take the path of nuclear deterrence."   With these harsh words, Advani was telling Pakistan's leaders that India was prepared to meet their advances toward nuclear capability and that, if they continued to mount incursions into Indian-held Kashmir or engage in other anti-Indian acts, they would face a very dangerous adversary because India would have nuclear weapons at its disposal.

Vajpayee's brief statement following his announcement that two rounds of nuclear bomb tests had taken place was directed to a worldwide audience because, in his words, "the tests have established that India has a proven capability for a weaponized nuclear program." It was also directed to the Indian people because the tests "provide assurance . . . that their national security interests are paramount and will be promoted and protected. Succeeding generations of Indians would also rest assured that contemporary techniques associated with [the] nuclear option have been passed on to them in the 50th year of Independence." Vajpayee's statement was elaborated by his principal secretary, who went on to say that, in conducting the tests, the government had merely carried out what it had said it would do in the National Agenda and that now "the message is clear that the people have a nuclear deterrent." A day later, India's minister of science and technology added to what the prime minister had said by informing the press that India would cap its missiles with nuclear warheads "as soon as the situation requires."

Following the second round of tests on May 13, the world was notified that the current testing cycle had been completed. Whereas the first round of tests had involved high levels of explosive power, including a type of hydrogen bomb that was called a "city buster," the explosions resulting from the second round were much reduced in scale, indicating that these tests were preparatory steps toward the development of battlefield nuclear weapons. During the forty-eight hours that had elapsed between the first and second round of tests, India had heard indignant words of condemnation from President Clinton and other world political leaders, had seen several diplomatic representatives withdrawn from their posts, and had been threatened with economic sanctions by the United States, Japan, and several other nations. Sri Lanka was the only country that had openly commended India for carrying out the tests, a response that was almost inevitable from a tiny neighbor that was anxious to maintain good relations with the giant across a narrow strip of water that had dispatched troops to Sri Lanka's soil a decade earlier in an attempt to suppress Tamil insurgents.

That the second set of tests had taken place in the face of the worldwide disapproval of the first set showed that India was prepared to defy the international community in order to join the "big five" countries with nuclear weapons. Vajpayee characterized the economic sanctions that would be imposed on India as part of the price that would have to be paid to safeguard the country's security. "We have come to understand that we will be denied aid, credit and other assistance and that we will face problems. But in the event of such steps, the country will have to face them squarely. If the path ahead is a difficult one, we will not shy away from it." Leaders of the political parties opposing the BJP who heard his words found it difficult to avoid the feeling that, while he genuinely regretted that India would suffer from the negative political and economic reactions emanating from other countries, he took comfort from knowing that these reprisals would become a rallying point for unifying the Indian people behind his government because it had stood up to a hostile world in order to safeguard their security.

Much to the delight of the Vajpayee government, the BJP, and the RSS, the Indian people's reaction to the tests was a euphoric outburst of national pride. There were enthusiastic demonstrations throughout the country, celebrating the tests as a demonstration that India was well on its way to joining the exclusive "nuclear club." The third day after the completion of the second round of tests was observed nationally as a "Day of Pride," and a Hindu fundamentalist organization that was an auxiliary of the RSS and the BJP announced that it would build a temple at the Pokhran test site. A public opinion poll conducted in Mumbai, Delhi, Calcutta, Chennai, Bangalore, and Hyderabad on the day following the first series of tests showed that 91% of the respondents applauded the government's action and that 82% thought India should go forward and build nuclear weapons. But the finding that brought the greatest satisfaction to the Vajpayee regime was that 67% of those polled said they were now reassured that the government was strong and would safeguard their security.

Even the great grandson of Mahatma Gandhi, the apostle of *ahimsa*, stated that "he was proud that it had been done in India and by Indians." The head of the Shiv Sena party expressed his support in more earthy language: "We have to prove that we are not eunuchs." But it was Prime Minister Vajpayee who expressed the nation's pride most simply and succinctly when he told BJP members of the Lok Sabha meeting on the day before Parliament was convened for the first time following the explosions at Pokhran: "Because of the tests we are now among the great powers." He underlined this point the next day, when he addressed not only BJP MPs but also MPs representing the other parties belonging to his coalition government and cited the nuclear tests as his government's "greatest achievement." This achievement was, in his words, the "continuation of the solid national consensus which has marked India's policy all along. The cornerstone of this policy until now was to keep India's nuclear option open. All we have done is to exercise that option." MPs representing all of the BJP's coalition partners responded to his words by passing a resolution congratulating the prime minister, the nuclear scientists, and the army personnel for successfully conducting the nuclear tests that had made "India the sixth nuclear weapons state in the world."

Indian newspapers expressed unanimous approval of the government's action in conducting the tests, although they were more measured in their support than the Indian populace and more aware of the price that India would have to pay to become a "nuclear weapons state." Almost all of the opposition parties joined the laudatory chorus. Only the two Communist parties broke ranks by expressing their disapproval of both the tests and the government's branding China as India's "Number One enemy." The opposition parties did couple their approval with expressions of unhappiness because they had not been included in the deliberations that had led up to the decision to "go nuclear" and did insist on learning why the first tests had taken place on May 11 rather than at a later date. But, after their leaders had met with Vajpayee to discuss these relatively minor complaints, they soon fell silent.

The Congress Indira Party, because it had been in power during most of the years between 1974 and 1998 when no nuclear tests had been conducted and had been the party that had headed the governments which had backed off in 1983 and 1995 from carrying out the tests that had been planned for those years, might have been expected to raise some serious questions about Vajpayee's decision, but it did not. It said little and what it said through Sonia Gandhi was supportive: "I would like to place on record in this meeting of the Congress Working Committee the pride we feel in the achievement of our nuclear scientists and engineers for putting India's nuclear capability in the front rank. We recall with equal pride that successive Congress governments have ensured that India's nuclear capability remains up-to-date, so that our security is not compromised. The nuclear question is a national matter, not a partisan one. On this every Indian stands united."

Given the extent and degree of national support for the nuclear tests, Vajpayee was able to use it to the full to back up his continuing defiance of world opinion and to take the credit for his government and his party. When the United Nations passed a May 14 resolution deploring India's action because the second set of tests had been carried out "despite overwhelming international concern and protests," he responded by asserting: "We conducted tests for our national security. . . . We want our borders secure. We want to live in our house safely. . . . We do not have aggressive designs. We believe in the policy of live and let live." Speaking for himself and his party, he went on to say: "I have been advocating the cause of

India going nuclear for well over five decades. My party, the BJP and earlier the Bharatiya Jan Sangh had been raising the demand consistently and forcefully for long. Now that we are in the government, people expect us to translate our long standing realities [*sic*]."

In written responses to questions asked by reporters for the news magazine *India Today*, Vajpayee stated unequivocally that his government intended to proceed with the production of nuclear weapons: "We do not want to cover our action with a veil of needless ambiguity. India is now a nuclear weapons state. We have the capacity for a 'big bomb' now, for which a necessary command and control system is also in place." He then went on to adopt a defiant, almost aggressive tone: "Yes, our actions have entailed a price. But we shall not worry about it. India has an immense reserve of resources and inner strength. If we tap this reservoir, the benefit will be a hundred times more than any price that we may have to pay in the short term. . . . India has never considered military might as the ultimate measure of national strength. It is a necessary component in overall national strength. I would, therefore, say that the greatest meaning of the tests is that they have given India *shakti* [power], they have given India strength, they have given India self-confidence." His final word was that India would counter economic sanctions with a "sanction of her own past glory and future vision to become strong—in every sense of the term."

The first serious barrage of parliamentary criticism came two weeks after the Pokhran tests had been conducted, when it was announced in the Lok Sabha on May 28 that Pakistan had conducted a series of five nuclear tests. This news led to an uproar in which opposition MPs accused Vajpayee of having launched India on a nuclear arms race with Pakistan. His defense was to go on the offensive by stating that "these Pakistani tests vindicate our policy" because it was now clear that India's suspicions that Pakistan had nuclear weapons capability were correct. Facing this threat, the prime minister proclaimed that "India is ready to meet any challenge. . . . People must stand united to face the new situation. . . . We may have our differences but if the challenge is from abroad, then that challenge must be met with a united House and a united nation." Discomfited as they were at the prospect that Pakistan's nuclear tests would further strengthen both Prime Minister Vajpayee's government and his party, leaders of opposition parties could not avoid acceding to his appeal for a "united House."

The Vajpayee government's first opportunity for using its post-Pokhran political muscle on the domestic front came on June 2 when it introduced its 1998–99 budget. It proposed a budget conveying the message that providing India with nuclear weapons capability would not mean its people would have to go through the painful economic transition that Pakistan's leaders had predicted when they proclaimed that Pakistanis were prepared to eat grass if necessary to provide the resources needed to implement Pakistan's nuclear weapons program. The budget did include an increase of 14% in conventional military expenditures and increases of 62% and 68% respectively for the atomic energy and space programs that would be involved in developing nuclear weapons and the missiles to deliver them. But even with these substantial increases in funding, the total for these three programs rose to just over 20% of total budgetary expenditures, not much more than three percentage points higher than their 1997–98 budget share. Compared with the virtual doubling of defense expenditure that had taken place during each of the two years following India's defeat in the 1962 border war with China, a 3% plus rise in budget share could hardly be called a radical increase. Taking into consideration the inflation rate that was already edging well above 8% and the fall in the value of the rupee that would boost the rupee cost of importing high-tech defense hardware, it was obvious that budgetary increases of such a modest order were not going to produce substantial increases in military capability measured in real terms. This point was emphasized by Mulayam Singh Yadav, who had served as defense minister under the United Front governments, when he argued that the 1998–99 conventional defense expenditures should be double those included in the previous year's budget. When he had managed to incorporate an 11% increase in these outlays in the Deve Gowda government's budget for "pre-nuclear" 1996–97, it was no wonder that he was not impressed with Vajpayee's "post-nuclear" 14%.

The message that India would experience a relatively easy transition to its "post-Pokhran era" was repeated in the budget's silence on ways and means of coping with the economic sanctions that followed the Rajasthan desert tests. Stating that those sanctions would not have a significant impact on economic development, the finance minister included figures for foreign assistance and investment that took no account whatsoever of the cutback in foreign funds that would begin to take effect during 1998–99. His ignoring of the sanctions was so complete that he projected an increase of 43% over 1997–98 in the amount of foreign grants and economic assistance that would be received, and estimated that the 1998–99 fiscal year would see private foreign investment receipts continue at the previous year's level of approximately $3 billion.

Making the 1998–99 budget's message of "business as usual" even louder and clearer were the major increases that were included in expenditures for economic and social development programs that the Vajpayee government's National Agenda had promised would receive special attention. Infrastructure, energy, and transport would receive 35% more funds, as would efforts to promote education and social development. The farm sector and rural development would be funded at a level 50% higher than the previous year. Although increased funding was badly needed to deal with India's social and economic problems, committing the government to provide substantially more money for this purpose at a time when the country was embarking upon an expensive nuclear arms program raised a serious question regarding the government's ability to deliver on its budgetary promises. Looking at the budget's income and expenditure figures, one of the United Front's MPs described the budget for the first year of India's nuclear weapons era in words that were both simple and damning: "No budget in 50 years has ever been shrouded in such an atmosphere of utter unreality." But, given the

BJP-led coalition's post-Pokhran political muscle, it proved possible to push the 1998–99 budget through Parliament despite its "utter unreality."

8

Golden Jubilee Economic Scene

To put it mildly, free India's Golden Jubilee Year—the twelve months between August 1997 and August 1998—was not a golden year for its economy. It did not begin as a bad year, when viewed from the perspective of the economy's long-term record since 1947, but even during its opening months the evidence was clear that the 1991–96 boom had ended and that progress, while it was still being made, was slowing down. As the year took shape, the increase in Gross National Product (GNP) fell to 5% from the record high of 7% attained during 1996–97, and the rate of increase in industrial production went down from 7.5% to 6%. The most disquieting statistic was the 2% decline in agricultural output, coming as it did after an increase of 7% in 1996–97. While this fall in agricultural production was troubling from an economic point of view, it was even more worrisome from a human point of view because of what it said about feeding the nation's people. Population was continuing to increase at the prevailing annual rate of just under 2%, and agricultural production would have to increase by at least the same amount if a setback in the food situation was to be avoided. Any movement in a negative direction, however small, was a matter of concern.

While a decline in a single year's production did not constitute a crisis on the food front any more than one swallow makes a spring, note had to be taken of the Central Government's estimate that the 1998 wheat harvest would be 3% less than the previous year, because it was that estimate that triggered its decision to import 2 million (metric) tonnes of wheat from Australia. Two million tonnes do not represent a large consignment when compared with India's annual domestic wheat production figure, which had reached the 100 million tonne level by 1997, but procuring even a relatively modest amount of grain from abroad meant that, at least during 1998, India would be a food importing nation. Ever since 1996, the Central Government had made much of its claim that India had achieved "self-sufficiency" in food, pointing to its exporting of several million tonnes of wheat and rice as evidence that its production of food grains had increased to the point where there was now more than enough available to meet the demands of the domestic market. During the Golden Jubilee Year, that claim could no longer be made, which explains why there was no public announcement of the planned purchase of Australian wheat and why there was a great deal of political uproar when it became public knowledge. The shift from the status of being a food exporting nation in 1997 to the status of a food importing nation in 1998 might turn out to be a temporary phenomenon, but it could be a pointer to a coming era of steadily increasing food grain imports that some experts predict will reach 48 million tonnes annually by 2030.

On the foreign front, in 1997–98 the economic signs were also disquieting. Exports, which had fueled much of the 1991–96 boom, had continued to increase but only at an 8% rate in 1996–97 and a 3% rate in 1997–98, compared with 21% in 1995–96. The export numbers for the first five months of 1998 were particularly worrisome because they showed that the dollar value of goods and services exported during January–February was 7.5% less than it had been during the same months in 1997. While the value of goods in April was 2.2% higher than in April 1997, the comparative figure for May was a whopping negative 17%. This dramatic slowdown in exports had negative repercussions in the domain of foreign exchange because it caused a fall in the demand for rupees. Reinforcing this downward trend was the $200 million net outflow of foreign investment which had taken place by the end of January 1998, after an unbroken and substantial net inflow during the previous five years. The result was that the value of India's currency fell from 35 to 42 to the U.S. dollar by June 1998.

The economic slowdown on both the domestic and foreign fronts during 1997–98 was not brought on by external economic forces stemming from the recession that was taking place in much of Asia but by conditions that prevailed within India. The internal forces producing negative impacts were as much political as they were economic. Power shortages, a decaying infrastructure, and limited irrigation systems continued to hamper the production, distribution, and export of industrial and agricultural products, but the ineffective and unstable Central Governments that were in office between 1996 and 1998 meant that the large-scale investments of public funds needed to begin the process of making good these infrastructural deficiencies had not been made. Ineffective and unstable coalition governments in Delhi and the high degree of uncertainty that characterized India's political future also dampened private sector investment, particularly from foreign sources. Foreign investment was also inhibited by the failure of the Deve Gowda and Gujral governments to continue the process of economic liberalization initiated in 1991 by the Narasimha Rao regime. Excluded from participation in the segments of the Indian economy that had not yet been "globalized," especially insurance and financial services, and unsure of the complexion and *modus operandi* of future Central Governments, foreign investors were disinclined to commit additional funds, and, where they could, inclined to withdraw some of those already committed.

The prospects for future economic damage resulting from external economic forces were increased by the external political and economic events that followed the May nuclear bomb tests. One of the immediate political repercussions of this action was to bring into play the United States's 1994 Nuclear Proliferation Prevention Act. The provisions of this act made it mandatory for the Clinton administration to subject India to a number of economic sanctions that would result in a diminished inflow of governmental and private capital. Except for support for humanitarian programs, all American economic aid, which had amounted to several hundred million dollars a year, was cut off, and American banks were forbidden to make loans to Indian government agencies.

What would hurt the Indian economy more than the blocking of American government or government-guaranteed funds would be the repercussions of the Nuclear Proliferation Prevention Act's provision that the United States would oppose any future loans to India from the World Bank. India had been the Bank's largest borrower, having already obtained a total of $44 billion and expecting to receive an additional $3 billion during the remaining months of 1998 and another $8 billion during the next five years. While the United States could not veto further loans to India, its voting power, combined with the highly negative way in which Japan and several of the other countries represented on the Bank's board had reacted to the nuclear tests, made it highly unlikely that India would be granted additional World Bank loans over American objections unless these funds were to be used for humanitarian purposes. The first step in the direction of a World Bank sanction occurred as early as a fortnight after the second set of nuclear tests. When the fifteen foreign ministers of the European Union countries voted to "work for a delay" in consideration of future World Bank loans to India, the World Bank's executive director announced that a decision on lending $865 million to India to upgrade its power grid had been postponed indefinitely. A second step was taken a short time later when the Bank decided to defer action on a second package of loans to India, bringing the total held in abeyance to $1.7 billion.

Japan, which heretofore had been the country that supplied the largest amount of public and private investment to India, also took action to block further grants and loans, including $1 billion that had been promised for 1998. Germany stated that it was suspending its program of providing India with economic assistance. Adding to these losses of government funds coming from major foreign economic players, India was also subjected to economic sanctions that took the form of cutoffs by a number of smaller donor countries: Canada, Denmark, Norway, Sweden, Holland, Australia, and New Zealand. While the BJP-led government in Delhi had initially taken heart from President Clinton's failure to persuade the leaders of the world's largest industrial nations, the so-called "Group of Eight," to adopt joint economic sanctions against India identical to those imposed by the United States, its leaders were soon reminded that the Group of Eight meeting in Birmingham had left it open to individual members to take punitive economic actions on their own.

They decided a few weeks later to do just that. On June 12, the United States, Japan, Russia, Britain, France, Germany, Italy, Canada—the entire "Group of Eight"—agreed individually and severally to postpone all governmental loans to India except for those designated for funding of humanitarian programs and to use their votes to enforce a similar policy with respect to World Bank funds. Three days later, the members of the European Union agreed to delay consideration of all nonhumanitarian loans to India and to block further loans from the World Bank. In addition, they warned the Indian government that they would impose additional sanctions if India did not ease tensions with Pakistan and sign the NPT and CTBT. All in all, it was estimated that India would lose approximately $6 billion in government and government-guaranteed funds during the coming year as the result of the sanctions imposed following its nuclear tests and that its long-term loss could be as much as $20 billion.

The negative economic developments that followed the May 11 and May 13 nuclear bomb tests did not put an immediate brake on an economy that was already slowing down, but the harbingers of possible trouble ahead were worrisome. To the surprise of many Indian politicians, the finance minister did not show any signs of worry when he presented and defended the 1998–99 budget, and the Vajpayee regime continued to maintain a "whistling in the dark" position so far as its economic policy was concerned. As the Golden Jubilee Year ended, the BJP-led government was living in a state of economic denial. The attitude that it projected was to defy the world community that had imposed economic sanctions, to insist that India "cannot be bullied," and to express confidence that the Indian people would "withstand" whatever troublesome economic repercussions came their way.   Its finance minister characterized these troublesome economic repercussions as "minor roadblocks" that would have little effect on India's corporate sector or its future economic development. He assured Parliament and all those members of the public who might be worried by the loss of foreign public and private investment that "alternative sources" of foreign capital would be found in sufficient quantity to make up any shortfall.

9

Taking Stock in August 1998

When the Implementation Committee announced in June 1997 that the observance of free India's 50th anniversary would be continued throughout the year following August 15, rather than confined to the day itself, it designated this extended period, which came to be called the Golden Jubilee Year, as a time for rekindling a spirit of patriotism and cultivating cultural harmony, national integration, social justice, and political freedom. Although these were certainly ambitious goals, the Anniversary Day dawned with the hope that, in the words of the familiar Chinese proverb, the following twelve months would see India taking "the first step on the journey of a thousand miles" that would have to be completed if the goals were to be achieved. At the beginning, it looked as though this "first step" might be taken and that it might take a constructive form. A special four day session of Parliament was called so that MPs could take a hard look at the country's problems and discuss what might be done to alleviate them. Unfortunately, it was poorly attended, inconclusive in its findings, impotent as far as legislative action was concerned, and soon forgotten.

Disheartening as was this well intentioned but futile parliamentary gesture toward national reform, its failure to produce tangible results came as no surprise. Taking that "first step" would have amounted to nothing less than reversing the direction that free India was following as its first half century was coming to a close—the course leading to the "old" India of Hindu rule and defiance of its Muslim adversary. Reversing direction would have meant leaving that road and heading instead toward the "new" secular India that Jawaharlal Nehru had envisaged when he gave his "Tryst with Destiny" speech. He had set that vision before the eyes of free India at the time of its birth, but during the five decades that had followed, the power of the "old" India had gradually prevailed, and the country had continued down the path that was leading it toward Hindu India. When that half-century journey had come to a close on August 14, 1997, India had found itself governed by a shaky coalition government led by a "do nothing" prime minister, plagued by communal conflict, increasing lawlessness, and political corruption, and faced with an economy that was beginning to lose steam. From all points of view—political, social, and economic—the country was in no state to undertake the monumental task of making a fundamental change in the direction in which it was headed.

The developments that took place as its second half century dawned were no more propitious for the working of what would have been nothing short of a historic miracle. The second United Front government had collapsed only seven months after the fall of its predecessor, a general election had been held, and in April 1998 another coalition government had been installed in Delhi, this one headed by a Hindu fundamentalist party. Within a period of less than one year, free India had moved from being guided by a "secular" hand at the helm of its affairs to being guided by a "communal" hand. Within a period of less than twenty years, the concept of the secular state which was central to Mahatma Gandhi's and Jawaharlal Nehru's vision of the "new" India had become, according to a leading journalist, "a sham" and, for the leader of the Samyukta Party who had become India's defense minister, a joke: "There are secular people in this country and there are normal people," was the way that he had put it in a mocking tone of voice.

In the words of an editorial in the *Hindu*:

Secularism has become Orwellian double-speak. It says one thing and means exactly the opposite. Our politics is not divided between secularists and communalists, but between different brands of communalists. . . . On some page or other of the morning newspaper, it will be reported that some politician or other has uttered the term secularism at the drop of the metaphorical hat. What gives one a sense of profound irritation is that various politicians religiously utter the word as if it were a "mantra" [incantation] to rescue them from their particular predicament. More disturbing is the increasing vulgarization the concept of secularism has been subjected to in our public life. Politicians guilty of massive corruption reach for secularism as if it were an alibi for all acts of omission. . . .

When opportunistic alliances have to be formed between parties which otherwise have nothing in common, simply because they want to stake a claim to power by bringing down the existing governments, they legitimize each other on the ground of secularism. . . . Though the Congress is not the RSS, surely its claim to be the guardian of secularism has been deeply compromised by its involvements in the events of the last two decades. But then secularism becomes a useful tool when staking a claim to a monopoly of power. . . . No sophisticated and skilled practitioner of the politics of the Sangh Parivar [Hindu fundamentalist coalition of which the RSS is the principal member] would claim that he does not believe in secularism. In fact, he would claim that he is the true secularist; [that] the rest of us are pseudo-secularists at best. The party does not want to lose out in the race when it comes to secularism. Therefore, the BJP is secular. Committed secularists shudder in consternation. What on earth, they ask, has happened to secularism?

If there had been any doubt at the time of the 1998 election about the BJP's continuing to be committed to implementing its "Hindutva" agenda, it had been dispelled within a few weeks of the Vajpayee government's installation. In early May 1998, the BJP had held its National Council meeting, attended by 2,500 delegates from all over the country. Vajpayee and Advani had explained to the participants that, because the BJP-led coalition government was dependent upon support by parties that did not share its Hindu fundamentalist agenda, it would be guided by the National Agenda for Governance, which did not include building a Ram temple at Ayodhya, the enactment of a uniform civil code, or the termination of Jammu and Kashmir's special constitutional status. But they had assured them that the BJP-led government's following this pragmatic course of action did not mean that the party had abandoned its ideological goal of making India a Hindu nation.

That this and nothing less remained the BJP's ultimate goal had been made clear by Kashabhau Thakre, who had succeeded L. K. Advani as the party's president. He had reminded the delegates that India had evolved a common way of life that was rooted in a shared cultural heritage. "It is this common way of life that we call Hindutva or cultural nationalism. You can call it any other name—Indianness or Bharatiyata—but the core remains the same." According to Thakre, this was the fundamental reason why the BJP proclaimed that "India is one nation, one people, and one culture" and why its political collaborator was the RSS, which had been formed to make that ideology a reality in everyday life. Thakre had not gone on to explain that characterizing Hindutva as "cultural nationalism," and using the term "one culture" to describe India's "core," was tantamount to excluding from the "one nation" and "one people" the Muslims, Christians, and Sikhs whose cultures differed from the Hindu way of life. It was this omission from the BJP president's remarks that had troubled one of the *Hindu's* editorial writers, who warned: "That the leaders—including Prime Minister, Mr. Atal Behari Vajpayee—took pains to convey to the National Council their commitment to the party's core principles and that the compulsion of coalition politics will in no way deter them from carrying forward the party's agenda clearly shows that there is no way that the BJP leaders in the Government can insulate themselves from the aims of the Sangh Parivar and their divisive company. It is in this context that one cannot but feel apprehension about the shape of things to come."

His editorial was followed by an article that traced the BJP's ideology back through the Jana Sangh to the RSS in order to show its anti-minority roots. The article quoted from the 1939 writings of M. S. Golwakar, at that time the lifetime head of the RSS, who had branded Gandhi as the traitor who wanted "all Hindus to become Muslims":

In Hindustan [land of the Hindus before the Muslim invasions and the coming of the Europeans] exists and must needs exist the ancient Hindu nation and nought else but the Hindu nation. . . . So long, however, as they [Muslim and other non-Hindus] maintain their social, religious and cultural differences, they cannot but be only foreigners. . . . There are only two courses open to the foreign elements, either to merge themselves in the national race and adopt its culture, or to live at the sweet will of the national race. . . . The non-Hindu peoples in Hindustan must either adopt the Hindu culture and language, must learn to respect and hold in reverence Hindu religion. . . . in one word, they must cease to be foreigners, or may stay in the country, wholly subordinate to the Hindu nation, claiming nothing, deserving no privileges, far less any preferential treatment—not even citizens rights. . . . In this country, Hindus alone are the Nation and the Muslims and others, if not actually anti-national, are at least outside the body of the Nation.

Although this uncompromising statement of Hindu fundamentalist belief was written almost sixty years ago, it has remained imbedded in the thinking of contemporary members of organizations like the RSS, the Vishwa Hindu Parishad, and the Bajrang Dal. To their minds, the installation of a BJP-led government in Delhi gave a stamp of political legitimacy to this ideology, and the most fanatical and violent among them began to feel that the government would back them if they translated it into action. Fortunately, instances of this had not been widespread during the Golden Jubilee Year, but, following the swearing in of the Vajpayee regime, they had reared their ugly heads in several places in north and central India in the form of attacks on Christian churches and church workers located in areas where conversions were taking place. The perpetrators of these acts of violence had characterized the victims as "missionaries" in order to gain support from the antiforeign sentiments harbored by Indians of other political persuasions, but the reality was that those who had suffered were Indian Christians. Although BJP officials had condemned the anti-minority violence, some leaders of Hindu fundamentalist groups had defended those involved on the ground that they were seeking vengeance for decades of Christian domination of their Hindu homeland.

Second in political importance to the emergence of a Hindu fundamentalist-led coalition Central Government had been the movement that had taken place during and after the 1998 election campaign toward a two-party system. The political events of the first three months of 1998 had destroyed the United Front as a third force in Indian politics. Although the Congress Indira Party had not emerged from the 1998 contest stronger in terms of parliamentary seats, it had survived as a significant political force. It now had a clearly defined leader who had saved the party from what, without her, would have been a disastrous campaign and who was seen as its prime ministerial hope for the future: Sonia Gandhi. Two days after the final polling had been completed, Sitaram Kesri had announced his intention to resign as party president, declaring, "I have said a number of times that the post of Congress president should be graced by Sonia Gandhi." That his decision had been the result of the demeaning treatment that had been meted out to him during and after the election campaign had been made plain by some other words that he had spoken at the time he had offered to resign. When asked why he had taken this radical step, he had responded in a bitter tone, "Have you not seen how things took shape during the last two months? No man with self-respect could tolerate this."

The Congress Working Committee had thereupon passed a resolution appointing Sonia Gandhi as the party president to replace Sitaram Kesri, who, according to the committee, "had resigned." Despite Kesri's objecting to their action on the ground that his resignation would become effective only after it had been submitted to and accepted by the All India Congress Committee and despite the fact that, as a primary party member, Sonia Gandhi was not eligible under party rules to become its president, she had accepted the appointment. She had given as her reason for doing so her perception that the nation was passing through critical times in which its democratic and secular fabric was being tested. As she assumed the party presidentship, she had called upon party workers to work together to make the Congress Indira Party a powerful tool in the nation's service. "All our people need the benefit of economic growth and prosperity and India must move forward toward a place of primacy and honor in the comity of nations."

Although Kesri had reacted to her acceptance by maintaining that he was still the party's president, his only concern had been to leave the post "in a dignified manner." The Congress Working Committee had agreed to assuage his hurt feelings by arranging for a meeting of the All India Congress Committee that would be held in early April to accept his resignation. This concession obviously had mollified him because he had responded in a cooperative mood by moving that Sonia Gandhi also be elected chairman of the Congress Parliamentary Party even though she was not a member of either the Lok Sabha or the Rajya Sabha (Upper House). His motion had been declared to be in order and had been passed, but only after the Parliamentary Party's constitution had been hurriedly amended to allow a person who was not a member of either house of Parliament to hold the chairman's post. In assuming both the Congress Indira Party presidentship and the chairmanship of the Parliamentary Party, Sonia Gandhi had become the party's unchallenged leader, much as her mother-in-law, Indira Gandhi, had become the unchallenged leader of the Congress Party, which she called the Ruling Congress Party, in 1969 and of the Congress Indira Party in 1980. The status of a party member had been changed in the process from that of a building block in a political organization to that of a "sheep led by a shepherd," just as it had been changed by Indira Gandhi twenty-nine and eighteen years earlier. At both the top and the bottom levels of the Congress Indira Party, the opening months of the Golden Jubilee Year had seen a reversion to the party's earlier history of personal rule by a member of the Nehru family.

The request made to Sonia Gandhi to become Congress Indira Party president and chairman of the Parliamentary Party Committee was based on her status as the surviving member of the Nehru family, not upon any political qualifications that she shared with her late mother-in-law. It was the product of the party's desperate need to find someone to fill its leadership vacuum, a desperate need reflected in the way that a party rule was set aside and a committee's constitution hurriedly amended to make way for Sonia Gandhi to take charge. It reflected the party's desperation, not only in the understanding that its regular leadership cadre did not include anyone who could rise above Sitaram Kesri's level of incompetence, but also in the understanding that the results of the election had showed that the attributes that qualified Sonia Gandhi in the eyes of the party's leaders for the party's top positions were not going to produce sweeping political gains for the party among the populace.

The first and foremost of these attributes was her membership by marriage in the Nehru dynasty. Voters' responses during the 1998 election, however, had revealed that they were not interested in what the Nehrus had done for them in the past but in what the Congress Indira Party would do for them in the future. The political truth that the Nehru dynasty no longer commanded the allegiance of the Indian people had been reflected not only in the overall results but also in what had happened in two particular constituencies. Despite Indira Gandhi's and both her sons' having been elected to Parliament from Amethi in Uttar Pradesh and that constituency's having been regarded for years as a "safe seat" for a Congress Indira Party candidate, the party's latest candidate had been defeated. Standing as an independent, Maneka Gandhi, Sanjay Gandhi's widow, had won a parliamentary seat in another constituency even though she had been on the Nehru dynasty's blacklist since 1980 when Indira Gandhi had ordered Maneka and her children out of the prime minister's residence immediately after her husband's death in an airplane accident.

The second attribute was the success that Sonia Gandhi had achieved as a campaigner who could attract huge crowds to party rallies. Her "exotic" characteristics as a Roman Catholic Italian woman who had become an Indian citizen in 1984 and had only recently left political seclusion had proved during the campaign to be assets rather than liabilities. But functioning as an effective leader of the Congress Indira Party at both the organizational and the parliamentary levels was "a horse of a different political color." In playing this new political role, the peripheral position that she occupied in Indian society because of her lack of a regional, linguistic, and caste identity and her limited experience in Indian politics would be liabilities. While she had caught the fancy of the crowds when she was a mysterious foreigner who descended from the skies in a helicopter—an Italian woman, dressed in a sari, speaking rudimentary Hindi with an Italian lilt, whisked away after a short stay on the ground—her "mystique" would begin to be lost when she came to earth on the dusty floor of the political arena and became engaged in the hurly-burly of everyday political strife with BJP leaders like A. B. Vajpayee and L. K. Advani.

As a reminder that Sonia Gandhi's standing in the political world was subject to serious challenge on moral grounds, the Bofors guns scandal, which she had succeeded in keeping in abeyance during the election campaign, had reared its head within a month of the BJP-led government's taking office. Although the news that her Italian friends, Mr. and Mrs. Ottavio Quattrocchi, were among the recipients of funds paid by Bofors, the Swedish company that had sold India 400 artillery pieces, to "agents" who had helped to persuade the Indian government to buy their guns had been revealed almost a year earlier, the Gujral government, fearful that embarrassing the Congress Indira Party would lead to withdrawal of its support from outside the government coalition and the government's fall, had refused to reveal any additional information until the Central Bureau of Investigation's inquiry had been completed. The BJP-led government had not been shy about adding new chapters to the Bofors story, and, within a fortnight of Sonia's Gandhi's election as Congress Indira Party president, those chapters had begun to make a public appearance. In a legal proceeding involving Ottavio Quattrocchi's attempt to persuade the Delhi High Court to quash a warrant for his arrest, the Central Bureau of Investigation (CBI) had filed an affidavit that, for the first time, laid out his dealings with Bofors in some detail and explained how he, along with his wife, had managed to receive a substantial payoff when the gun deal was closed.

According to the CBI affidavit, the Indian army had begun as early as 1984 the process of deciding which of the world's arms manufacturers should be the supplier of 400 artillery pieces that would cost approximately $1.4 billion. Negotiations continued off and on for several months, and a French company emerged as the front runner. In November 1985, with Quattrocchi acting as the middleman, Bofors took steps to improve its competitive position by entering into an agreement with a firm called A.E. Services. The agreement provided that, if Bofors received the contract for supplying the guns by March 31, 1986, A.E. Services would receive a percentage of the price paid by the Indian government. In and of itself, the conclusion of this agreement was a violation of the rules laid down by the Indian government for the gun procurement program, which provided that no third party commissions should be paid by the company that received the contract. On March 15, 1986, during a visit with the Swedish prime minister, Prime Minister and Defense Minister Rajiv Gandhi announced that India would purchase from Bofors all of the 155 millimeter howitzers that its army needed. A few days prior to his departure from Delhi, a hectic bureaucratic race had been run to finalize the "letter of intent" covering the purchase, during which the signatures of eleven high-ranking officials serving in several different ministries had been obtained within forty-eight hours. The contract between the Indian government and Bofors was not actually signed until nine days after the public announcement.

Having met the deadline stipulated in the agreement, Bofors paid a commission of $7,340,000 to A.E. Services three months after receiving the first installment of the $1.4 billion due from the Indian government. A short time later, $7,120,000 of this amount was transferred by A.E. Services to Colbar Investments Ltd., a front company set up by the Quattrocchis, who, in turn, immediately withdrew the $7,120,000 from Colbar Investments and deposited the money in a Swiss bank account, giving a fictitious New Delhi address as their residence. When the Swiss bank later revealed that the Quattrocchis' account had been one of these that had received Bofors money, the Quattrocchis moved their funds to a bank in the Channel Islands and thereafter to banks in Geneva and Vienna. As early as July

1993, the Swiss police had informed the CBI that the Quattrocchis were among the bank depositors who had taken legal action to prevent their names being revealed to the Indian government as recipients of Bofors money. Tipped off by an official of the Narasimha Rao Congress Indira Party government that ruled in Delhi at the time and fearful that they would be detained and questioned, they had fled India for Malaysia less than a week after the Swiss information had been received. Since the Malaysian government had continued to refuse to extradite them, the Quattrocchis had remained beyond the reach of the Indian authorities even after the most recent CBI information had become public knowledge.

The bottom line of the CBI's April 1998 affidavit was its conclusion that "only because of his [Quattrocchi's] close proximity to the then Prime Minister and his family and the perception generally of bureaucrats and Ministers that he was in a position of vast influence [was he able] to determine the fate of a contract of this nature going into millions of dollars." The CBI's investigation had revealed that, although no evidence had surfaced to contradict Rajiv Gandhi's statement to Parliament that neither he nor any member of his family had received any part of the Bofors payoff, their close friends, the Quattrocchis, had benefited handsomely by virtue of their close friendship with the Gandhis. Given these revelations, it would be difficult for the member of Rajiv Gandhi's family who had become the new Congress Indira Party president to maintain for very long the position of total innocence that she had taken during the 1998 election campaign.

Apart from her ability to weather the Bofors guns scandal, Sonia Gandhi's success or failure in her new and politically more significant role as the head of the Congress Indira Party would depend upon the political skill and wisdom she displayed in meeting its demands. These demands would be heavy because of the state of her party. The Congress Indira Party had come out of the 1998 election in a shambles. Its plight had been covered up by the spectacular glitz of Sonia Gandhi's campaign, which had been financed, not by the party treasury or by contributions from its members, but by contributions from leading Indian businessmen who wanted to have access to the new "queen" of Indian politics if she came to power. A great deal of money had been spent on expensive transportation and communication equipment and on campaign decorations and publicity but virtually nothing on activities and resources   that would have strengthened the party organization. Rather than running a campaign that built upon the party's institutional framework, the Sonia Gandhi faction had taken over the campaign and conducted it in a way that had run roughshod over the party president, an "organization" man whose skill lay in managing its "nuts and bolts." The message of the campaign strategy was that the party's fate depended, not upon its members and its organization, but upon its "star" performer who was a member of the Nehru dynasty.

The "blitzkrieg"methods that had put Sonia Gandhi in power had reiterated the message that only the party's new leader mattered and that its personnel and structures were to be subjected to whatever manipulation was necessary to clear the way for her to take over. Pushing the party's institutional well-being even lower on its list of priorities was the fact that this particular leader was the surviving remnant of a family dynasty that had headed the party for almost forty of its last fifty years. Instead of envisaging a future that focused upon revitalizing the party as a political organization, the party's leaders had seen the restoration of the Nehru dynasty as the way to reverse the decline. Even though India's voters had said through the results of the 1998 General Election that the Nehru dynasty no longer dominated their political lives, the Congress Indira Party had refused to shake off its grip.

If Sonia Gandhi had emerged from the 1998 election as the clearly identified leader of the Congress Indira Party, A. B. Vajpayee had done the same for the BJP. During the run-up to the election and during the campaign itself, Vajpayee's leadership role had been shared with L. K. Advani, who had acted as Hindu fundamentalism's hardliner while Vajpayee had donned the party's moderate "mask." From the campaign's outset, Vajpayee had been designated as the BJP's candidate for prime minister. He would take the high road by ignoring Sonia Gandhi, while Advani would take the low road by counterattacking when she attacked the BJP's "star." When he became the prime minister heading a BJP-led coalition government, Vajpayee had completed his ascent to the preeminent position within his party's ranks. While Advani continued to hold second place by assuming the home minister's post in Vajpayee's cabinet, the two voices that formerly spoke authoritatively for the BJP became one voice—that of the new prime minister.

Thanks to Sonia Gandhi, the Congress Indira Party had emerged from the 1998 election no worse off than before it had entered the fray, but it had been in no position to undertake an early initiative to form a new coalition Central Government. Its only viable option had been to play the leading role in opposition to the BJP-led government. With the BJP playing the role of the governing party and the Congress Indira Party playing the role of its principal opposition, Indian politics had begun to take the shape of the two-party system which has been regarded as a necessary ingredient of a healthy democracy. Although a large number of smaller regionally based parties were still on the political scene, the BJP and the Congress Indira Party had emerged from the 1998 election as the only parties that had won as much as 25% of the popular vote and had placed more than 140 of their candidates in the Lok Sabha. These votes had been secured and these electoral victories had been won in almost all parts of the country, and at the head of each of the two major parties stood a nationally known and recognized leader. In both these ways, the political picture that had developed during the Golden Jubilee Year looked more like the British and American version than had been the case during the years when the Congress Party had been dominant in a one-party system or when United Front coalitions had come to power only to disappear within two years.

At the same time that two major national parties had emerged to face each other, the political system as a whole had experienced further fragmentation. The United Front had splintered into a mélange of separate parties. The Rashtriya

Janata Dal, the Biju Janata Dal, and the Lok Sakthi had broken away from the Janata Dal, and a second Telegu Dasem Party had emerged in Andhra Pradesh. In West Bengal, the Trinamool Congress had abandoned the Congress Indira Party. The 1998 election had produced MPs representing thirty-eight different parties, the highest number that had found their way into the Lok Sabha since Independence. While the political system had been consolidating at the top, it had been fracturing at the bottom.

Such was the situation that had prevailed on the surface of Indian politics in April as the Vajpayee government had begun its tenure in Delhi. But under that turbulent but not unprecedented spate of relatively ordinary political activity, the makings of a radical political change were being assembled in the form of the preparations to conduct the Pokhran nuclear tests. When Prime Minister Vajpayee announced that the first round of those tests had been completed and that India had "gone nuclear," India's political landscape had taken on a new look almost overnight.. The fragile BJP-led coalition government's potential for survival had been strengthened despite the slim majority that it enjoyed in the Lok Sabha and the continuing difficulty it faced in retaining the support of its coalition partners.

That the conducting of the nuclear bomb tests had increased the Vajpayee government's popular support was evidenced by the country's reaction to the performance of the BJP-led coalition government during its first 100 days in office. Except for creating a mechanism for handling the Cauvery waters dispute and submitting an unrealistic 1998–99 budget that took little or no account of the fiscal consequences of embarking on a nuclear weapons program, the Vajpayee regime had accomplished little or nothing on the domestic front. Despite the fact that it had concentrated its attention on the defense and foreign policy fronts and had failed to address mounting economic, social, and environmental problems, the coalition government and its prime minister had won the support of the majority of the Indian people.

Proof of that support surfaced in a post-100 day poll conducted by the news magazine *India Today* in Mumbai, Chennai, Delhi, Calcutta, Bangalore, and Hyderabad. Fifty-two percent of those polled responded that the Vajpayee regime had compiled a "good" record, 29% called it "neither good nor bad," and only 17% characterized it as "bad." Seventy-six percent supported its decision to embark on the nuclear weapons road, while 21% expressed their opposition. When asked which of India's political leaders would make the best prime minister, 59% named A. B. Vajpayee and only 13% Sonia Gandhi. These numbers contrasted sharply with the responses to the same question that had been elicited at the close of the 1998 General Election campaign. At that time, only 22% of the respondents had opted for Vajpayee against 14% for Sonia Gandhi.

The 52 % of the *India Today* poll respondents who characterized the Vajpayee government's performance during its first 100 days as "good" and the 76% who supported its decision to enter a nuclear arms race reflected a general feeling among the Indian populace that the government had made the right decision when it turned its immediate attention to national security concerns rather than to concerns emanating from the home front. These respondents were saying that they agreed with the BJP-led government's position that dealing with the foreign security threat should take precedence over dealing with the domestic security threat. This reaction on the part of the Indian public was not one that could have been taken for granted because there had been no imminent foreign threat from Pakistan or China staring India's citizenry in the face at the time that the Vajpayee regime had taken over, whereas there had been a serious security threat on the domestic front that had been glaringly apparent for several years to Indians living both in cities and in the countryside. That was the threat posed by the breakdown in law and order that had taken place nationwide, but especially in India's urban centers.

Although the problem was concentrated in major cities, violence and lawlessness had become common throughout the country by the time that the Vajpayee government assumed office. In July 1998, the Parliamentary Standing Committee on Home Affairs presented its annual report. The report characterized the nationwide internal security picture as "dismal." Of the 535 districts that made up the country, 210 were plagued by some sort of security crisis. In the Northeast Region, 48 of the 49 districts were experiencing insurgencies and ethnic violence. Ten of Kashmir's districts suffered from gunfire, armed attacks, and terrorist raids, and 23 of Assam's districts were affected by religious conflicts, tribal clashes, or antigovernment uprisings. In Uttar Pradesh, internal security problems arose from communal clashes and in Bihar from communal wars and widespread criminal activity. Disruption of law and order in Tamil Nadu came from the clandestine activities of members of Muslim fundamentalist organizations and from intercaste rioting.

The serious threat to public safety posed by the countrywide violence and lawlessness that was reported by the Parliamentary Committee was not a problem that had developed overnight. It had been a subject of debate during the 1998 General Election. The BJP had taken the position that this problem, along with India's other domestic problems, would be dealt with in a decisive way by the strong and stable government that it would put in place under Prime Minister Vajpayee. When the BJP had emerged as the party that would lead the new coalition government, it had been expected that one of its initial major efforts would be to apply a firm hand to bring about a major improvement in the country's badly deteriorated law and order situation. This expectation had been reinforced when the hard line politician L. K. Advani had been appointed as home minister. Instead of living up to the expectation, Vajpayee's government had begun its tenure by turning a blind eye to the domestic front and focusing its attention on what it portrayed as the dire threat to India's national security posed by China and Pakistan.

Despite his government's failure to come to grips with the increasing level of crime and violence to which the Indian people were subjected, Vajpayee had convinced them within the first 100 days of his government's taking office that he was a strong prime minister who had what it took, not only to lead a coalition government and keep its constituent parties together, but to mobilize the support of the Indian people behind its defense and foreign policies. His personal standing, combined with the weakness of his political opponents, gave his government the potential to extend its tenure beyond the few months that had been the lifespan of both of its immediate predecessors. Even though India would still be under a fragile coalition regime, it appeared in August 1998 that the two year era of short-lived, do-nothing Central Governments had come to an end and that the country would approach the 21st century with a government strong enough to carry out at least a part of the platform on which it had campaigned. The question that had to be answered was no longer the one that the Vajpayee government had faced when it took office—Would it last long enough to accomplish any-thing?—but the question which it faced after it had conducted the nuclear bomb tests—In what direction had the Vajpayee regime led the Indian people when its major accomplishment during its first 100 days in office had been to embark upon a nuclear weapons program?

Any attempt to frame an answer to that question has to sketch three possible national security scenarios, each of which could conceivably emerge from the Vajpayee government's decision to embark upon a nuclear arms race with Pakistan but each of which had a different degree of likelihood of becoming a reality. Sketching these possible scenarios has to be prefaced by laying out some political "givens" that would be a part of each one of them. The first of these "givens" is that India would proceed to implement a nuclear weaponization program. Although it was by no means clear just how extensive that program would be, Defense Minister Fernandes had stated that, having conducted successful nuclear bomb tests, it would not make sense for the government to refrain from building nuclear weapons and the missiles to deliver them. Prime Minister Vajpayee's principal political advisor had announced to the nation that "all defense-related programs including development of long range missiles will continue" and that the nuclear tests had been undertaken to "provide assurance to the Indian people that their national security interests are paramount and protected."

India adopted a defiant tone in responding to the joint Chinese-American declaration made during President Clinton's July 1998 visit to Beijing. When the leaders of the world's two superpowers called upon India to refrain from building nuclear weapons, to sign the NPT and CTBT, and come to an understanding with Pakistan over Kashmir, their requests were categorically rejected by India's External Affairs Ministry on the grounds that they were assuming a responsibility for maintaining peace and stability in South Asia which was not theirs and that their statement reflected "the hegemonistic morality of a bygone age in interna-tional relations that was completely unacceptable and out of place in the present day world." A fortnight later, Prime Minister Vajpayee reiterated India's rejection of the Chinese-American diplomatic initiative, which he characterized as "highly objectionable and unwarranted." In his first statement to members of the Lok Sabha regarding ongoing post-Pokhran discussions with the United States, he went on to declare that India would not allow outside parties to place any limitations on its program to develop a nuclear weapons capability, describing the steps that it would take as "sovereign functions, not subjects for negotiation." Any discussions with leaders of foreign countries would go forward on "the fundamental premise" that "India will define its own requirements for its nuclear deterrent on its own assessment of the security environment."

According to the prime minister, those requirements were the deployment of "a deterrent which is both minimum and credible," the development of ballistic missiles, and the production of more bomb grade uranium. Dominated as the government was with determination that India should take its rightful place among the world's nuclear powers and that it would not bend to pressure from other countries to refrain from entering into a nuclear arms race with Pakistan, it was almost certain as the Golden Jubilee Year came to an end that the Vajpayee government would neither sign the Non Proliferation Treaty and the Comprehensive Test Ban Treaty nor take the lead in developing a national consensus that India should sign them.

Adding to the danger posed by India's and Pakistan's embarking on nuclear weapons programs was the certainty that India would refuse to make territorial concessions to Pakistan in order to reach a settlement of the long-standing Kashmir dispute. The demarcation of the Line of Control (LOC) separating the Pakistani- and the Indian-held territories had been incorporated in the 1972 Simla Agreement that had tied up the loose ends left by the Bangaladesh war. That LOC was virtually the same as the cease-fire line that had marked the relative positions of the armed forces when the initial fighting had ended in 1949. Both sides had pledged themselves at Simla to honor the LOC and to refrain from using military force to change it. This "interim" arrangement was worked out on the understanding that it was without prejudice to the terms of a final settlement of the Kashmir dispute that would be reached through negotiations between the two belligerents without the intervention of any third party. Almost a quarter century later, Simla's "interim" arrangement had hardened into a stand-off in which both India and Pakistan steadfastly refused to recognize the other's claim to a single bit of the territory that it had held for almost fifty years. Both the Congress Party and United Front governments that had preceded the Vajpayee regime had taken similarly intransigent stands on the Kashmir issue as well as the CTBT issue, and any move by the BJP-led government to reverse this long and strongly held position under pressure from the United States, China, and the world's industrialized countries would lead to its repudiation by both the Indian people and the political parties that represented them.

Taking these political "givens" into account, three possible national security scenarios for the coming years can be envisaged, all of them with outcomes that would be bad for India and its people. The first would be the least damaging and is the most probable, and it would run as follows: According to this minimum damage scenario, the Indian government would maintain a defensive stance in carrying out its internal and external actions even though it was engaged in developing its nuclear weapons capability. Substantial central government resources would be diverted into building nuclear weapons, developing long-range delivery missiles, and setting up a command and control system to manage their disposition. Economic sanctions and reduced foreign investment would cause a reduction in the GNP's growth rate, and India's standard of living would suffer. The poor would be the major sufferers because, with the slowdown in economic development and the diversion of public sector resources to the nuclear weaponization program, fewer new jobs would be created and fewer rupees would be available to fund programs designed to meet the needs of those living at the bottom of the socioeconomic ladder. If the degree of economic deprivation reached the point where political and social unrest developed, the government would be forced to revert to authoritarian means to maintain law and order. Here again, it would be the poor who would bear the brunt of a law and order crackdown because they would be the main driving force behind this antigovernment agitation.

The level of military conflict in Kashmir would be maintained at its present level of sporadic firing of conventional weapons across the LOC and sorties by raiders into Indian-held territory in order to attack Indian security forces and members of the Hindu minority living there. A policy of restraint in the face of these provocations would be continued even though they had produced over 9,000 fatalities within Kashmir since 1995. India would not respond by instituting a "forward policy" against Pakistani troops, similar to the one implemented in 1962 against Chinese forces in Ladakh and in the North East Frontier Agency, in order to suppress shelling and small arms fire from the Pakistani side or undertake "hot pursuit" of raiders operating out of Pakistani-held territory. Participation in a nuclear arms race with Pakistan would increase the level of suspicion and animosity directed toward the country which India regarded as a growing threat to its security, and the domestic result would be an escalation of anti-Muslim feeling on the part of the Hindu majority. Given this growing anti-Muslim sentiment among the populace, the Indian government would not take action to stem the resulting increase in communal tension but would act decisively to counter violent actions taken by India's Muslims to defend themselves against a heightened level of interreligious conflict.

A second possible national security scenario takes on a configuration that is worse than the first but is less likely to become a reality. According to this scenario, the Indian government would use its developing nuclear weapons potential to back an aggressive policy vis à vis Pakistan. India's forces in Kashmir would adopt a "hot pursuit" policy in which they would follow Pakistani raiders into Pakistani-held territory and a "forward policy" directed toward the Pakistani troops facing the Indian army along the 450 mile LOC. The aim of the latter would be to push the Pakistanis back far enough to prevent their firing small arms and artillery into Indian-held territory. Shifting from a defensive to an aggressive posture in Kashmir would lead to heightened military conflict with Pakistan, but only conventional weapons would be used and fighting would be confined to Kashmir.

This escalation in the level of military operations against Pakistani forces in Kashmir could not fail to have internal economic and political repercussions. More government funds would have to be spent to cover its cost, and, consequently, less would be available for dealing with economic, social, and environmental problems. On the political front, the Indian government would institute a crackdown on Muslims in order to prevent their playing the role of a "fifth column" that would work to aid Pakistan. Since upwards of 120 million Muslims would have to be kept under control, such a step would produce widespread political and social turmoil, especially in states like Uttar Pradesh, West Bengal, Kerala, and Andhra Pradesh which have large Muslim populations.

India's playing out the third possible national security scenario would result in the greatest damage to India and its people but it is the least likely to become a reality. Reacting to the casualties resulting from intensified fighting in the area of the LOC and spurred on by its desire to realize its goal of bringing all of Kashmir within India's domain, the Indian government would launch a campaign to drive Pakistani forces from the whole of Kashmir. Pakistan, on its part, would launch a full-scale attack against the Indian forces, not only to prevent Kashmir from being overrun, but to show its solidarity with fellow Muslims who were being repressed within India. It would turn to radical Muslim states like Afghanistan and Iran for support, but their response would be limited and slow to come. Since India's conventional armed forces would be far stronger than Pakistan's and could be mobilized in short order, Pakistan would be faced very soon with the prospect of a fourth military defeat in its continuing struggle with India and one that would lead to a loss of land which it has claimed as part of its national territory since British India was partitioned in 1947. In order to avert such a disaster, Pakistan would resort to using the battlefield nuclear weapons which it had at its disposal as a means of offsetting India's superiority in conventional weapons. That Pakistan would be prepared to initiate a nuclear war with India if such a dire situation were to arise was made clear in a statement made by its foreign minister shortly after Pakistan had conducted its own nuclear tests: "One hopes that it never goes nuclear but Pakistan will not lose a war, and we will not give ground."

Pakistan's use of battlefield nuclear weapons to defend Kashmir would lead to India's introducing battlefield nuclear weapons of its own, and what began with conventional fighting over Kashmir would become an all-out war between the two countries in which nuclear weapons were used. At this point India and Pakistan would be faced with a monumental choice. In order to avoid inflicting terrible damage upon each other by escalating from battlefield to strategic nuclear weapons, they could arrange a truce and work out some territorial settlement involving Pakistan and Kashmir that would be acceptable to both sides. Or they could opt to proceed to the ultimate level of destruction by attacking each other's cities with strategic nuclear weapons, thus destroying millions of their citizens, large areas of their lands, and all of their economies. If fighting did reach the stage where both countries considered using strategic nuclear weapons, Pakistan would be more likely than India to initiate the nuclear exchange. Pakistan's urban centers and much of its population lie relatively close to India's borders. A large-scale invasion of Pakistan by India's superior conventional forces would place the bulk of Pakistan's citizenry and most of its cities in jeopardy very soon after hostilities began. Faced with such a crisis, Pakistan's leaders could very well come to the conclusion that the only way to head off total defeat and unconditional surrender would be to deliver a blow to India's cities that would be so devastating that it would cause India to pull back from overrunning Pakistani territory. If Pakistan were to launch such a "first strike," India would respond in kind and "mutually assured destruction" would follow. That Pakistan's leaders recognize that Pakistan would have a greater need than India to launch a "first strike" was evidenced by their refusal to sign the "no first strike" agreement that India had proposed.

This Armageddon-like scenario is least likely of the three to become a reality, but it cannot be ruled out. A former member of the United States Arms Control and Disarmament Agency has described the possibility that Pakistan and India might come to nuclear blows as "the most dangerous since the beginning of the nuclear age," except for the Cuban missile crisis. Ved Mehta, one of the best informed and most astute observers of the Indian scene, has characterized the Indian nuclear tests as probably the most dangerous events in the subcontinent since Independence in 1947. He points out that "India's real enemy has always been Pakistan and vice versa" because the underlying conflict between India and Pakistan is rooted in religion rather than ideology and territory. For that reason, the danger that it could lead to nuclear war is greater than in the case where the United States and the Soviet Union faced each other with nuclear weapons but did not put them to use. In Mehta's words, "Religious passions, once inflamed, are uncontrollable and the capitals of India and Pakistan are only a few minutes away from contact by missiles."

Given the slow pace of social change, little was noticeable when one looked for the significant developments that had taken place in India during the Golden Jubilee Year. While the shape of its technological and other surface trappings was different on August 15, 1998, from what it had been on August 15, 1997, the underlying social strata were substantially the same as they had been a year earlier. A Dalit had been chosen as the speaker when the 12th Lok Sabha had met in April but, since he had replaced a speaker who was a member of a "Scheduled Tribe," his election did not constitute a significant breakthrough in the direction of raising the political status of the untouchable order in Indian society. So far as its sociopolitical significance was concerned, it was a repetition of the Indian political parties' policy of providing token rather than meaningful recognition to India's dispossessed, the policy that had led to the July 1977 installation of K. R. Narayanan as India's first Dalit president. Political, economic, regional, religious, and caste conflicts had continued much as they had done during the previous years, but in different places and under different circumstances.

So far as rank and file Dalits were concerned, any attempt by Delhi to cut back on their "affirmative action" benefits would have caused agitations and demonstrations in those parts of the country where "Scheduled Castes and Tribes" were concentrated, especially when they now had a political voice in the Bahujan Samaj and Samajwadi Parties and were led by Dalit activists like Uttar Pradesh's Mayawati and supported by "Other Backward Classes" leaders like Laloo Prasad Yadav and Mulayam Yadav Singh. For very good political reasons, the BJP-led government did nothing to restrict the scope of this aspect of governmental social policy. When Prime Minister Vajpayee was questioned as to how his government would deal with the expiration in the year 2000 of the fifty year time limit imposed by the Supreme Court on the validity of the constitutional provision granting "reserved" legislative seats for candidates who were members of "Scheduled Castes and Tribes," he replied that his government supported a continuation of this provision. The vice-president of the BJP followed up his statement by specifying that its continuation would be for a period of ten years.

The BJP-led government reiterated its commitment to resuscitate the United Front's proposal to "reserve" 33% of all legislative seats for women candidates. But Prime Minister Vajpayee did not use the full weight of his heightened political standing to make this proposal a reality. When Prime Minister Gujral had introduced a "women's reservation" bill in the 11th Lok Sabha, he had been shouted down by MPs belonging to his own Janata Dal party, and the uproar that had followed had showcased the highly controversial nature of any steps that might be taken to implement this kind of "affirmative action" for women. The bill was introduced again in July 1998 by the Vajpayee government, but the unruly scenes that it sparked showed that the "women's reservation" proposal was as controversial as ever. MPs representing the RJD and Samajwadi parties, which had taken a firm stand from the days of the Gujral government that the bill must be amended to include a special quota for women candidates who were either Muslims or members of "Other Backward Classes," once again shouted their opposition. This time two of them went so far as to snatch the copy of the bill held by the law minister and the order sheet held by the speaker, to tear both documents to shreds, and to throw the pieces into the air. Faced with a storm of opposition that took physical as well as verbal form, the speaker had no recourse but to adjourn the Lok Sabha until the next day.

When the next day dawned, it became clear that a large question mark had been placed over the ultimate fate of the bill. Although the prime minister's words set forth the BJP's official position that the government which it led would support passage of the bill, ample evidence had come forth by this time that the Vajpayee government was not going to spend a great deal of political capital to make "women's reservation" a feature of India's future legislatures. The day after the bill had been snatched from the law minister's hands and torn to shreds, the prime minister admitted to newsmen that it might be "difficult" to bring the bill up again during Parliament's current session. He later expanded upon this remark by saying that his government would not be able to bring the bill up again until the various political parties had reached a consensus on the form that the bill should take. Knowing full well that it would be a long time, if ever, before such a consensus would develop, these words were tantamount to saying that, while the BJP-led regime's "official" position on the "women's reservation" issue would be one of support, its "unofficial" position would be to refrain from taking any legislative action that would resurrect the bitter controversy that had produced ugly scenes in the Lok Sabha Sabha both times that the bill had been introduced.

The "mother"of India's domestic problems—an exploding population—cannot be ignored when looking for noteworthy happenings that had taken place during the Golden Jubilee Year. To no one's surprise, population increased throughout the year in more or less unabated fashion. Maintaining the prevailing annual rate of increase (1.9%) and starting with a population exceeding 960 million, some 16 to 18 million people were added to the population by year's end, bringing the total that much closer to the 1 billion mark. One of the many critical areas of public policy in which neither of the United Front governments had done anything effective was family planning. Their inaction in this vital area of domestic concern was a continuation of the "do nothing" approach that had been pursued by successive governments since Sanjay Gandhi had given family planning a bad name by implementing a draconian crash program during his mother's 1975–77 Emergency. The Narasimha Rao government had made a token gesture in the direction of addressing the problem by setting up a commission to draft a national population policy. By May 1994, that commission had produced a draft report, but it was never adopted by Parliament. The Gujral cabinet had approved a subsequent draft report in November 1997, but it could not immediately be placed before Parliament because the Lok Sabha was in recess. Before it could be taken up for a vote, the Lok Sabha had been prorogued and a general election had been ordered.

The Vajpayee government had not done any better in taking decisive action to address the population problem. Despite the National Agenda's statement that "a suitable and judicious mixture of incentives and disincentives for population control shall be presented early so that national commitment on this issue is obtained," the health minister had to confess on July 9 that a new draft of a national population policy had not yet been finalized. Before it could be completed and presented to Parliament, the draft would have to be reviewed by demographic experts, and an unspecified amount of time would be required to carry out the review process. In the face of almost total inaction on the part of the Vajpayee government, any progress that was made in reducing the number of births during the Golden Jubilee Year had been a by-product of the attainment of higher levels of literacy and family income rather than a product of an effective government-sponsored family planning program. Unfortunately, the positive impac of socio-economic improvements on the population situation was limited to the southern states. In the north, where many more Indians lived, continuing illiteracy and poverty caused the birth rate to remain as high as ever.

The same "little or no progress" report has to be made with respect to coming to grips with the increasing deterioration of India's natural environment. Except for a token effort to put pressure on a limited number of factories to cease discharging their untreated industrial effluents directly into adjacent streams, the pollution of India's air and water continued unabated, its untreated solid waste continued to pile up, and its trees continued to be cut down without respite. This failure to slow down the rate of environmental deterioration and to make good some of the damage that has already been done brought the Indian people, especially the almost one-third who lived in cities, that much closer to the time when they would be facing an environment that was barely tolerable for human habitation.

A survey of the broad expanse of the Indian landscape during the year following the 50th Anniversary of its Independence revealed conflicting evidence regarding whether or not the political, economic, social, demographic, and environmental developments that had taken place had moved the country closer to achieving the goals set by the Golden Jubilee's Implementation Committee—rekindling the spirit of patriotism and promoting cultural harmony, national integration, and social justice. One of the areas of national life where movement in a positive direction had occurred was the political arena, although even here the democratic bright spots stood out against the gloomy background of a drift toward Hindu fundamentalism. On the political bright side, India had maintained its tradition of democratic government. Civilians, not military men, had headed state and local governments. Free and fair elections had been held, and voters had been able to cast their ballots as they saw fit. New parties had been organized, and all parties had operated free of governmental restraint. The lower orders of Indian society had made their voices heard, and their votes had been sought after as never before. Newspaper reporters and editors had written what they wanted to write about politicians and their policies without fear of censorship or arrest. The Indian people had told the world during its Golden Jubilee Year that their country continued to be a democracy, despite the fact that its democratic way of political life faced demographic, environmental, social, and economic problems that were daunting enough to tempt them to give up on popular rule. They had successfully resisted that temptation during a year in which they had carried out another general election and had ushered in another Central Government.

The Vajpayee government's decision to conduct nuclear weapons tests and to follow them with a nuclear weaponization program had "rekindled" a spirit of patriotism, but it was a brand of patriotism different from the one that the members of the Implementation Committee had in mind. They were thinking of the patriotism exemplified by free India's founding fathers—Mahatma Gandhi and Jawaharlal Nehru—self-sacrificing service for the well-being of India and its people. Far from being remembered, honored, and imitated, Nehru and Gandhi had been forgotten in the former case and denigrated in the latter. The secular state which Nehru had championed and for which Gandhi had died had been replaced by a Central Government led by a Hindu fundamentalist party that was dedicated to creating a Hindu India. The significance of secularism had degenerated to the point where it was serving as a cover for the communalism practiced in varying degrees by all political parties. The socialist economic system which Nehru had constructed had come to be blamed for free India's slow economic development during its first three decades, and free market capitalism had replaced it as the guiding light of economic policy. In keeping with this post-Nehru economic model, discussion was under way preparatory to beginning privatization of the state-owned industries which he had created as the backbone for his socialist economic order.

Gandhi's Golden Jubilee Year fate had been even worse. During the fifty years following Independence, Gandhi's moral and political influence had waned to the point where, like Nehru, he no longer mattered to the day to day happenings in the political world. But, in a tragic way, after the BJP had come to the fore following the 1998 General Election, his memory had come back to life for a short period. On July 17, a group of Congress Indira Party supporters in Mumbai went on a rampage to force the closure of a theater in which a play with the title, *This is Nathuram Godse Speaking*, was being performed. They were outraged because the play portrayed Nathuram Godse, Gandhi's assassin, as the patriotic hero and Mahatma Gandhi as the villainous traitor in much the same way that they had been pictured by the RSS ever since the time of Gandhi's death. The Congress Indira Party agitation was called off when, following the recommendation of Home Minister Advani, the Maharashtra government banned further productions of the play. But the fact that a play denigrating Gandhi had been written and staged to the delight of audiences made up of members of the Shiv Sena and other pro-BJP parties testified to the degree to which he had become a target for political attack rather than an object of national veneration.

The final words on the closing of *This is Nathuram Godse Speaking* were said by a group of leading cinema and theater personalities who issued the following public statement:

We would like to express our sense of revulsion at the hooliganism that has greeted the presentation of the Marathi play, "This is Nathuram Godse Speaking," in Mumbai and the advice of the Central Government to the Maharashtrian government to prohibit the staging of the play. Carefully orchestrated disruption of law and order to get a work of art banned or a public event stopped is becoming a regular and dangerous feature of our social life. The Constitution of India guarantees every citizen the freedom of expression, and it is incumbent upon all parties to see that this freedom is ensured. Whatever its critique of Mahatma Gandhi, we all have a right to see the play and decide for ourselves the merits of the playwright's arguments.

While these leading cinema and theater personalities made a valid point when they maintained that the closing of the play in response to a "disruption of law and order" was a blow to freedom of expression, they expressed no regrets that the playwright, by portraying Mahatma Gandhi as a traitor rather than a patriot, had slandered the man who had been honored for fifty years as the father of the Indian nation. Apparently they, like the members of the Shiv Sena, BJP, and RSS who had cheered the play's performances, no longer saw him as a historical figure whose style of patriotism needed to be "rekindled" in the hearts of the Indian people.

The Pokhran tests and their aftermath most certainly had not "rekindled" the founding fathers' brand of patriotism. They had created a new kind of patriotism—aggressive to the point of being jingoistic, boastful that India now had to be counted among the preeminent countries of the world because it had developed nuclear weapons. This post-Pokhran patriotism would not provide the positive results that the Implementation Committee was looking for when it called for a "rekindling of patriotism." Instead of leading to a better life for the Indian people and an India that lived in harmony with its neighbors and the rest of the world, the patriotism that was ignited by India's entry into a nuclear arms race would cause economic loss for those living within India's boundaries and increased conflict with surrounding nations and the international community. The most dangerous point of conflict with a neighboring state would be in Kashmir where an intensification of fighting could act as a flash point that could produce another war with Pakistan. For it must be remembered that the brand of patriotism espoused by the BJP and ignited by India's decision to crash the nuclear club called not only for the return of the one-third of Jammu and Kashmir that had been "seized" by Pakistan but also for the reunification of what in ancient times had been called "Bharat," the land that had included both present-day India and present-day Pakistan.

On the social justice front, the political events of the Golden Jubilee Year had moved India in a positive direction. The 1998 General Election had provided one more important opportunity for the poor to voice their demands for social justice through the parties that represented them in the campaign. Even more important in giving the lower socioeconomic orders a say in the formulation of government policy was the election's outcome—a coalition government in which the dominant high caste party depended for its continuation in office upon the backing of small regional parties, some of which counted numerous Dalits and members of Other Backward Classes among their supporters. But neither the general election campaign nor the emergence of the BJP-led coalition government had brought the extension of India's "affirmative action" program to the fore as an important political issue that merited serious attention.

Wholly negative results had been produced on the economic side of social justice. India's poor, 50% of the population, were not going to enjoy an enhanced degree of social justice unless, in addition to giving them more of a political voice, the Central Government and the state governments took steps to improve their economic status by providing them with additional educational and job opportunities. Additional educational opportunities would come only if more schools and teachers were provided, and if poor students were given the financial support that they needed in order to go to school rather than to work. In order for this to happen to a significant degree, governments would have to spend much more money on their educational programs, but this was not done during the Golden Jubilee Year. Nor was it likely that a Vajpayee government would improve on this record of nonperformance during the remainder of its time in office. Large amounts of governmental resources would have to be used to mount a nuclear arms program and governmental income would not increase at a rate sufficient to compensate for this higher level of defense expenditure. Far from being able to allocate more money to raising the educational standards of India's poor, the BJP-led government would be hard pressed to maintain its existing programs.

Additional job opportunities for the poor would be created only to the extent that the Indian economy grew. During the height of the post-1991 economic reform boom when the annual rate of increase in GNP had reached the 7% level, it had looked as though India was on the way to providing the millions of new jobs needed to provide for its expanding labor force. But by 1998, the GNP's annual rate of increase had fallen to 5%, three percentage points below the level needed to maintain the current rate of employment. It might well be that the downturn in the rate of economic growth would not last for long. But it was certain that, whatever its duration, the poor would bear the major share of the economic hardship it brought.

Commenting on the impact on the poor of the BJP-led government's decision to "go nuclear," the director of the Institute of Social Studies in Delhi had this to say:

To the historical and social factors which hold the poor captive an acute adverse economic factor has been added. The argument is not that without foreign assistance India cannot survive. But rapid economic and social development in the present international context or even the trickle down effect of economic growth cannot be expected in the present economic isolation. . . . With the funds at the disposal of the government, whether even the status quo could be maintained is a big question. In all probability, the situation may deteriorate for the vulnerable sectors. . . . A domestic factor which pushes the social sector to a corner is obviously the escalation of defense expenditures in keeping with the BJP's nuclear calculations. The Prime Minister has said that no price is too high for ensuring national security.   But there can be no national security without building the people's security. And that does not come by adding to the burdens of the poor majority.

The Vajpayee government had made plans for a joint nationwide celebration of the end of the Golden Jubilee Year and the beginning of the fifty-first year of Independence, to take place on August 14 and 15. The August 15 meeting in the Central Hall of Parliament differed from observances during the first decades following Independence. During these earlier observances of the anniversary of Indian Independence, the nation's founding fathers had been identified as a triumvirate made up of Mahatma Gandhi and Jawaharlal Nehru, as the principals, and Sardar Patel as the third but less important member. The 1998 Anniversary celebration also honored a triumvirate of founding fathers. It included Mahatma Gandhi and Jawaharlal Nehru, but the third and most important member was Subhas Chandra Bose. Bose—the nationalist firebrand who, because he had advocated using violence to end British rule in India, had been Gandhi's principal adversary in the Congress Party during the 1930s and, after being expelled from the party in 1939, had gone on to lead the Indian National Army which had fought together with the Japanese in their attempt to drive Mountbatten's forces out of Assam—and who had died in 1945 as he sought political refuge in the face of Japan's impending defeat.

Bose's memory had been relegated to the trash heap of history during the decades immediately following his death, but he took pride of place among the founding fathers who were honored as the Golden Jubilee Year came to a close and the observance of the fifty-first year of Indian Independence got under way. Along with words spoken by Gandhi and Nehru during the heyday of their political ascendancy, the audience gathered in the Central Hall of Parliament heard Bose's 1940 exhortation to Indians to take up arms against the British: "The hour has struck and every patriotic Indian must advance toward the field of battle. Only when the blood of freedom loving Indians begins to flow will Indian attain its freedom." Not only had Bose been added to the triumvirate of founding fathers, but it was he rather than either of the other two who was showcased. A cinematic presentation of the deeds that had made the nation's founding fathers famous followed the president's address. It was made up of clips showing each of them at a high point of their respective contributions to India's freedom struggle and its life as an independent nation. The final clip showed Bose, dressed in his uniform as the commander of the Indian National Army, raising his arm and shouting "Long Live Free India." It was this picture and these words, rather than Gandhi as the champion of nonviolence and Nehru as the builder of a secular India, that roused the audience to the enthusiastic and prolonged round of applause that ended the meeting. It was the image of Bose rather than that of Gandhi and Nehru that they carried in their minds as the members of the audience returned to their homes thinking about the champions of Indian freedom.

Several factors need to be cited in explaining why the combined celebration of the end of the Golden Jubilee Year and the beginning of the fifty-first year of Independence assumed the shape that it did, but the most important was undoubtedly the fact that India in 1998 had crashed the nuclear club. During its Golden Jubilee Year, India had embarked upon a nuclear weapons program and that radical step had made it a nation with a very different self-image and a very different view of how it would deal with other nations. It was no surprise that such a marked change in political orientation would produce a marked change in the way that the end of the Golden Jubilee Year would be publicly observed. What was a surprise was that this change in the mode of celebration had not been accompanied by a marked increase in the degree of celebration that accompanied it. The events in Delhi had been well organized and had received extensive television coverage, but, whereas the conducting of the May 11 and May 13 Pokhran nuclear bomb tests had produced exuberant demonstrations of national pride throughout the country, this exhilaration of national spirit had largely dissipated four months later when the nation reflected upon what had been accomplished during the Golden Jubilee Year. The writer of a *Deccan Herald* article covering the events of August 14–15 encapsulated a rather dismal story with the heading: "Golden Jubilee celebration failed to glitter." The article went on to say that what "began with a whimper, ended with a sigh." Many of India's cities and villages had failed to follow Delhi's example and had made no effort to celebrate. An official of the Central Government's Ministry of Human Resources Development, which had been given the responsibility of orchestrating the national observance, lamented that "enough funds had been granted but not enough enthusiasm had been generated."

As the August 15, 1998, observance came and went, it was impossible to come up with a balanced overall measure of the degree to which the political, cultural, and social goals identified by the 50th Anniversary Implementation Committee had been furthered by what had happened during the preceding twelve months. In addition to the complexity of the components that make up political freedom, patriotism, national integration, cultural harmony, and social justice and the various forms which they take, there is the difficulty of establishing their relative importance for India's national life. A simpler and more feasible way of measuring what the developments that had taken place during the previous twelve months had meant and would mean for India was to focus upon the series of events that overshadowed everything else that had happened—the carrying out of the May 11 and May 13 nuclear bomb tests as a first step in embarking upon a nuclear weaponization program. Those events not only changed the face of India but shortened the appropriate time frame for focusing attention upon India's future. Before the Pokhran tests had taken place, one could confine oneself to a long term view and see that time frame as India's next half century. After the Pokhran nuclear bomb tests had taken place, one was forced to take the short term into account as well and also look at the next decade. While India's long-term future still had to be viewed in half-century terms, it was obvious after India had joined the nuclear club that what happened during the next decade would go a long way toward determining the shape that the country would take fifty years later. It was equally obvious that the most crucial decisions the Indian nation would make during the next decade would be those involving its behavior as a nuclear weapons state.

Indian President K.R. Narayanan stands for the national anthem at a Navy Day function in New Delhi Thursday, December 4, 1997, shortly after Narayanan dissolved parliament. Midterm elections are to be held within the next few months. (AP/Wide World Photos)

Indian Prime Minister Atal Bihari Vajpayee during the National Development Council in New Delhi Friday, February 19, 1999. Vajpayee will inaugurate the first passengers bus service on Saturday between the uneasy neighbors India and Pakistan. The meeting between Vajpayee and Pakistani Prime Minister Nawaz Shariff for peace talks is the first to be held on Pakistan soil in a decade. (AP/Wide World Photos)

Indian Home Minister L.K. Advani addresses an All Political Parties meeting at the parliamentary annex in New Delhi Friday, May 22, 1998. Advani, one of the most powerful members of the Indian government, has warned Pakistan and China not to interfere in Indian affairs. Advani, earlier this week, had harsh words for Pakistan, saying "Islamabad should realize that change in the geo-strategic situation in the region and the world [and] roll back its anti-India policy, especially with regard to Kashmir." Pakistan in turn accused Advani of "brandishing of the nuclear sword." (AP/Wide World Photos)

Jaswant Singh, foreign minister of India, addresses the 54th session of the General Assembly at the United Nations Wednesday, Sept. 22, 1999. (AP/Wide World Photos)

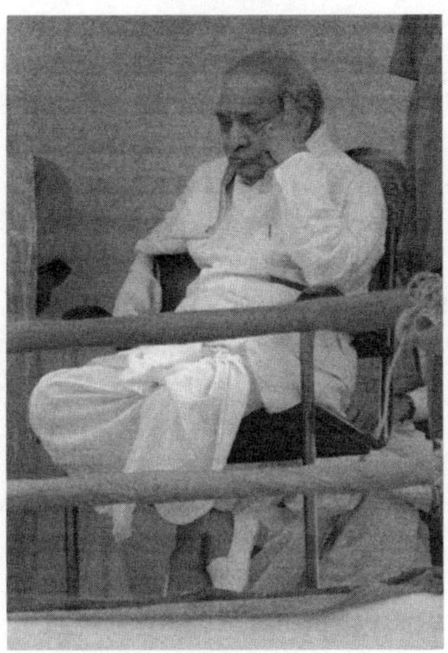

India's prime minister P.V. Narasimha Rao awaits his turn to speak at a Congress Party campaign rally in Gaya in the state of Bihar Saturday, May 4, 1996. Rao's beleagured Congress Party is behind in opinion polls for ongoing parliamentary elections. (AP/ Wide World Photos)

United Front prime ministerial candidate Inder Kumar Gujral seen in this April 9, 1997 photo. Gujral was appointed by the ruling UF coalition to replace outgoing Prime Minister H.D. Deve Gowda. During his 10-month tenure as Foreign Minister, Gujral was highly regarded for improving relations with India's historical enemy Pakistan. (AP/ Wide World Photos)

Sonia Gandhi, the widow of former Indian Prime Minister Rajiv Gandhi, presides over a Congress working committee meeting Saturday March 14, 1998 after she was unanimously voted new Congress party president in New Delhi. Gandhi's elevation to president was challenged by the man she replaced, Sitaram Kesri. Kesri had announced Monday he was stepping down and wanted Sonia Gandhi to replace him, but told reporters Saturday that he objected to the summary manner in which she was appointed by Congress's powerful Working Committee. (AP/Wide World Photos)

Laloo Prasad Yadav, president of Janata Dal, one of the major constituents of the Indian coalition government, facing prosecution by the federal police in an alleged theft of $138 million, is shown in a photo taken in New Delhi on April 12, 1997. The decision to prosecute Yadav and 55 other politicians casts a shadow over the government of new Prime Minister Inder Kumar Gujral, also from the same party, as the other accused belong to either of the coalition parties, or the main supporting party, Congress. (AP/Wide World Photos)

Nawaz Sharif takes the oath of the office of prime minister of Pakistan Monday, Feb. 17, 1997 at the Presidency in Islamabad. Lawmakers gave the Pakistan Muslim League an overwhelming vote of confidence in a secret ballot that automatically made Nawaz Sharif Pakistan's new prime minister. (AP/Wide World Photos)

Pakistan Army Chief Gen. Pervaiz Musharraf is seen in this undated photo. Musharraf overthrew the democratically elected government of Prime Minister Nawaz Sharif on Tuesday, Oct. 12, 1999, saying he staged the coup as a last resort to prevent the country's economic and political demise. (AP/Wide World Photos)

Jayalalitha Jayaram, leader of a group known by its Tamil acronym AIADMK, greets journalists in the traditional Indian style after holding talks with the Indian president in New Delhi Thursday, April 22, 1999. Jayalalitha, whose withdrawal of support to Prime Minister Atal Bihari Vajpayee's government precipitated the crisis, pledged the support of her 18 lawmakers to Sonia Gandhi and her Congress party. (AP/Wide World Photos)

10

Vajpayee's Roller Coaster Rolls

During the eight months following the August 1998 observance of the end of India's Golden Jubilee Year, the Vajpayee regime experienced a roller coaster ride that ended in a crash. Rather than proceeding on an even track to implement its agenda, the BJP-led coalition's performance rose to heights and fell to depths that at times followed each other and at times occurred almost simultaneously. An early high point was reached during September when Prime Minister Vajpayee traveled to New York to address the United Nations General Assembly and to meet with Pakistan's prime minister. He assured the General Assembly that India would not stand in the way of the Comprehensive Test Ban Treaty's coming into force in September 1999 and pointed out that India had declared a moratorium on future nuclear weapons tests. He qualified this statement by saying that India's action on the treaty would be linked to the United States's lifting the economic sanctions which it had imposed following the Pokhran nuclear bomb tests. During the course of his meeting with Pakistan's prime minister, Vajpayee agreed to the resumption of the talks on the Kashmir issue that had collapsed a year earlier, the renewal of a commitment for mutual adherence to the Line of Control (LOC) in Kashmir, and the setting up of a hot line that would make it possible for the two prime ministers to communicate directly with each other if a crisis situation arose. The two countries' foreign ministers did begin within a month the first dialogue on the Kashmir problem in thirty-five years, but nothing came of it except for an agreement to meet again during the following February.

Progress on India's foreign policy front suffered a setback during October when the Clinton administration issued a list of some 200 Indian agencies and companies that were involved in India's nuclear weapons and missile development program and forbade their American counterparts to do business with them. Additional downward movement in Indo-American relations came from the fact that, despite a series of discussions between Deputy Secretary of State Strobe

Talbot and External Affairs Minister Jaswant Singh, the two countries' positions on nuclear proliferation remained far apart. Secretary of State Madeleine Albright responded to Prime Minister Vajpayee's seemingly positive declaration to the General Assembly regarding India's signing the CTBT by declaring that "more steps had to be taken by India before the American sanctions could be lifted." Albright then went on to specify what India needed to do—sign the CTBT, cease producing raw material for nuclear bombs, institute a "restraint regime" on production of nuclear weapons, and control the export of nuclear material and technology. Vajpayee's remarks to the General Assembly and his agreement to return to the negotiating table with Pakistan may not have led to any foreign policy victories for India, but, coupled with the continuation of Jaswant Singh's talks with Strobe Talbot, they had softened the hawkish image that his coalition government had acquired in the world community as a result of its contribution to the nuclear proliferation problem.

At the same time that some progress was being made in foreign affairs, the Vajpayee regime was suffering a setback on the domestic front. Here the issue involved its dealings with Bihar. The state that had produced Gautama Buddha more than 2,500 years earlier had become by 1998 the worst regional blot on free India's record. During the decades since Independence, the social, economic, and political situation in Bihar had been steadily deteriorating. By the 1990s, the state's troubles had reached crisis proportions. Bihar had a negative rate of economic growth and the highest rate of illiteracy of any state in the Indian Union. While 200 Biharis had been killed in the twenty-four intercaste massacres that had taken place during the twenty years between 1970 and 1990, almost 400 had died in the thirty-five massacres that had occurred during the seven years following Laloo Prasad Yadav's 1990 takeover of political control of the state. Beginning in 1997, a series of caste battles had cost the lives of 300 men, women, and children, almost all of them Dalits. The most recent outbreaks of intercaste violence had been brought on by the efforts of Dalit landless laborers who had been organized by a militant leftist organization called the Peoples War Group to force landlords to give them land and pay them better wages. Landlords had responded by recruiting private armies to terrorize and kill Dalit villagers who were causing "trouble."

Continuing and violent social turmoil, coupled with a negative rate of economic growth that had seen the state's domestic product fall by 4% and its per capita income drop by 6% between 1990–91 and 1998–99, produced a situation in which well over 50% of the state's people lived below the poverty line. So far as government was concerned, the leader of the state's dominant Rashtriya Janata Dal, Laloo Prasad Yadav, had turned over the chief minister's post to his wife, Rabri Devi, because he faced criminal charges in the multi-million "fodder scandal." He now ran the state government from behind his wife's sari. Law and order were virtually nonexistent. Politics and criminal behavior went hand in hand. Commenting on this combination of social, economic, and political black marks, an article in the *Economist* summarized the dismal state of the state's affairs in a single sentence: "If anywhere deserves the smack of direct [Presidential] rule, it is Bihar."

Shortly before the Prime Minister left Delhi for New York, Governor Bhandari reacted to the rapidly deteriorating situation in Bihar by proposing that the Central Government's cabinet recommend the imposition of presidential rule on the state under Article 356 of the Constitution. The Central Government's cabinet agreed with the governor's proposal, and the prime minister presented to the president its resolution calling for President's Rule in Bihar. He expected that the president would follow the usual course by accepting the resolution and issuing the necessary proclamation. To his surprise, President Narayanan showed that he was not going to be a "rubber stamp" president but, as he styled himself, a "working" president. He returned the cabinet's recommendation with the comment that he did not agree that a constitutional breakdown had occurred in Bihar and advised the cabinet to reconsider its recommendation. As support for his position he could cite the fact that Rabri Devi's RJD government had shown a few days earlier that it enjoyed the support of the majority of Bihar's legislative assembly members.

While Prime Minister Vajpayee was still in New York, the cabinet met to consider the president's advice. Its initial decision was that its resolution should be submitted once again to the president, in which case he would have to accept it if he was to avoid the charge that he was attempting to assert his powers over those of the elected government. But final action could not be taken until September 30 when the prime minister returned to Delhi. Not wishing to enter into a constitutional dispute with the president, Vajpayee convinced his cabinet members that their resolution recommending President's Rule in Bihar should be rescinded. By persuading his cabinet to back down on this issue, Vajpayee not only avoided a showdown with the president but also blunted the attack that had been launched against his government's action by leaders of opposition parties. Sonia Gandhi, for example, had described the Cabinet's recommendation that President's Rule be imposed on Bihar as "utterly unconstitutional, undemocratic and [one that] smacks of very narrow political aims."

The Vajpayee government's September "downer" had come from the expected quarter of Bihar, but it did not raise serious questions about the government's viability. Its November "downer" came from the unexpected quarter of the onion market. During October, a serious shortage of onions had surfaced in Indian markets. The price of onions had shot up dramatically, to the point where it reached 60 rupees ($1.50) per kilogram in Delhi, seven times greater than it had been a year earlier and an astronomically high figure in a country where the per capita income was only a little over $1 per day. The primary cause of the onion shortage was a major drop in domestic production from 4,400,000 tonnes in 1996 to 3,650,000 tonnes in 1997. Vajpayee's government had not taken early action to avert a supply crisis because it was confident that an abundant harvest in September 1998 would increase availability and reduce the price.

India's recent experience with onion growing should have made it clear that this "do nothing" approach was risky. Following 1997's bad harvest, the price of onions had begun to rise steeply as early as January 1998. This increase continued during the ensuing months because heavy rains during the 1998 planting season, drought during the growing season, and more heavy rains at harvest time made it certain that the September crop upon which Vajpayee's Agriculture Department was depending for salvation would be another failure. Despite the meteorological indicators of trouble ahead, the minister of state for agriculture continued to base "onion" policy on the unrealistic assumption that the coming harvest would yield a bumper crop.

By October 1998, the Vajpayee government realized that it would have a serious political problem on its hands if it did not take quick action to deal with the onion shortage. Not only was the onion a basic ingredient in the Indian diet, but its price had been made a political issue by Indira Gandhi during the 1980 General Election when she had used the sharp price increase during the Charon Singh regime as a political stick with which to beat her opponents. Since that stick could be used again by her daughter-in-law in the coming state elections in Rajasthan, Delhi, and Madhya Pradesh, emergency steps had to be taken to increase the supply of onions, especially in the major cities. The import duty on onions was removed, and the pace of importation was rapidly accelerated. Truck loads of onions were rushed into cities, some under police protection, and sold from truck beds for 10 rupees (25 cents) per kilo. Even then, buyers had to wait hours in line, received only a few kilos, and often went away empty-handed.

Unfortunately for the BJP-led coalition, these emergency actions were not enough to alleviate the onion crisis quickly and effectively. Demonstrations against the government erupted, especially in Rajasthan and Delhi, where the BJP also controlled the state governments. The Congress Indira Party did an effective job of laying blame on the Central Government and its BJP party leaders for failure in a matter that was, for the moment, of greater concern to the average Indian household than India's new standing in the international community due to its nuclear weapons. The Congress Indira Party succeeded in turning the BJP-led Central Government's failure on the onion front into a symbol of the BJP's inability to perform effectively when its leaders were voted into power at the state level as well as at the center. Responsibility for failure to avert the onion crisis lay at the feet of the BJP-led Central Government, not the BJP state governments, but the popular mind did not draw this constitutional distinction and saw the culprit as the BJP, which had not lived up to its 1998 General Election promise to give India effective governance. Voters were determined to register their anti-BJP feelings as soon as they could, and the first opportunity would come on November 25 when they would cast their ballots for members of the legislative assemblies of Rajasthan, Delhi, and Madhya Pradesh.

While the BJP was headed for a serious defeat on the domestic front, the Central Government which it led scored a significant success on the foreign front. Following the sixth round of discussions between the United States's Strobe Talbot and India's Jaswant Singh, Washington announced on November 6 that it would ease some of the sanctions that had been imposed following India's nuclear bomb tests. It was stated that this action had been taken as a positive response to India's moratorium on further testing and as a way of encouraging it to take additional steps to prevent a nuclear arms race in South Asia. Although this easing of the sanction regime would do no more than enable India to participate in the American government's investment and trade promotion programs and although the existing ban on American exports to India of military equipment and high-tech and dual-use technology would be continued, this was the first hint that the United States had ceased to view India as a nuclear pariah and would henceforth approach its nuclear proliferation dealings with India on a quid pro quo basis. That the United States was keeping the door open for more progress on this front was indicated by the additional announcement that the Indo-American talks would be extended until January 1999. In the meantime, India would benefit economically as well as politically from the United States's November 6 actions because American governmental lending and granting agencies would now resume dealings with their Indian opposite numbers and make it possible for India to make up at least part of the 30% shortfall in foreign investment that had occurred during 1998. This economic benefit would be significant, but its impact would be limited because American opposition to World Bank and International Monetary Fund loans, India's principal source of foreign government funds, would continue.

A foreign policy victory for the Vajpayee regime was followed within weeks by serious defeats on the home front—direct defeats for the BJP state governments in Rajasthan, Delhi, and Madhya Pradesh and indirect defeats for the BJP-led Central Government. Although Prime Minister Vajpayee had assured the nation earlier that the coming state elections would not be a "referendum" on the performance of his government, he turned out to be wrong. With 590 state assembly seats up for grabs and 81 million people participating in the voting, the November 25 state elections turned out be a "referendum" in which the record of the Central Government as well as the records of the state governments involved would be on trial.

It was the voters of Rajasthan, Delhi, and Madhya Pradesh who proved Vajpayee wrong. The staggering cost of onions, accompanied by a sharp rise in the prices of other vegetables, that they had faced in October was still fresh in their minds. The voters saw the Central Government as the culprit and the BJP which led it as the party responsible for the nonfeasance and misfeasance that had caused the problem they had faced in putting food on the table. Unable to express their wrath by unseating the Central Government, they took vengeance on the BJP by voting against its candidates for legislative seats in the three states where November elections were held. The result was that control of both the Rajasthan and the Delhi state governments shifted from the BJP to the Congress Indira Party, and the Congress Indira Party maintained its hold in Madhya Pradesh where it had feared that it might lose its majority in the legislative assembly. Apart from the fact that the Congress Indira Party lost to regional parties in the small northern state of Mizoram, November 25 was a day of political triumph for the Congress

Indira Party and of serious defeat for the BJP in the first "referendum" on the performance of the Vajpayee regime since it had assumed office in March 1998.

While the results of the November state elections portended future trouble for the Vajpayee regime, they did not have an immediate unsettling effect. None of the BJP's coalition partners withdrew their support because they had lost confidence in the Central Government's ability to deal with the problems facing the nation. Even though Prime Minister Vajpayee admitted that he had been taken aback by the BJP's defeats in Rajasthan, Delhi, and Madhya Pradesh, he pointed out that his government still had the backing of the majority of the members of the Lok Sabha and that, with their backing, he would continue to lead it. He conceded that his Agriculture Department had made a mistake by failing to anticipate the onion shortage but argued that it had taken quick and effective action to deal with the problem when it had reached serious proportions.

However much the prime minister tried to put the best possible face on the results of the November state elections and his government's responsibility for them, he could not escape the fact that the Congress Indira Party had not only won, but had won big. The BJP attempted to take some of the sting out of its defeats by arguing that they were caused by the peculiar political situations prevailing in the states where voting had taken place rather than by dissatisfaction with the Vajpayee administration. The Congress Indira Party could not help but see the defeats as proof that the BJP-led coalition in Delhi was vulnerable to attack because of the BJP's current low standing in the eyes of the nation's voters. In addition, the Congress Indira Party's leaders viewed the results of the November elections as testimonials to the popularity of Sonia Gandhi, who had led the party's campaigns in the three states, and as a striking indication that she had the potential to become a prime minister heading a Congress Indira Party Central Government.

Sonia Gandhi had shown during the 1998 General Election that she could bring out the crowds but that she had limited effectiveness in helping Congress Indira Party candidates win election to the Lok Sabha. The favorable results of the November state elections proved to her Congress Indira Party lieutenants that she could lead the party in getting its candidates into office at the national level and making herself the country's prime minister. In order to groom her to be a successful candidate for this post, it was decided that she should take steps to soften her religious image as a Roman Catholic. She had spoken out already to diffuse the issue of her Italian nationality by emphatically declaring that she had been a citizen of India since 1984 and that she had regarded herself as an Indian ever since she had married into the Nehru family. Now she was forced to deal with her religious status as a Roman Catholic, which had come to the fore shortly after the November state elections when Hindu fundamentalist extremists made the charge that one of the purposes of the Christian churches' efforts, financed from abroad, to convert Hindus was to strengthen Sonia Gandhi's political clout as a Christian leader. Since she was the Congress Indira Party president, it was alleged that her party was refusing to join in the Hindu fundamentalist attempt to stop conversions because it was interested in promoting rather than curtailing them.

Knowing that there was no way that it could refute such a charge by compiling evidence from church sources to convince the Indian public that it was false, the route that the Congress Indira Party took was to showcase Sonia Gandhi as a Christian who saw her religion, not as a rival of Hinduism, but as one of many pathways to God. Supplementing this effort was an attempt on the part of the Congress Indira Party to make it clear that her party did not promote Christianity, because its commitment to secularism was based upon its commitment to the Hindu religion. The Congress Indira Party's Working Committee passed a resolution declaring that "Hinduism is the most effective guarantor of secularism in India." This committee action came a month after Sonia Gandhi's address to the Ramakrishna Mission, in which she had extolled the virtues of Swami Vivekananda and had commended the form of Hinduism that he represented. "India is secular," she had asserted, "because Hinduism, both as a philosophy and a way of life, has been based upon what our ancients said: 'Truth is one, the wise pursue it variously.'" She had followed this speech with visits to Hindu temples at Tirupati and Shirdi, during which she had received the blessing of the presiding deities. To make sure that the Indian people saw these words and actions as evidence that Sonia Gandhi was not an overzealous Christian who would attempt to undermine the Hindu religion if she came to power, a high-ranking Congress Indira Party leader who was a former speaker of the Lok Sabha stated emphatically for all to hear: "Sonia Gandhi is not a practicing Christian. She does not go to church."

If November had been a bad month for the BJP and the government which it led in Delhi, December was the beginning of a two month period during which its image became even more tarnished. November had seen a political backlash resulting from its failure to prevent the cost of onions and other vegetables from soaring to intolerable heights, but that backlash had been confined to three of India's states. December saw the beginning of a series of communal incidents that highlighted the BJP's character as a Hindu fundamentalist party, and the impact of these incidents spread throughout India and much of the Western world. They took the form of an escalation in attacks on Christian institutions and on church workers and members. These attacks had been going on ever since the BJP-led government had taken over in March 1998. The worst of the earlier instances of violence had occurred in September 1998 in Madhya Pradesh when four Roman Catholic nuns had been raped. By year's end, church buildings had been burned and church workers had been assaulted in more than forty places in Gujarat. Similar attacks in Uttar Pradesh and Maharashtra had brought the year's total to 86, many more than at any time since Independence.

Church leaders organized a rally in Delhi on December 4 to protest this violence against the Christian community, but despite this public display of outrage, the Christmas season that followed saw the demolition by militant Hindu mobs of churches, prayer halls, and schools in Gujarat. Instead of taking action to protect Christian institutions and personnel, the police department of the BJP-headed state government distributed a secret circular instructing its officers to find out where Christians lived, identify their leaders and the foreign countries that provided their financial support, ascertain if they had access to firearms, discover the "tricks" which they used to convert Hindus, and compile dossiers on any Christians with "criminal minds." It was apparent that Gujarat's BJP government regarded the Christian victims rather than those who attacked them as the culprits who were causing the trouble.

The BJP-led Central Government did not condone the December attacks on the Christian community. Prime Minister Vajpayee condemned them and said that they should stop immediately. He did not put the blame on the victims, but he implied that the trouble stemmed from the churches' evangelistic program, by calling for a "national debate" on the acceptability of the practice of converting Hindus to Christianity. His call had the effect of giving a degree of legitimacy to the campaign that was being waged by extremist elements in the Sangh Parivar, the family of Hindu fundamental organizations to which the BJP belonged, to convince the Indian people that such conversions should be outlawed. While Vajpayee did not endorse their violent actions, he made it clear that, in his view, the Hindu fundamentalist organizations had a case when they objected to the Christian churches' conversion efforts, a case that merited serious consideration. There was no evidence that Vajpayee's call for a "national debate" was intended to provide an excuse for the extremist Hindu fundamentalist groups that had been involved in or had defended the anti-Christian attacks, but it was clear that he was being careful to avoid taking a hard line against them because the core of the BJP's supporters came from their ranks.

Given the failure of the BJP-led Central Government and state governments to act decisively to deal with the problem, it was not surprising that attacks on Christians and their institutions continued into 1999. What was surprising was that they took an unbelievably gruesome turn on January 23, when an Australian missionary and his two young sons were burned alive by a Hindu mob that poured gasoline on and set fire to the van in which they were sleeping. This attack, which horrified both India and the world at large, occurred in a tribal area of Orissa where a number of Hindus had been converted to Christianity. Gordon Staines, who had lived and worked in this area for thirty years, had not been directly involved in this evangelistic work because he had devoted his time and energy to running a hospital and providing medical services for lepers. But he was a foreign missionary who had been a long-standing leader of the local Christian community, and he had been targeted for elimination by a Hindu fanatic who went by the nickname of Dara Singh.

Dara Singh had been active in the tribal area of Orissa for a number of years, attacking Muslim cattle traders and attempting to organize the young men of Manoharpur into a local contingent of the Bajrang Dal, a Hindu fundamentalist youth organization. During this time, Christians living in the vicinity had filed complaints against his high-handed communalist activities, but the local police had allowed him to remain at large. On January 23, he led a mob of 50 to 100 tribal youths shouting "Long live Hanuman" (the Hindu monkey god) in an attack which ended the lives of Gordon Staines and two of his three children. Following the murderous attack, Dara Singh fled into the forests of Orissa and hid there with local logistic support until he was finally arrested on February 1, 2000.

India's president and prime minister strongly condemned this outrageous mob action and promised that those responsible would be apprehended and punished. A team of cabinet ministers headed by the Christian defense minister was sent to the scene of the atrocity to ascertain whether or not the killings were locally instigated. After a brief visit to the area, the team returned to Delhi with the report that no local group had been involved. Even though no investigation of the incident had yet been conducted, Defense Minister Fernandes expressed the view that the killings had been prompted by unidentified "forces" in the nation and abroad that were intent upon bringing down the Vajpayee government. Fernandes and his fellow cabinet members might well have allowed this to become the final word on what lay behind the Staines killings, except for the demands made by leaders of opposition parties that a thorough investigation be conducted and the expressions of shock voiced by foreign diplomats and the world press. This foreign and domestic pressure combined to force the Vajpayee regime to appoint a Supreme Court justice to act as a one man commission to investigate the Staines killings and present within two months a report that would identify the individuals and/or groups that were responsible.

This action gave the impression that the Vajpayee government was determined to follow a policy of full disclosure regarding the Orissa incident. Supreme Court Justice Wadhwa was appointed without delay, but, during the six weeks that followed, he was given neither a staff of investigators nor an office out of which he could operate. Only after he had complained publicly about the absence of central government logistic support was he provided with the tools that he needed to carry on his work. The minor result of the "go slow" policy followed by the Vajpayee government was that it took the Wadhwa Commission five months instead of two months to produce its report. The major result was that Justice Wadhwa was given the message that he should not come up with findings that reflected badly on the BJP-led government or the Sangh Parivar organizations that supported it.

Supreme Court Justice Wadhwa submitted his 300 page report on June 21, and his findings were just what the Vajpayee regime wanted to hear. Long before the Wadhwa Commission had completed its work, Home Minister Advani had assured the nation that the Bajrang Dal had not been involved in the killings. Now that the commission's work was done, he could point to its report as evidence that confirmed his earlier statement. The commission found that neither the Bajrang Dal nor any other Hindu fundamentalist organization had been behind Dara Singh's violent action. According to Justice Wadhwa, it had been carried out by an individual who had no organizational affiliation. The commission described it as "a gruesome murder" and an "act of hatred" supported by a number of "disgruntled individuals." The killing of Gordon Staines and his two sons was portrayed as an expression of a personal determination to do away with a religious enemy rather than an expression of a Hindu fundamentalist organization's opposition to the conversion of tribal Indians to Christianity.

An editorial in the *Deccan Herald* argued that Justice Wadhwa had taken a "narrow view" of the incident:

It may be true that the Justice Wadhwa Commission of Enquiry that went into the gruesome killings of an Australian missionary and his two sons at Manoharpur in Orissa did not find any evidence of direct involvement of the Bajrang Dal or any such group. But, given the fact that most of the groups—the Bajrang Dal, the VHP [Vishwa Hindu Parishad] or other Sangh Parivar outfits—are hardly known to maintain records of their membership, it would have been difficult, if not impossible, to prove whether Dara Singh (the first accused) was at all formally associated with them. And in this sense, although the conclusion by the Wadhwa Commission may be held "technically" correct, to draw the implication that the Hindutva forces stand exonerated would lack credibility. For the murder was not an isolated incident but was certainly a fallout of the hate campaign carried out by the Bajrang Dal and the VHP in various parts of the country. There is sufficient evidence that a concerted propaganda [campaign] against Christian missionaries was organised at Manoharpur and in adjoining areas in Orissa, at least a couple of months before the killings took place on January 24, 1999.

It is rather strange that Mr. Justice Wadhwa refused to see this connection and ruled out any role in the incident for "any authority or organization" and instead treated the Manoharpur killings as merely an individual act by Dara Singh. Far more inexplicable is the report holding only Dara Singh responsible for "playing on the sentiments of the poor tribals in the region," describing him as a "rabid fundamentalist," and refusing to identify the link between his acts and the organised campaign carried out by the Bajrang Dal, the VHP and other Sangh Parivar outfits. After all, Dara Singh's activities were in no way different from the vicious propaganda by the Hindutva brigade—conjuring up images of the Hindu religion coming under threat from the Christian missionaries—which was endorsed by sections in the ruling party including some members of the Union Cabinet.

A revealing postscript to the BJP-led government's reaction to the large number of anti-Christian incidents that had taken place between December 1998 and March 1999 was written six months later. On September 9, the U.S. State Department issued its first annual report on religious freedom throughout the world. Mandated by Congress and based upon evidence supplied by embassy staffs, the report identified the various countries where religious freedom had been restricted or prohibited during the months between January 1998 and June 1999. Named among them was India, which was cited not only for the "deterioration of religious tolerance in many states" reflected in the numerous instances where Hindu extremists had attacked Christian personnel and property, but also for the "inadequate" response of state and local authorities to the violence that had been used in attempts to prevent minority groups from exercising their religious freedom. The section dealing with India included certain specific criticisms: "State governments initially downplayed a sharp upswing in violence perpetuated by extremists against religious minorities and their places of worship. Responses by state and local prosecutors to these events often were inadequate. In some cases, local police and government officials abetted the violence." The report went on to note that "members of the BJP (Bharatiya Janata Party which heads the coalition at the Center), the RSS (Rashtriya Swayamsevak Sangh) and other affiliated organizations have been implicated in violence and discrimination against Christians and Muslims."

The U.S. State Department followed up the release of the report by revealing that Robert Seiple, the ambassador for international religious freedom, proposed to visit the countries named in the report for "candid" discussions with government officials regarding what could be done to provide a greater measure of religious freedom for their peoples. Seiple explained the reason for his proposed trip to India by saying: "I will go to India before the end of the year. There are a lot of things that happened last year that are troubling." India's response to his proposal was swift and decisive. It took the form of a September 11 statement by the Ministry of External Affairs that slammed the door in his face. "The Government of India has no plans or intention to invite such an official to India or to engage in discussions with any foreign Government or agency on these matters." Pointing out that the Indian Constitution guarantees absolute religious freedom to its citizens, the statement concluded by saying emphatically that "the government and people of India reject any intrusive exercise in how we conduct our affairs."

A Congress Indira Party spokesman also objected to the State Department's report and Ambassador Seiple's proposal to visit India as an unwarranted "extra-regional endeavor," saying in so many words that the United States should mind its own business. At the same time, he could not resist the temptation to use the United States's "extra-regional endeavor" as a political club to attack Prime Minister's Vajpayee's party: "It is bad enough that the BJP has systematically fostered an atmosphere of religious intolerance that is unprecedented. It is worse that the BJP has opened another formal front against India and this time by a country with which Mr. Vajpayee is allegedly conducting a strategic dialogue." The RSS dismissed the report as a "cheap propaganda gimmick aimed at frightening away the Muslim and Christian voters from voting for BJP." The assertion that the RSS bore much of the responsibility for encouraging the anti-Christian attacks produced a defiant response from its general secretary: "We refuse to place ourselves in the dock as the accused whenever every Tom, Dick, and Harry comes up to say something irresponsible about us. I am really sorry to see the U.S. embarked upon this disinformation campaign at a time when in the wake of Kargil, the people of Bharat had come to have a bright opinion about its impartiality on the whole affair. It is also high time the U.S. saw the reality of the Bharatya situation. The charge about the attack on the so-called religious freedom of minorities is like rubbing salt into the already wounded Hindu psyche."

With his personal record and the record of his BJP party tarnished at home and abroad by the outbreak of violence against Christians since the BJP had come to power in Delhi, Vajpayee needed to find a way to rebound if his regime was to project a positive image. As had been the case during September 1998, his opportunity came in his foreign policy dealings. At the end of January, the eighth round of the discussions on nuclear weapons that had been going on for almost a year between Strobe Talbot and Jaswant Singh came to a close. During the course of this eighth round, Talbot had invited the ambassadors of the G-8 countries to a luncheon where they discussed the possibility of resuming World Bank loans to India. At the luncheon's conclusion, the State Department for the first time publicly expressed its satisfaction at the way the talks were going: "There is encouragement on the part of our negotiators. There are some indications that the Indians are going to move in a direction that will allow us to respond with moves of our own."

These hopeful words obscured the fact that the United States and India still had a long way to go before the gap in their positions on nuclear weapons was closed. Its persistence had become apparent during the eighth round of talks when President Clinton called Prime Minister Vajpayee and urged him to sign the CTBT. Vajpayee was still in no position to agree to take this step because to have done so would have exposed him to charges by opposition parties that he had both undermined India's national security and given in to American pressure. Even though Prime Minister Vajpayee could not say what President Clinton wanted to hear, the State Department's encouraging statement and the meeting of the G-8 ambassadors gave him grounds for claiming that India was making progress toward getting the Americans to lift the economic sanctions imposed under the Glenn Law following the nuclear bomb tests at Pokhran.

A few days into the new year, Prime Minister Vajpayee was able to achieve a much greater success on the foreign policy front when he announced that he had accepted the Pakistani prime minister's invitation to a meeting where the two would discuss the issues which separated the two countries. Both prime ministers had agreed on the need for such a meeting when they met in New York the previous September. Almost five months had gone by before it was held, but a number of events that had taken place during this time had helped bring it about. Most importantly, both countries had been under continuing pressure from the United States to engage in a dialogue that would ease tensions between them, particularly with respect to Kashmir. With foreign exchange reserves exceeding $25 billion, India was not immediately vulnerable to the economic sanctions that had been imposed by the United States. Pakistan, on the other hand, with foreign exchange reserves of only slightly over $1 billion, faced a potential financial crisis that made it imperative to open channels for receiving American and World Bank assistance. So it was neither an accident nor a display of goodwill when Pakistan's prime minister issued the invitation for a meeting with India.

Prime Minister Vajpayee not only accepted the Pakistani prime minister's invitation to a meeting but announced that he would do so by riding the first bus to Lahore. He arrived on February 20, the first visit to Pakistan by an Indian Prime Minister since 1989, and only the third since Independence. His first words were: "I bring the good will and hopes of my fellow Indians who seek enduring peace and harmony with Pakistan." As described by a reporter from the *Minneapolis Star Tribune*, his meeting with Prime Minister Nawaz Sharif at the border crossing was a truly spectacular event: "Bunting was strung on both sides of the crossing station. The roadways were a burst of color, with newly planted flowers, and freshly painted stripes. Red carpets had been unfurled. Indian and Pakistani flags stood side by side. As the bus crossed into Pakistan, Sharif stood at the door and waited for Vajpayee. The two greeted each other with a double handshake. It didn't seem enough for those cheering. Vajpayee initiated a hug. Then the bus was slowly emptied of the diplomats, businessmen, athletes and film stars who had joined the journey. . . . After juice was served, a color guard saluted Vajpayee. Finally, the two leaders left together aboard a helicopter for Lahore and a day and a half of talks and highly choreographed pomp."

The *Minneapolis Star Tribune's* reporter did not include in his description one detail that was noted by a reporter for the *Deccan Herald*. Absent from the Pakistani dignitaries who assembled to greet Vajpayee at the border crossing were the commanding officers of Pakistan's military forces: "The three service chiefs were not there. I wonder if they were supposed to be. I came to know about it when, on arrival at the hotel, a newspaperman asked me for my reaction to a story published that the three service chiefs had refused to salute the Indian Prime Minister." Neither the *Deccan Herald* reporter nor the more than 300 other newspapermen who covered the Vajpayee-Sharif meeting made much of this one sour note in the festive scene at the border crossing, because the Pakistani service chiefs did attend the state banquet that was held in Vajpayee's honor after he had reached Lahore. But looking back from the vantage point of the outbreak of the Kargil "war" only three months later and the imposition of military rule in Pakistan during October, it was clear that the Pakistani military chiefs' failure to join the welcoming party at the border crossing was a sign of something much more ominous than a lack of good manners. The military brass were not the only Pakistanis who showed their displeasure at Vajpayee's arrival. Organized by a militant Islamic group, hundreds of Pakistan's citizens took part in violent demonstrations in Lahore. A general strike was called. Shops were closed, and roads were blocked. When the demonstration got out of hand, the police had to resort to the use of firearms, and a number of casualties, including a dead policeman, resulted.

Despite these signs of opposition to any rapprochement with India, the meeting between the two prime ministers went on smoothly and ended with signed documents and public declarations that gave the impression that Indo-Pakistani relations would experience substantial improvement in the days ahead. Both countries pledged themselves to attempt to resolve their long-standing disputes, to continue the moratorium on further nuclear bomb tests, and to reduce the threat of nuclear war between them. In furtherance of the last mentioned aim, a mutual commitment was made to continue diplomatic talks at the foreign ministerial level. A Memorandum of Understanding was signed. Under its terms, the two countries would undertake "confidence building measures," would give each other advance warning of any ballistic missile tests that they might carry out, and would notify each other of any "accidental, unauthorized, or unexplained incident that might lead to a nuclear fallout or a nuclear war." Finally, the "Lahore Declaration" was issued, in which it was stated that resolution of the Kashmir problem was "essential" for the restoration of good relations between Pakistan and India and that both countries would intensify their efforts to achieve this goal.

During his stay in Lahore, Vajpayee once again put on the liberal "mask" of Hindu fundamentalism that he had worn during the 1998 General Election campaign. In order to make a gesture that would go down well with India's Sikhs, he visited the memorial to the 19th century Sikh king who had ruled Afghanistan, Kashmir, and Ladakh, as well as what is now Pakistan. To please India's Muslims, he spent a few minutes at the spot where, during the 1940 meeting of the All India Muslim League, Mohammed Ali Jinnah had issued his call for the creation of Pakistan. For the head of a party that claimed Pakistan as a part of ancient "Bharat" that had to be reunited with India, this visit, brief though it was, bordered on the ideologically sacrilegious. But Vajpayee's Sangh Parivar supporters were reassured that Vajpayee had not abandoned his Hindu fundamentalist principles when he refused to take part in a tour of a mosque built by Aurangzeb, the Mogul emperor who had ordered the erection of the mosque at Ayodhya that had been demolished by Hindu fundamentalists in 1992.

Both prime ministers recognized the validity of the *New York Times*'s evaluation of the results of their meeting as "long on good intentions but short on detente." They agreed that discussions between officials of the two countries should continue and that they should begin by talking about the less contentious issues of visa rules, trade relations, and release of prisoners and detainees. They were clear that, when all was said and done, the meting at Lahore could do no more than break the ice of hostility between the two countries. It could not sweep the ice away in one grand gesture. If any tangible and lasting improvement in Indo-Pakistani relations was to result from Sharif's initiative and Vajpayee's bus ride, much hard work would have to follow. All that could be achieved at Lahore was to display to the world that both prime ministers had come to the conclusion that, in Vajpayee's words, "We can change history but not geography. We can change our friends but not our neighbors. Now friendship must be given a chance."

Even while Vajpayee was basking in the limelight created by his Lahore bus diplomacy, serious trouble was brewing on both his domestic and his foreign fronts. He had been aware of the domestic trouble for some time, and it would have to be dealt with as soon as he returned to Delhi. He was unaware of the foreign trouble, which would not become fully apparent for another three months. Once again, the trouble at home was the chaos that continued to plague Bihar. On January 25, twenty-two Dalits had been killed by a landlord-supported private army called the Ranbir Sena. The state government had reacted by requesting that the Central Government send paramilitary forces to help maintain law and order.

Although two companies of reserve police were dispatched, the Ranbir Sena struck Narainpur village on February 10 and 12, and more Dalits were slaughtered in their sleep. These attacks represented only the tip of the iceberg in Laloo Prasad Yadav's Bihar where, according to *India Today's* summary description of the almost total absence of law and order, "a cognizable offense is committed every four seconds, a murder every two hours, a kidnaping for ransom every three hours and a rape every four hours, while the loot of the treasury is a year round activity. Sheer lack of governance has seen, among other things, extremists and private armies of landlords establishing parallel administration in nine of the state's 55 districts."

The killing of another twelve Dalits in Narainpur, followed by the retaliatory slaughter of eleven villagers belonging to the landowning caste, brought the January total to thirty-four deaths within three weeks. As it had five months earlier, the Central Government's cabinet recommended on February 12 that President Narayanan institute President's Rule in Bihar. Since the fatalities that had occurred during January and February had convinced Narayanan that law and order had broken down in the state, instead of returning the recommendation with the request that the cabinet reconsider its position as he had on the previous occasion, he issued the necessary proclamation and the Rabri Devi (Laloo Prasad Yadav) government was replaced by Central Government authority. The very next day, 16,000 central government paramilitary troops were dispatched to restore order in Bihar.

The Constitution provided that, in order for President's Rule to be continued, both houses of Parliament would have to approve the president's action within sixty days of its having been taken. Prime Minister Vajpayee was visiting Jamaica when President Narayanan issued his proclamation, but the prime minister was confident that he could obtain the necessary parliamentary endorsement when he returned to Delhi. He had majority support in the Lok Sabha and, although opposition parties dominated the Rajya Sabha, he had every reason to think they would agree that the situation in Bihar was so bad that it cried out for President's Rule. Sonia Gandhi, the president of the opposition party that held the balance of power in the Rajya Sabha, had already indicated that the Congress Indira Party would endorse Vajpayee's government's move by stating publicly that Rabri Devi had no moral right to rule in Bihar.

These words convinced Vajpayee that, with the votes of the Congress Indira Party's representatives added to those of the representatives of parties that belonged to his coalition, he would have no difficulty getting the Rajya Sabha as well as the Lok Sabha to approve the issuing of the President's proclamation. As events unfolded, it became apparent that he was mistaken in thinking that he could gain the approval of the Rajya Sabha. He was proved wrong when Sonia Gandhi's supportive statement was reversed by the Congress Working Committee's taking the position that the Congress Indira Party would oppose President's Rule in Bihar. The Committee's "about-face" did not prevent Vajpayee from gaining the approval of the Lok Sabha by a comfortable margin of twenty-nine votes. But, with only 80 of its 250 members representing parties that belonged to his coalition, Congress Indira Party opposition was bound to lead to a defeat if the matter came to a vote in the Rajya Sabha.

Taking advantage of the sixty days allowed by the Constitution for obtaining Parliament's endorsement of action taken under Article 356, the Vajpayee government agonized for more than a fortnight over how best to react to the dilemma that it faced. Should it back down and recommend that the president withdraw his proclamation or should it press for a vote in the Rajya Sabha and, after being defeated there, force the Congress Indira Party to take the political heat for having guaranteed the continuation of chaos in Bihar? Since both of these courses constituted bitter political medicine that the Vajpayee government was extremely loath to swallow, it was decided, as the sixty day time limit approached its end, that the prime minister should make a last minute personal appeal to Sonia Gandhi that she live up to her earlier statement that Rabri Devi had no moral right to rule Bihar, by placing her party's votes behind the imposition of President's Rule.

Vajpayee met Sonia Gandhi on March 8, but, after a forty-five minute discussion of the issue, she refused to budge from the stand that her party had taken a fortnight earlier. Her refusal to relent made it certain that the Vajpayee government would be defeated in a Rajya Sabha vote. Rather than face a humiliating defeat, the Cabinet voted the next day to recommend to the president that he revoke his proclamation of President's Rule in Bihar. The president's compliance with this recommendation constituted the first case of such an action in the 115 instances where Article 356 had been invoked since the Constitution had come into force in 1950.

For obvious reasons, the Congress Indira Party could not state publicly that its decision to oppose President's Rule had been taken to protect its political interests in Bihar, where it had allied itself with the RJD, which controlled the state government. It was forced to explain itself on constitutional grounds by saying that the party was in principle opposed to the use of Article 356 to depose a duly elected state government which, as was the case in Bihar, still enjoyed the support of a majority of the members of the legislative assembly. No thinking Indian who knew the political history of free India could believe that this was the party's real reason, because 96 of the 115 instances in which Article 356 had been invoked had occurred under Congress Central Governments. Adding an additional measure of hypocrisy to the Congress Indira Party's action was the fact that it flew in the face of the contention voiced over and over again by Sonia Gandhi and her lieutenants that their party was the protector of Dalits and the other oppressed groups in Indian society. When an opportunity came to translate these words into action by supporting a move by the BJP Central Government that would have provided greater protection for the Dalits and other depressed groups in Bihar, the Congress Indira Party had played a leading role in seeing that it came to naught. It was to be expected that the Dalits and Other Backward Classes of Bihar would remember the party's hypocrisy when it attempted to campaign in the next general election as the guardian of the poor and downtrodden.

The determination showed by Sonia Gandhi and the other leaders of her party to pay whatever political price they had to pay to support Laloo Prasad Yadav's RJD was the first public hint of a shift from long-term strategy to short-term tactics as a guide for the party's future. Up to this point, their public posture had been that they were acting in their long-term interest, taking the position that their party should be in no hurry to take over the Central Government and should concentrate upon strengthening the party's organization and increasing its popular support. Their reaction to the Bihar situation showed that, rather than waiting for the ruling coalition to fall apart on its own, they would begin to shift to short-term tactics, pursuing ways and means of weakening the Vajpayee government in order to bring it down as soon as possible, even if this involved taking steps that ran the risk of producing consequences that would work against the party's long-term interests.   Sonia Gandhi had hinted earlier that the party's thinking had undergone such a change after its victories in the November 1998 state elections, but only to members of her party. The February 1999 issue of a publication put out by the All India Congress Committee for Congress Indira Party members contained the report of an interview in which she was quoted as having predicted that "the country's responsibility will fall on the Congress sooner rather than later."

Bihar's continued bleeding kept alive the memory of what Vajpayee's government had tried to do to end it and what the Congress Indira Party had done to keep the wound open. Sonia Gandhi's about-face on the issue of whether or not the Rabri Devi government should remain in power showed that the surviving member of the Nehru dynasty was a politician who would sacrifice principle for political expediency.   Her party's unconvincing explanation that its action was taken to uphold a constitutional position that it had earlier violated many times in practice stood in sharp contrast to Prime Minister Vajpayee's justification of his government's action in an interview that was reported in the news magazine, *India Today*:   "Bihar is a jungle.   Three C's—casteism, corruption, and criminalization—have replaced the other C—Constitution. Bihar has become a killing field for Dalits and the poor. You can't remain blind to the plight of Bihar. It would amount to abdicating my responsibility. . . . My government acted with courage knowing full well that the numbers were stacked against us. The Lok Sabha is the House of the People. Had it not been for the Congress refusal to act in the interests of the Dalits merely to embarrass us, we would have secured the Rajya Sabha's approval too.   The Congress is free to think that they have embarrassed us. The truth is that they let down the Dalits of Bihar. They stand exposed for putting political opportunism above morality."

11

Vajpayee's Roller Coaster Crashes

Ten days after it was forced to back down on the Bihar issue, the BJP-led government observed the first anniversary of its taking office. The observance began on March 17 with a television program entitled "Pokhran to Lahore —Journey to Destination," which highlighted the accomplishments of the Vajpayee regime. This nationwide broadcast was followed in Delhi by a "Concert of India" in which more than 300 artists performed for an audience of 3,000 invited guests and a combined laser, *son et lumière*, and dance spectacular. Although the BJP spent a great deal of money on these productions, a Bangalore newspaper observed that "the birthday party, with so much thoughtless investment, concluded anti-climactically." Even within the ranks of the BJP, a number of party leaders were displeased because they had not received invitations to the Delhi performance.

The president of the RSS had taken it as a good omen that the BJP-led government's first anniversary had fallen on the day of the Hindu New Year, but the news magazine *India Today* reported that "this auspicious coincidence failed to enthuse the Hindu Parivar [family of Hindu fundamentalist organizations] which appeared singularly apathetic about the entire jamboree." The major reason for this lack of enthusiasm was that the ups and downs of the Vajpayee roller coaster during its first year of operation failed to constitute a record of accomplishments that would promote cheering among its supporters. Another reason was that the Vajpayee regime had been forced to struggle for survival in the face of a series of threats by one or another of the partners in its coalition to withdraw its support. Its friends and well-wishers could not help wondering, as its first anniversary gala was being staged, "How much longer can it survive?" Little did they realize that the answer to the question that troubled them was beginning to emerge even as they asked it.

The primary cause of the turn of political events that provided an answer within a month involved, not surprisingly, the political fortunes of the Anna DMK's Jayalalitha. She had kept the BJP-led government on tenterhooks from the days preceding its formation through its first year in office. She had threatened on a number of occasions to withdraw the support of her eighteen Anna DMK MPs upon whom the Vajpayee regime depended to maintain its majority in the Lok Sabha. She had made various demands on the prime minister and his cabinet, but the one that really mattered to her and that underlay all the others was her demand that the prime minister and cabinet use the power granted to the Central Government under Article 356 of the Constitution and replace M. Karunanidhi's DMK government in Tamil Nadu with President's Rule. Karunanidhi was Jayalalitha's mortal political enemy; after his victory and her defeat in the 1996 state election, he had succeeded in jailing her for a short time on a series of corruption charges and had instituted special courts to hear the cases against her.

According to Tamil Nadu's DMK government, she stood accused of the following:

- Receiving kickbacks of 8.53 crores of rupees ($2,030,000) from manufacturers who sold television sets to the Tamil Nadu government;
- Acquiring for almost nothing 3.1 acres of prime state government land for the use of her Jaya Publishing Company, resulting in a loss of almost 4 crores of rupees ($950,000) to the state treasury (In January 2000, a Madras High Court judge dismissed this charge, but Tamil Nadu's prosecuting attorney appealed his verdict to the Supreme Court. The following month, the Supreme Court stayed the Madras High Court's judgment and ordered a special court in Chennai to proceed with the trial with Jayalalitha as one of the accused);
- Exempting a hotel built by a group of her supporters in the rapidly developing hill station tourist center of Kodaikanal from the Hill Area Development Rules (Jayalalitha was convicted on this charge and sentenced to one year in jail. She appealed the verdict and was allowed to remain free pending disposition of her appeal);
- Amassing over 100 properties and other assets worth 66.65 crores of rupees ($15,875,000) during the time when her salary as chief minister was 1 rupee (less than 3 cents) per month;
- Receiving 39 crores of rupees ($9,285,000) for granting granite quarrying licenses to private exporters;
- Laundering a check for $300,000 received through Bankers Trust as a gift from friends in the United States;
- Concealing 1993–94 income of over 1 crore of rupees ($240,000) from tax authorities;
- Waiving a fee of 2 crores of rupees ($480,000) due from Meena Advertisers;
- Causing a loss of 6.5 crores of rupees ($1,560,000) to the Tamil Nadu government on 2 million tonnes of coal imported from Australia (She was initially acquitted of this charge by a Chennai Special Court, but its decision was appealed by the Tamil Nadu government to the Supreme Court. The Supreme Court subsequently ruled that " the [Chennai special] court would not and should not have discharged Jayalalitha at this premature stage" and that she should stand trial on the charge).

Not only had Karunanidhi's government succeeded in having these charges laid against Jayalalitha, but it had set up special state courts to try them in order to increase the chances of obtaining convictions. From the time that Jayalalitha had been bailed out of jail and had been able to resume her political activities, her overriding preoccupation had been to escape conviction on the charges that had been laid against her by inducing the Vajpayee government to replace Karunanidhi's government with President's Rule. With Tamil Nadu's courts being directed from Delhi rather than from Chennai and the accused being able to deal with a friendly central government chief executive rather than a hostile state chief minister, there was every chance that she could get the charges dropped or, if she came to trial, secure an acquittal.

Knowing that his government did not have the necessary votes in Parliament to sustain the imposition of President's Rule in Tamil Nadu, Prime Minister Vajpayee was in no position to accommodate Jayalalitha by taking such a radical step. He was willing to help her by doing what he could to delay proceedings against her in Tamil Nadu's special courts, and, when legal matters reached the trial stage, enhance the possibility that she would be acquitted. In forming his cabinet, he had appointed a member of Jayalalitha's Anna DMK party as the minister who supervised the nation's courts. On February 5, 1999, his Ministry of Personnel, also headed by an Anna DMK member, issued a notification that the corruption cases pending against Jayalalitha would be heard in Tamil Nadu's regular court rather than in the special courts presided over by judges appointed by the Karunanidhi government with instructions to obtain convictions. This change in jurisdiction, if it were carried out, would mean that Jayalalitha would be protected from a judge who was sure to be unfriendly. But the Ministry of Personnel's notification was rejected by the special courts' judges, who maintained that they operated under the authority of the Madras High Court and were not bound to comply with central government legal directives. Dissatisfied with the steps that the prime minister had taken to ease her legal predicament, Jayalalitha decided as the Vajpayee regime's first anniversary celebration came and went that her only hope lay in initiating an effort to bring the government down and replace it with one led by the Congress Indira Party.

Such an effort could succeed only if the Congress Indira Party was ready to cooperate. Fortunately for Jayalalitha, the aggressive attitude that Sonia Gandhi and her lieutenants had adopted following their victories in the November state elections and their success in forcing the Vajpayee government to withdraw its recommendations that President's Rule be imposed in Bihar provided the powder needed to make it possible for Jayalalitha's spark to touch off the political explosion that would cause the crash of the Vajpayee roller coaster. Sonia Gandhi had begun her second year as Congress Indira Party president three days before the Vajpayee regime had begun celebrating its first anniversary. The day that the celebration ended, a meeting of the Congress Working Committee was held to inaugurate her new year as president. It was decided at the meeting that the party should abandon its strategy of waiting for the BJP-led government to fall apart and then step in to pick up the pieces in order to forge a Central Government under its own control. It would now take the initiative to unseat the BJP-led government by attacking it on two issues that had to do with national security.

On December 30, 1998, Defense Minister Fernandes had dismissed Admiral Vishnu Bhagwat from his post as chief of naval staff on grounds of insubordination. Fernandes had defended his action by arguing that one of the essential elements of Indian democracy was that its military functioned under civilian control and that he had been forced to take action against Bhagwat when the admiral refused to carry out Fernandes' order. Rejecting this argument, the Congress Indira Party launched a campaign to force the BJP-led government to reinstate Admiral Bhagwat and remove Fernandes from his position as defense minister, and sought to obtain the support of other opposition parties in pressing its demands. Mustering the support of all opposition forces in pressing these demands was not an end in itself. It was to be the opening gambit in a strategy to bring down the Vajpayee regime.

Even though reinstating Admiral Bhagwat and removing Fernandes from the defense minister's post were not matters on which the fate of the nation depended, and even though Bhagwat had difficulty justifying his insubordination and Fernandes made a good case for the action that he had taken, Sonia Gandhi and her Congress Indira Party lieutenants saw these issues, in the words of the Polish proverb "if you want to beat a dog, you can always find a stick," as political sticks that could be picked up to beat the Vajpayee regime to death. Since both demands involved India's national security, they could be raised by the Congress Indira Party "for the good of the nation rather than for narrow partisan reasons." Having been forced by the Congress Indira Party to back down on President's Rule in Bihar, the BJP government could not give in to the new demands without showing itself to be so weak in the face of opposition that it could not govern effectively. To accomplish its ultimate objective of causing the Vajpayee roller coaster to crash, the Congress Indira Party's leadership needed the help of a "fifth column" within the BJP-led government's coalition that would assist the opponents of the government outside the coalition by withdrawing its support in the Lok Sabha and putting the government's majority at risk. That "fifth column" appeared during Vajpayee's "Ides of March" in the form of Jayalalitha and her eighteen Anna DMK MPs.

All that was needed now was a catalytic hand that would put Jayalalitha's spark to the Congress Indira Party's powder and produce the necessary explosion. That hand was applied on March 29 by Dr. Subramaniam Swami. Subramaniam Swami was the president of the minuscule Janata [People's] Party who, although once one of her severest critics, had become during recent years a close confidant and ardent supporter of Jayalalitha. Since he had taught economics at Harvard University, he felt that he was eminently qualified to serve as finance minister in the BJP-led government that had been formed in March 1998. Jayalalitha had agreed with him and initially had made his appointment to this important post a part of her price for providing the support of the eighteen Anna DMK MPs that

Vajpayee needed in order to cobble together a majority of Lok Sabha members to back his government. While Vajpayee had not been willing to satisfy this particular demand on her list and while Jayalalitha had tendered to the president a letter of support despite his refusal, her attempt, albeit unsuccessful, to win Subramanian Swami the high office that he coveted made him a political ally who was ready and willing to return her favor. No opportunity to do so came his way during the first year of the Vajpayee regime, but, by the time that first year had come to its close, the political situation was ripe for him to provide the catalyst that would join Jayalalitha's political fortunes with those of Sonia Gandhi.

Subramaniam Swami organized a reception in Jayalalitha's honor to be held in Delhi and to which Sonia Gandhi, as well as leaders of some of the other opposition parties, would be invited. To everyone's surprise, the Congress Indira Party President accepted the invitation. Surprise was the common reaction for more than one reason. Heretofore, those who wanted to interact politically with Sonia Gandhi had had to comply with her "dynastic style" and travel to her heavily guarded bungalow at number 10 Janpath to pay their respects. By turning up at Jayalalitha's reception, she was leaving her "court" and coming to a political function at which another political leader would be the person to be honored. Up to this point, Sonia Gandhi and Jayalalitha had had little to do with each other politically or socially. Sonia Gandhi had kept aloof from Jayalalitha and had appeared to regard her with disdain because of Sonia's emphasis on correct political behavior and Jayalalitha's reputation for political corruption. Jayalalitha had reacted to Sonia Gandhi's emergence as a major political figure during the 1998 General Election by likening the possibility of her becoming prime minister to "a national tragedy." Surprising as it was that Sonia Gandhi was willing to attend the March 29 reception, it was even more surprising that she and Jayalalitha chatted amiably with each other for ten minutes and that Sonia Gandhi said afterwards of their relationship: "We are old friends."

For her part, Jayalalitha described their ten minute conversation as a "political earthquake." When these words gushed forth, newspaper reporters and other political observers denied their political importance on the ground that they were nothing more than another example of Jayalalitha's hyperbolic way of speaking. The two political leaders had talked for only ten minutes and both had maintained that politics was not the subject of their conversation. But, as political events unfolded during the weeks immediately following the reception, these political observers came to see that, so far as the fate of the Vajpayee regime was concerned, Jayalalitha's characterization of that brief episode of "chit chat" as a "political earthquake" was apt. Even though Sonia Gandhi, in contrast to Jayalalitha, had downplayed the political importance of the reception honoring Jayalalitha, saying that it was nothing more than "a social gathering," her brief talk with Jayalalitha was the beginning of a political alliance, the aim of which was to cause the collapse of the BJP-led coalition government.

Jayalalitha produced the first aftershock of the March 29 "political earthquake" the very next weekend when she issued a public demand that the prime minister reinstate Admiral Bhagwat as chief of naval staff and transfer Defense Minister Fernandes to a "less sensitive" post on the ground that, as defense minister, he posed a threat to national security. It was obvious to all, including Vajpayee and his cabinet ministers, that she was echoing the position of the Congress Indira Party as part of a collaborative strategy to bring down the existing Central Government and replace it with a Congress Indira Party regime that would finally grant Jayalalitha the long sought boon of imposing President's Rule on Tamil Nadu. Neither of the issues that Jayalalitha raised was a matter of overriding concern to her party or to the Tamil people, and her status as the leader of a regional party did not give her the political standing that would qualify her to play a leading role in matters of defense policy. Such obvious political considerations did not trouble her, and she happily assumed the role of the champion of Admiral Bhagwat and the enemy of Defense Minister Fernandes.

Despite the disconnection between the issues and the person voicing them, Jayalalitha was well chosen as the party leader to make demands from within the BJP-led coalition, and these two issues were well chosen as the demands for her to make. She was in a position to act as a "fifth column" that could cause the Vajpayee regime to collapse if her demands were not met. The issues involved national defense and civilian control over the military, and any Central Government that was forced by a leader of a regional party that was a member of its coalition to change the stand it had taken in dealing with matters of such fundamental importance would proclaim to the nation that it had lost the power to rule. So it was clear from the outset that the demands Jayalalitha made were demands that Prime Minister Vajpayee had to refuse.

In commenting on Jayalalitha's challenge to the Vajpayee regime, a Congress Indira Party spokesman hinted that it reflected a new political reality, namely, that Jayalalitha was now collaborating with the Congress Indira Party in an attempt to unseat the existing government in Delhi. Asked about the significance of an opposition party like the Congress Indira Party and a party that was a member of the ruling coalition like the Anna DMK making the same demands on the Central Government, he replied: "If both of us are demanding the same thing, then cooperation between the two is an obvious inference." He was careful to deny that this "cooperation" had begun with the ten minute chat that had taken place on March 29, by repeating Sonia Gandhi's characterization of the reception that had been held to honor Jayalalitha as merely a "social gathering." A fortnight later, another Congress Indira Party spokesman went further, in trying to hide the fact that Sonia Gandhi and Jayalalitha had become collaborators, by denying that the Congress Indira Party and the Anna DMK party were working together to destabilize the BJP-led government. The plot was under way, but the plotters did not want the public to know what was afoot.

After meeting with and receiving the support of some of the leaders of the BJP's coalition partners, Prime Minister Vajpayee refused to take either of the steps demanded by Jayalalitha and defied her and the Congress Indira Party, declaring: "We are prepared to welcome a trial of strength in the house [Lok

Sabha]." He was confident that his government would retain majority support even if Jayalalitha withdrew the votes of the eighteen Anna DMK MPs because he thought that none of the parties—opposition or government—wanted to face another general election. Given this reluctance to go to the polls, he was sure that new allies would join his coalition to replace any old ally who deserted him.

Jayalalitha responded to his defiance on April 2 by addressing him with fighting words: "If you try our patience for too long, we will throw out the driver and run the train ourselves." She went even further with her metaphor by saying that "if necessary, we shall even remove the driver and reach our destination and attach our engine to another train." Although she did not name it, the other train that she had in mind was the Congress Indira Party. Within days of issuing her threat and after predicting "interesting days to come," she instructed the two Anna DMK members of the Vajpayee cabinet to resign their posts. A week later she withdrew from the regime's Coordinating Committee. On April 12, accompanied by an entourage consisting of almost two dozen personal and security staff and forty-eight pieces of luggage, she traveled to Delhi and installed herself in one of the largest suites of one of the city's most elegant hotels. Here she would hold audience and confer with opposition party leaders regarding ways of bringing down the BJP-led coalition. Based upon the outcome of these meetings, she would decide whether or not to take the final step of withdrawing her Anna DMK MPs' support in order to bring the Vajpayee government's majority in the Lok Sabha to an end.

Desperate to head off such a disaster and to show its defense minister in a positive light, the BJP-led government beat Jayalalitha's expedition to Delhi by one day by launching a successful test of the Agni II missile. The Agni II missile was a decided advance over the Agni I version because its range had been increased from 900 to 1,250 miles. It was capable of reaching all of Pakistan and parts of interior China with a full payload and even Beijing and Shanghai with a reduced payload. Its testing had been delayed for several months, but on April 11 Defense Minister Fernandes could finally proclaim: "With today's launch we have reached a point where no one from anywhere can threaten us." Claiming that India now enjoyed "an unchallengeable national security position," he boasted that "as a government, first there was the Pokhran tests, now by operationalizing Agni II, no one can put pressure on us. . . . I don't think that we need to be told by anyone to practice restraint."

A British Foreign Office spokesman differed with Defense Minister Fernandes, saying: "We continue to believe that restraint in developing missiles and nuclear weapons is in India's long term interest." The United States seconded the British by expressing its "regret" at India's aggressive move: "We believe that concrete restraints by India would create a more positive atmosphere for improving relations among the various countries concerned and for addressing international nonproliferation issues. The flight test appears to be out of step with positive developments in the political sphere, including the recent summit in Lahore and the resumption of Sino-Indian dialogue. We hope that India will provide tangible indications that it is prepared to practice restraint consistent with its declared intentions."

Prime Minister Vajpayee reacted to these expressions of international displeasure by assuring Pakistan, China, and the rest of the world that Agni II had been developed only for defensive purposes. In order to reap whatever domestic political benefit might accrue, he accompanied these reassuring words with a claim directed to his Indian audience that the successful testing of Agni II had shown the world that India was moving in the direction of becoming a nation that could take care of itself so far as its security was concerned. "In a rapidly changing security environment, India cannot depend on others to defend her. We have to develop our own indigenous capabilities. Agni is proof that resurgent India is able to say: 'Yes, we will stand on our own feet.'"

Unfortunately for the prime minister, his words of assurance addressed to the world did not satisfy his British and American critics. Their displeasure re-surfaced a month later when preparation for the 1999 meeting of the India Development Forum (IDF) failed to materialize. The United States and other developed countries who were the donor countries of the IDF were disinclined to hold the meeting because of their negative reaction to India's missile development program. Expressing their opposition in this way meant that India would be hurt economically as well as politically because the loss of IDF funds, which had been averaging approximately $7 billion per year, would seriously impede implementa-tion of the badly needed infrastructure projects they had been underwriting.

Even more important was the political fact that Vajpayee's words to the Indian people did not succeed in bringing to a halt the attack that was being mounted to destroy his government. Three days after the successful Agni II test, Jayalalitha met President Narayanan and informed him that the eighteen Anna DMK MPs would no longer support the BJP-led government. Sonia Gandhi and her lieutenants in the Congress Indira Party took the next step by meeting to work out the strategy for ensuring that Jayalalitha's withdrawal from the Vajpayee coalition would guarantee its collapse and lead the way to an alternative government under their party's control. They opted for a Congress Indira Party government which, since their party had only 140 seats in the Lok Sabha, would need the outside support of other opposition parties with at least 132 representatives. Although some party leaders argued unsuccessfully for a Congress Indira Party–led coalition government, no difference of opinion was expressed on the question of who should be the prime minister if a Congress Indira Party minority government came into being. The party leaders' unanimous choice was party president Sonia Gandhi.

President Narayanan acceded to the request made by leaders of the opposition parties and directed Prime Minster Vajpayee to seek a vote of confidence in the Lok Sabha to show that his government still commanded a majority despite the loss of the support of the Anna DMK's eighteen MPs. Since Vajpayee was loath to create a constitutional crisis by refusing to comply with the president's directive and waiting for the Congress Indira Party to move a vote of no-confidence in his government, and since he felt certain that he could win a vote of confidence, he took the necessary steps to carry out the president's directive. His confidence stemmed from three developments that had taken place since Jayalalitha had left his coalition. The first was that Jayalalitha's withdrawal of support had produced an opposite reaction by her arch rival and the head of the DMK, M. Karunanidhi. He had declared that his party would play no part in an alternative coalition government that included the Anna DMK. Taking such a position meant that almost certainly the six DMK members of the Lok Sabha would vote in favor of the vote of confidence. The second was that Vajpayee had convened a meeting of the leaders of the parties that were still his coalition partners, during which they had expressed continuing support for his government. The third was that Mayawati, the parliamentary leader of the Bahujan Samaj Party (BSP), had stated that her party's five MPs would abstain when the motion of confidence came to a vote. Taking into consideration the facts that the BJP-led government's second attempt to impose President's Rule in Bihar had cleared the Lok Sabha by a margin of twenty-nine votes, that Jayalalitha's defection would add only eighteen votes to the total recorded against the government, that six of these negative votes would be offset by DMK MPs who supported the confidence motion, and that the total against the motion would be five fewer than it would be if the five BSP members did not abstain, Vajpayee was sure that the numbers were in his favor.

Opposition parties worked feverishly to put together the votes necessary to defeat the confidence motion. Jayalalitha conferred with Sonia Gandhi and other party leaders to consider the form that an alternative government might take. Members of the Congress Working Committee met to discuss the same topic. Subramaniam Swami talked with the president of the BSP in an unsuccessful attempt to persuade the latter to align his party with the opposition. Only when Mayawati received an appeal from Sonia Gandhi during the morning prior to the Lok Sabha vote did she agree to withdraw her abstention order and instruct the BSP MPs to vote against the Vajpayee government. The result of these political maneuvers was that, when the Lok Sabha votes were counted on April 17, the motion of confidence failed by one vote—269 in favor, 270 against. If the five BSP members had abstained, the Vajpayee regime would have survived by a margin of four votes. But a defeat by even a single vote was enough to cause the prime minister and his Council of Ministers to resign after only thirteen months in office. Following the customary constitutional procedure, the president accepted their resignations and asked them to remain in office as caretakers until a new government could be formed.

Their one vote victory was enough to propel the leaders of opposition parties into frantic motion to cobble together the votes needed to form an alternative government from the membership of the 12th Lok Sabha. The Congress Indira Party took the lead in this enterprise, its spokesman predicting that "a new government will be in place within two or three days." Laloo Prasad Yadav, the leader of the RJD, was even more euphoric, reducing the time required to "five minutes." The only element of order in the midst of this political chaos was an agreement arrived at between the caretaker government and the opposition parties that resulted in a special session of Parliament being held in which the 1999–2000 budgets were passed, thus averting a governmental financial crisis.

The BJP-led coalition's immediate reaction to losing the confidence vote was to strengthen its solidarity and to seek to prevent the Congress Indira Party from forming a minority government. A delegation led by Defense Minister Fernandes lost no time in meeting the president and urging him to follow the same procedure that he had followed in the establishment of the Vajpayee government, namely, to insist that a party leader demonstrate that he or she had the support of more than 270 members of the Lok Sabha before being asked to form a government. A BJP meeting produced a statement reiterating the position taken by the coalition delegation that had met the president the previous day: "It is incumbent on the President that when and only when some party makes claim to form a government, if he invites a party to form a government, to ask that party to furnish similar letters of support [similar to those required of Prime Minister Vajpayee before he formed his coalition government]. And that support should add up to more than 270. Anything less than this would bring into question the legitimacy of any so-called alternative arrangement." The meeting also called upon all non-Congress-supporting and non-Communist parties to help thwart the Congress Indira Party, the Communist parties, and the Anna DMK, which had "betrayed" the mandate of the Indian people, and designated April 23 as a time to observe a national "anti-betrayal" day during which the public could show their continuing support for the Vajpayee regime.

The most confident voice heard at this time when India's immediate political future appeared uncertain was that of Sonia Gandhi. As she emerged from an April 19 general meeting of the Congress Parliamentary Committee, she announced to all and sundry: "We will certainly form a government." But, when newspapermen asked her to describe what shape this government would take—a minority Congress government, a Congress-led coalition, or a coalition government supported from outside the coalition by the Congress Party— she parried the question. A Congress Indira Party spokesman later clarified her statement by saying that all that was clear at the moment was that his party had the second largest representation in the Lok Sabha, that it expected an invitation from the president to form an alternative government, but that it would not take the initiative by approaching the president with a request for such an invitation.

Pending the arrival of this invitation, Sonia Gandhi carried on hurried consultations with leaders of other opposition parties with a view to obtaining their agreement to provide outside support for a Congress Indira Party minority government. As she continued her efforts, two flies appeared in the ointment. Both Jayalalitha and Mulayan Singh Yadav insisted that their respective parties, the Anna DMK with eighteen seats in the Lok Sabha and the Samajwadi Party with twenty-one seats, should have important places in the new cabinet. To make matters worse, both refused to support the position taken by other opposition party leaders that Sonia Gandhi should be the prime minister, suggesting instead that the post should go to Jyoti Basu, the Communist Party (Marxist) chief minister of West Bengal.

Despite these harbingers of trouble ahead, Sonia Gandhi and her lieutenants remained firm in insisting that the new government should be a Congress Indira Party minority government, not a Congress-led coalition. To retain for herself the status of the opposition parties' sole candidate for the prime minister's post, she met with Jyoti Basu and announced after their meeting that he had rejected the idea of becoming a prime ministerial candidate. Thinking that she had all her ducks lined up in a row, Sonia Gandhi responded to President Narayanan's invitation to form a new government by announcing on April 21 that she would form a Congress Indira Party minority government with sufficient outside support from other opposition parties to give it the backing of 272 members of the Lok Sabha. To validate her claim, she assured the president that she would provide him within two days letters from at least that many members of the Lok Sabha documenting their support.

At this point, most of India and much of the world thought that the die was cast —that India's new government would be a Congress Indira Party minority government with Sonia Gandhi at its head. But it was also at this point that the strategy that had been initiated with Subramaniam Swami's March 29 reception for Jayalalitha began to unravel. Mulayan Singh Yadav announced that his Samajwadi Party would give only "conditional and issued-based support" to a Congress Indira Party minority government, indicating that his party's twenty-one MPs would not be willing to provide the letters of unconditional support that President Narayanan required. More serious trouble soon appeared on the political horizon when a group of opposition party leaders met at Mulayam Singh Yadav's residence in Delhi to discuss what shape the new government should take and who should be its prime minister. The outcome was a decision to depute Jayalalitha and Laloo Prasad Yadav to meet Sonia Gandhi and convey the meeting's recommendation that the new government should be a coalition with Jyoti Basu at its head.

Sonia Gandhi's immediate reaction was to say that she would discuss these proposals with her party lieutenants and provide a response the next day. The brief response was that the Congress Indira Party had rejected both proposals. Faced with the Congress Indira Party's intransigence, Mulayam Singh Yadav refused to instruct his Samajwadi Party MPs to write letters of support for a Congress Indira Party minority government. His negative stand was reinforced by a similar refusal on the part of two smaller parties which between them held seven Lok Sabha seats. Losing these 28 MPs and a dozen others along the way, a chagrined Sonia Gandhi met with President Narayanan on April 23 and informed him that her list of members supporting a Congress Indira Party minority government totaled only 233, 39 short of the promised 272.

The president responded by granting Sonia Gandhi an unspecified amount of additional time to produce the missing thirty-nine letters of support. During the forty-eight hours that followed, leaders of various political parties engaged in a frantic effort to arrive at an alternative government that could be constructed from the membership of the 12th Lok Sabha. Laloo Prasad Yadav met with Mulayam Singh Yadav in an attempt to persuade him to withdraw his objection to a Congress Indira Party minority government. Efforts continued to convince the leaders of the Congress Indira Party that they should give up their insistence on forming a minority government and, instead, seek to garner support for a coalition government which they would lead. The Communist Party (Marxist) pursued but ultimately rejected a proposal made by a group of party leaders who had gathered at Mulayam Singh Yadav's residence that Jyoti Basu head a "secular" coalition government that would include the Congress Indira Party.

As a last resort, the idea was floated of creating a "secular Third Front" coalition government that would not be headed by the Congress Indira Party. Picking up on this proposal, the mercurial Jayalalitha, who had earlier allied herself with the Congress Indira Party, changed her position by announcing that her party would support neither a Congress Indira Party minority government nor a coalition government under its leadership. She would now back a "secular Third Front" government with Jyoti Basu at its head and supported from outside by the Congress Indira Party This was a proposition that the leaders of the Congress Indira Party were bound to reject since it would preclude their enjoying any of the benefits of the ministerial power which they craved after three years of playing the role of the opposition.

Commenting on the political consequences of the developments that had taken place between April 14 and April 25, only one of which—Parliament's passage of the 1999–2000 General and Railway Budgets—moved governmental affairs forward, newspaperman Nitish Chakravarthi focused on the crucial role that had been played by Sonia Gandhi:

Where she can be faulted is in her priorities. If communalism was on top of her agenda, why was she averse to giving support to a secular front? Once she realized that a Congress government was out of the question, why did she not say that the Congress would support from outside the government of secular parties? Sonia Gandhi's "no" ended every conceivable alternative. She may blame others, but she is not free from it. She too has lost. For the first time she was seen functioning independently and found wanting. She went to the President alone. And, with a flourish, she said outside Rashtrapati Bhavan [the president's residence] that the Congress had secured the names of 272 members. Her claims were made by a country bumpkin and not by a person mentioned as the country's Prime Minister.

The political events that took place between April 14 and April 25 not only produced the fall of the third Central Government within three years and the promise of another general election but also brought about changes in the Indian political scene that would have impacts over the longer term. Sonia Gandhi emerged from her behind the scenes role as head of the Congress Indira Party to become a national political leader. On April 24 it looked as though she was on the verge of becoming India's next prime minister. When she acquired this more formidable political presence, her nationality and her political experience became salient issues. These issues had been raised but not driven home by her political opponents during the time when she had acted as a Congress Indira Party campaigner and functionary. After April 24, Indian voters saw her as a potential prime minister, making it necessary for them to decide whether or not they wanted to live under a government that was headed by a woman of foreign origin who had entered politics only in 1997 and had never held a governmental office. Her unimpressive, almost bungling performance during the hectic days of April would not enhance the prospects of an affirmative answer to this question.

Prime Minister Vajpayee, on the other hand, had improved his standing in the eyes of large segments of the Indian public. Quite apart from the question of whether or not his regime had performed creditably during its thirteen months in office, many Indians saw the downfall of his regime, not as just retribution for its failure to perform, but as the result of a conspiracy hatched by opposition parties whose primary motive was to get their hands on the power of the Central Government. Vajpayee had reacted with dignity to his government's one vote defeat on the motion of confidence and had not resorted to political machinations in an attempt to keep himself and his Council of Ministers in office. He had not attacked President Narayanan for showing a pro-Congress bias by allowing Sonia Gandhi more time to find additional MPs who would support a Congress Indira Party minority government. Vajpayee's coalition constituency and his BJP supporters did not turn against him when he became a "loser" but, except for Jayalalitha, remained solidly behind him. Nor did he lose support among members of the Indian public. On the contrary, public opinion poll results showed that his standing among India's citizenry had improved. In a poll conducted in December 1997, 27% of the respondents had favored Vajpayee for prime minister. In an April-May 1999 poll, the percentage in his favor had risen to 43%. During the sixteen months that had elapsed between polls, Sonia Gandhi's favorable percentage had remained much the same at just over 30%. All in all, it was an enhanced Vajpayee and a diminished Sonia Gandhi who emerged from the April struggle for control of the Central Government and who would enter the 1999 General Election campaign as their respective parties' "star" performers.

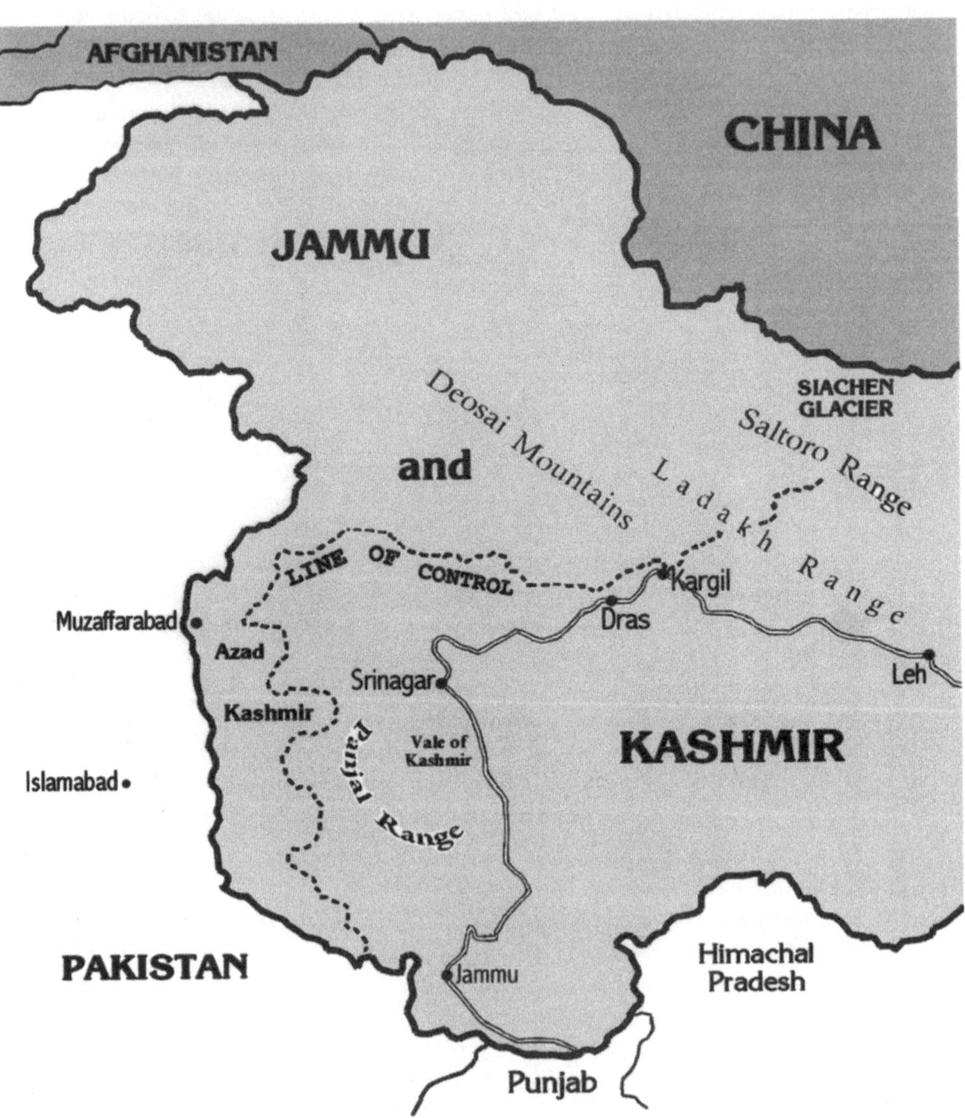

Kargil "War" Scene
May–July 1999
AFGHANISTAN
CHINA
JAMMU
SIACHEN GLACIER
Deosai Mountains
Saltoro Range
and
Ladakh Range
LINE OF CONTROL
Kargil
Dras
Muzaffarabad
Leh
Azad
Srinagar
Kashmir
Vale of Kashmir
KASHMIR
Panjal Range
Islamabad
PAKISTAN
Jammu
Himachal Pradesh
Punjab

12

Kargil "War" Operations

While the April political drama was being played out in Delhi, a mixed force of almost 1,000 Pakistani and Afghan Mujahideen (freedom fighters) and Pakistani army troops were infiltrating Indian territory in three sectors along a 150 kilometer stretch of the Kashmir Line of Control (LOC) in Kargil District. The infiltrators were establishing and supplying a large number of fortified posts and bunkers 6–7 kilometers inside Indian-held territory. Since the terrain in these areas consisted of mountains that rise 16,000 to 18,000 feet and since there were no roads leading to the high ridges that the Pakistani force occupied, planning for this invasion must have begun well before the February meeting between the Pakistani and Indian prime ministers at Lahore. The movement of ammunition, equipment and supplies by mules and on the backs of the infiltrators must have taken place during the two months that had followed the issuing of the Lahore Declaration.

It was only during the first week of May that Kashmiri shepherds encountered a contingent of the Pakistani force and reported their presence to the Indian army's command post in Kargil. Thinking that the intruders were no more than a patrol that the Pakistani army had sent in to reconnoiter the Indian side of the LOC, an Indian patrol was sent to investigate. Its members made contact with the Pakistani contingent, were met with a hail of gunfire, and were killed to a man. When the Kargil command post learned that the patrol had been wiped out, the Indian army realized that the intruders were more than a handful of Pakistani scouts and that it had something more than a routine military problem on its hands. As subsequent events unfolded, it became clear that the shots fired at the Indian army patrol were the first shots fired in a Kargil "war" which would last for the next two and a half months.

Pakistan embarked upon this invasion of Indian-held territory in Kashmir, at the very time that its prime minister would be meeting with India's prime minister to talk about resolving their countries' differences, for a number of military and political reasons. So far as the military reasons were concerned, it has to be remembered that Indo-Pakistani relations since the time the two countries came into being in 1947 can be summarized as one long cold war punctuated by three short hot wars. Militarily speaking, the Kargil "war" became the fourth hot war. It was a successor to the previous hot war that had been fought in 1971. Pakistan had never accepted its defeat in the Bangladesh war, which had dismantled the bifurcated Muslim country that had emerged from Partition. It regarded the Simla Agreement of 1972, which had tied up the loose ends of the Bangladesh war and had established the location of the LOC in Kashmir, as a pact that had been imposed upon a defeated Pakistan by a victorious India. Rather than agreeing that the LOC should be where the Simla Agreement said it was, Pakistan had accepted its location only until such time as it could be moved southward in Pakistan's favor.

From the time of the country's inception, Pakistan's military had played a dominant role in determining the country's relations with India. Although Indian Defense Minister George Fernandes went too far when he suggested that Pakistan's Prime Minister Sharif did not know at the time of his Lahore meeting with Prime Minister Vajpayee that a Kargil invasion was being planned, there can be no doubt that the Pakistani military was the invasion's prime mover and little doubt that Prime Minister Sharif was asked to give his authorization only when the plan was ready to be made operational. The military goal of the plan worked out by the leaders of Pakistan's armed forces was to improve the status of two of their operations that had been going on for some time but had not been going well. The first was the campaign to wrest control of the 14,000 feet high Siachen Glacier and its surrounding 15,000 feet high mountain peaks from the Indian army. Fighting in this portion of Ladakh had been going on since 1984, but it had its roots in events that had taken place in Kashmir thirty-five years earlier. The military confrontation that had erupted between India and Pakistan in Kashmir at the time of Partition had ended with a cease-fire and a 1949 agreement signed in Karachi that delineated a Line of Actual Control (LOAC) separating the opposing armies. This line extended for over 460 miles, but its precise location ended 40 miles short of the Chinese border. All that the Karachi Agreement said about this undelineated stretch of the LOAC was that it extended "north to the glaciers." The Siachen Glacier occupied the most strategic spot among these "glaciers." The LOAC was reviewed at the time the Simla Agreement was signed and, with minor adjustments, was defined as the Line of Control (LOC) in the nineteen maps that were appended to the agreement. The result was that the imprecise definition of the LOAC in the Siachen Glacier area was carried over into the LOC that became part of the Simla Agreement.

For thirty-five years after the Karachi Agreement was signed, Pakistan regarded the Siachen Glacier and its surrounding peaks as a part of Kashmir that was under its control. Its jurisdiction was recognized by a world atlas published in 1959 and by maps printed in the *National Geographic Magazine* in the early

1980s. Western mountaineering organizations whose members wished to climb peaks located in the Siachen Glacier area during the 1960s and 1970s applied to and received permits from Pakistani authorities. In 1984, this period of peace and quiet ended abruptly when, despite the provision contained in the Simla Agreement that neither country would use military force to change the division of territory in Kashmir, Indian troops occupied the Siachen Glacier and its adjacent mountain peaks. This occupying force took control of an area of approximately 1,000 square miles that for thirty-five years had been treated as a Pakistani preserve. As was to be expected, Pakistan reacted by sending its soldiers into the occupied area in an attempt to drive out the Indian "intruders." Since the Indian troops had seized control of the high ground, the Pakistani\ counterattack did not succeed. Indian troops retained their hold on the Siachen Glacier and the adjoining Saltoro mountain range.

During the next fourteen years, Pakistan had applied unremitting military pressure on the intruding Indian force, and India had maintained a dogged defense of the territory it had seized. Artillery exchanges had continued and, from time to time, infantry clashes had taken place. India had maintained a force ranging from 3,000 to 4,000 men in the Siachen Glacier area, and had spent about 5 crores of rupees ($1.2 million) per day to fund its defensive operation. Casualty figures have never been officially released, but newspaper accounts have estimated casualties at 500 dead and as many as 10,000 sick and injured. The conditions under which Indian troops had to operate explain the disproportion between the estimates for "dead" and for "sick and injured." Since Indian soldiers had dug in to protect themselves against artillery fire and since infantry clashes had involved small numbers of troops and had occurred only sporadically, only a limited number of Indian soldiers had been killed. But carrying on military operations in rugged mountainous terrain where the heights rose to 15,000 feet and encountering temperatures that fell to -40°F meant that injuries and sickness would be commonplace.

To American eyes, the fourteen year struggle between Pakistan and India over the Siachen Glacier made no military or political sense. The only source of the conflict that American observers had been able to suggest was the two countries' mutual hatred. According to an article in the *Minneapolis Star Tribune*, "Their combat over a barren, uninhabited world of questionable value is a forbidding symbol of their lingering irreconcilability." Stephen Cohen of the Brookings Institute likened the conflict to "a struggle between two bald men over a comb. Siachen is a symbol of the worst aspects of their relationship." But Indian and Pakistani eyes have seen the struggle quite differently. The commanding officer of the Indian troops stationed in Leh, the command center for Siachen Glacier operations, viewed his troops as defenders of their homeland: "Nobody can win, no matter how long we fight. But this is our land. It is part of our nation state and we will not cede it."

For Pakistani generals, the exact opposite was the truth. They saw the Siachen Glacier area as Pakistani land that had been stolen by Indian soldiers. They would continue the fight to drive out the Indian aggressors for as long as it took to regain the territory that had been lost. During the years between 1984 and 1998, the battle for the Siachen Glacier had become the strategic fulcrum and the principal bone of contention between the Pakistani and Indian armies. India's seizure of the Siachen Glacier area had become a black mark in the history of the Pakistani army, a black mark like the loss of the Bangladesh War and one that Pakistan was duty bound to do its utmost to expunge. Pakistan's continuing struggle to regain control of the Siachen Glacier area took on a new saliency in 1989 when an insurgency broke out in Kashmir aimed at freeing the state from Indian rule. It was the Indian army's responsibility to suppress this insurgency, which was centered in Srinagar and the Kashmir Valley. The more the Indian army was forced to disperse its men and equipment westward into Ladakh, the more difficult it would be to meet that responsibility. One way to force India to move its contingents away from the Kashmir Valley and into Ladakh was to make it more difficult for its forces to hold the Siachen Glacier and the peaks around it.

The Indian forces holding the Siachen Glacier area could be hurt by interdicting shipments of supplies coming to them over the Srinagar-Leh road. In the Dras sector of Kargil District, that road ran close to a series of mountain peaks that rose to heights of 16,000 to 18,000 feet. By taking control of and placing artillery on peaks located six or seven kilometers on India's side of the LOC, Pakistani forces could observe and shell road traffic that was moving only four kilometers away. Such close proximity would enable the Pakistani guns to attain a degree of accuracy that could delay Siachen Glacier supply shipments and even bring them to a halt. An additional means of isolating the Siachen Glacier from the rest of Kashmir would be to cross the LOC and occupy heights in the adjacent Batalik sector. These heights were some distance from the Srinagar-Leh road, but they dominated the overland approaches to the Siachen Glacier area. Occupying them would make it easier for Pakistan and harder for India to move men and material to the combat area.

Crossing the LOC in the Mashkoh Valley sector of Kargil District and taking over heights located some five kilometers within Indian-held territory would facilitate the infiltration into the Kashmir Valley of badly needed Mujahideen reinforcements for the Kashmiri insurgency. The Kashmir insurgency against Indian rule, the goal of which was to make Kashmir an independent state, had been going on since 1989. After seven years of hostilities during which, according to the Indian army, some 30,000 people and, according to Kashmiri insurgent sources, some 70,000 people had lost their lives and 250,000 refugees had been forced to move to other parts of India, the insurgency had begun to flag. beginning with the 1996 General Election. By 1998, the Kashmir Valley was relatively quiet. Only some 2,000 Kashmiri militants organized by the All Party Hurriyat Conference were still active. Schools and markets were open once more, and for the first time in years tourists were beginning to visit the Kashmir Valley. Taking control of the Mashkoh Valley and diverting the attention of Indian forces to coping with Pakistani incursions further west in the Dras sector would make it possible for Pakistan to bring in large numbers of additional Pakistani and Afghani fighters to join the remaining Kashmiri insurgents. This additional manpower would provide the "shot in the arm" which was badly needed to keep the insurgency going.

Insurgent operations would be able to do more damage not only because insurgent forces would have been strengthened but because Indian defenses would have been weakened. The Indian army had been doing an effective job of coping with insurgents' attacks. If Indian army contingents were moved to the LOC to counter Pakistani intruders, they would be replaced by paramilitary forces who would not have the personnel, training, or equipment to maintain the army's level of efficiency in keeping the insurgency under control. Facing a less formidable foe, the Kashmiri insurgents would be encouraged to act more aggressively in carrying on their campaign for independence. Their morale would also be enhanced because a show of force along the LOC would remind them that Pakistan stood behind them, that Pakistan had not lost its military clout, and that Pakistani forces could wrest Kashmiri territory from the Indian army.

These military goals were accompanied by a number of political goals that could be pursued by crossing the LOC at several crucial points. A Pakistani military force moving into Indian-held territory would proclaim to India and the rest of the world that Pakistan did not accept the LOC as a permanent boundary dividing Jammu and Kashmir between Pakistan and India. Increased fighting along the LOC and stepped-up insurgent activities within Jammu and Kashmir would also increase the chances that other powers would intervene in an effort to keep a South Asian regional problem from getting out of hand. While this danger to the international community had existed for decades, it had become much more acute now that the disputants had nuclear weapons at their disposal. From the early days of the Kashmir dispute, Pakistan had recognized that its hope for preventing India from making two-thirds of the state of Jammu and Kashmir a permanent part of the Indian union depended not only upon its military forces but also upon the support that it received from other countries who felt that Kashmir's predominantly Muslim population vitiated India's claim that it belonged to India. During the 1950s, the United Nations had tried to settle the dispute through a plebiscite in which the Kashmiri people could express their preference for joining Pakistan or India, but unending distrust between the two countries had prevented the plebiscite from being held. Since the United Nations continued to regard Kashmir as a "disputed" territory, Pakistan had persisted in its efforts to "internationalize" the Kashmir question.

India had taken the position that the dispute should be settled by the disputing parties and that other nations should not interfere. Accepting this approach automatically tilted the scales to India's advantage because India occupied twice as much territory in the state of Jammu and Kashmir and had a military establishment twice the size of Pakistan's. Since the start of the Kashmir insurgency in 1989, Pakistan had hoped that the insurgents' struggle for an independent Kashmir and their battles with the Indian army would renew international interest in a plebiscite, but this had not happened. When the Indian authorities had by 1996 brought the insurgency under control for the time being, Pakistan had to make a radical and risky move in an attempt to persuade the international community to become involved in finding a peaceful settlement to the Kashmir problem.

The portion of the LOC running through Kargil District had never been a point of military contention between Pakistan and India. The immediate area on the Indian side was dominated by ridges, rising as high as 18,000 feet, that, because of the forbidding terrain and bitterly cold winter climate, were uninhabited. The Indian army took advantage of the warmer months to send patrols into the mountainous area on its side of the LOC and establish observation posts there. These operations were halted when the snows came, at which time the observation posts were abandoned until spring. The spring of 1999 looked to be a time when the Indian army would have no difficulty reestablishing its outposts along the LOC as soon as the snow had melted. But when its soldiers returned to the Dras, Batalik, and Mashkoh Valley sectors in April, they found that a Pakistani invading force had crossed the LOC and occupied ridges that extended as far as seven kilometers inside Indian-held territory and brought Pakistani forces within four kilometers of the Srinagar-Leh road.

The Pakistani invading force was well equipped, well entrenched in fortified bunkers, and armed with rifles, machine guns, and mortars. It was obvious from their number and their equipment that planning for the invasion had begun as early as January and, given the difficult terrain into which the invading force had been moved, that implementation had been under way from the time that the two prime ministers had met at Lahore. Routes supplying the Pakistani outposts had been carefully laid out and tied into the Pakistani army's logistical network, and staging points had been established in all of the three sectors that the invaders had entered. Throughout the fighting in Kargil District, Pakistan admitted that artillery firing from the Pakistani side of the LOC provided cover for their outposts on the Indian side but steadfastly maintained the official line that the intruders were "freedom fighters" who had entered Indian-held territory to support Kashmiri insurgents fighting for independence and that no Pakistani army regulars were among them.

During the fighting, this official line was breached when Pakistani authorities accepted the bodies of three Pakistani soldiers who had been killed. After the invading force had been withdrawn, the Pakistani army chief of staff acknowledged in a July 17 BBC interview that Pakistani troops had been engaged in "aggressive patrolling" across the LOC during the preceding two and a half months. Pakistan used the good offices of the International Red Cross to recover the bodies of two Pakistani army officers who had died on the Indian side of the LOC. While tacitly admitting by these actions that Pakistani military personnel were included in the invading force, Pakistan's official line prevented it from giving any information regarding what proportion of the invading force was made up of its troops. A rough idea was provided by India's report that papers found on their bodies showed that 240 of the 850 invaders who were buried by Indian soldiers were members of Pakistan's army.

By the last week of April, Pakistani preparations had been completed for an extended occupation of positions on the Indian side of the LOC in three sectors of Kargil District. Pakistan's major military effort would now focus on defending these forward posts against Indian attack. At the same time, a secondary effort would renew pressure against Indian forces occupying the Siachen Glacier area. Between September 1998 and April 1999, Pakistan strengthened its forces in the Siachen Glacier sector and launched fifteen attacks on the Indian posts established there. It was at this point that the general commanding Indian troops described his front as a "war-like situation. Here it is a free for all and our troops have to be vigilant all the time keeping in view the evil designs of our neighbors."

During the first weeks of the Kargil "war," Pakistan fared well in its attempt to hold the posts that had been established by its invading force. When the Indian army, thinking that it was faced with a small-scale Pakistani penetration, launched an infantry attack against the Pakistani position on Jubar Ridge in the Batalik sector, it was met by heavy machine gun and mortar fire and concentrated shelling from the Pakistani side of the LOC. The resulting casualties—34 killed, 131 wounded, and 12 missing—were considered unacceptably high for the size of the Indian force involved. Reluctant to continue such costly ground operations, India's military decided to turn to air power as a means of expelling the invaders. Air strikes were launched on May 16, and two Indian fighters were lost, one shot down by a ground to air missile and the other a victim of engine failure. Despite these losses and the subsequent downing of an Indian helicopter, air operations continued. It quickly became evident that air strikes alone were not going to drive out the well entrenched and determined Pakistani invaders and that an Indian ground force of at least 25,000 men would have to carry most of the load. On May 31, Prime Minister Vajpayee acknowledged that India now realized that it had to undertake a large-scale army–air force combined campaign to retake the Kashmir territory that had been lost to Pakistani invaders, by announcing for the first time that India faced a "war-like situation" in Kargil District.

It had become clear by now that frontal attacks against the Pakistani positions would result in substantial casualties and that the Pakistani defense was being bolstered by a steady stream of supplies coming from its side of the LOC. Given this tactical situation, it was obvious to the leaders of India's armed forces that a less costly way to force the Pakistani force to withdraw would be to order Indian troops to outflank the Pakistani positions, cross the LOC into Pakistani-held territory, and cut the invaders' supply lines. Prime Minister Vajpayee resisted the temptation to take the route dictated by military strategy. While he realized that India's crossing the LOC into Pakistani-held territory would result in military gains, he was also aware that it would result in diplomatic losses. Pakistan would accuse India of engaging in aggression in Kashmir and use that accusation as the basis for appealing to the United Nations, the United States, and other members of the international community to intervene on its behalf.

Prime Minister Vajpayee's prognostication that this would be the result of India's crossing the LOC was confirmed by a diplomatic move that Pakistan made immediately after the loss of the Indian aircraft. Its foreign minister tried to intensify world fears that the fighting in Kargil District could end in nuclear war by declaring that Pakistan would use "any weapon" in its arsenal to defend its territorial integrity. He went on to say that, instead of merely expressing "verbal concern," the international community should pressure India into settling the Kashmir problem by diplomatic rather than by military means. His words were followed by a letter from Pakistan's prime minister to the secretary general of the United Nations (UN) requesting that the UN intervene in the Kargil conflict to halt "dangerous escalation" of the fighting in South Asia. The letter suggested that, as a first step, the UN should send a representative to investigate India's aggressive actions in the Kargil combat zone. The reaction of the UN and the United States to Pakistan's "dangerous escalation" warning was to call upon both countries to take steps to keep the fighting from spreading and to find a peaceful solution for their conflict in Kashmir.

On June 3, Prime Minister Sharif gestured in this "confidence building" direction by ordering the release of the pilot of the Indian fighter that had been shot down and by calling for a renewed effort to defuse hostilities along the LOC, which he blamed on India's "intention to mislead the world and deflect international focus from the crux of the matter." To define the "crux of the matter," he pointed to the secretary general's statement that a resolution of the Kashmir dispute was urgently needed and assertion that "the centrality of the Kashmir issue to peace and security in South Asia is indeed recognized by the whole world." A further gesture in the direction of using the diplomatic route to bring the Kargil fighting to an end came on June 8 when Pakistan offered to send its foreign minister to Delhi to discuss ways and means of stopping the bloodshed. After initially hesitating to accept the offer, India set June 12 as the day when the two foreign ministers would meet. In hope of taking advantage of Pakistan's and China's long-standing cooperation in matters of defense to line up China as an ally, Pakistan's foreign minister preceded his visit to India with a stop in Beijing. According to a press release put out in Islamabad at the time of his departure, "Pakistan and China enjoy close and friendly relations which have stood the test of time. Both countries coordinate and consult with each other regularly and the foreign minister's visit is a part of this tradition." Unfortunately for Pakistan, this episode of "coordinating" and "consulting" produced no word of support from its erstwhile ally.

Whatever foreign policy mileage Pakistan might have hoped to gain from Chinese backing must have been offset by a sharp rebuff which came at the same time from the United States: "We think that the LOC has been clearly demarked over the years. The two sides have not previously had significant differences about where the LOC is. Those who have infiltrated from the Pakistani side must go back." Not surprisingly, India's old ally, Russia, called in Pakistan's ambassador at this time and told him the same thing. Pakistan received additional bad news through diplomatic channels when Britain reiterated the message that had been received from the United States. The penultimate diplomatic blow came when the G-8 industrialized nations accused Pakistan of having violated the LOC and called upon it to withdraw its invading force. The final blow was delivered when the UN continued to refuse to place the Kargil conflict on the Security Council's agenda.

To no one's surprise, the June 12 meeting between Pakistan's and India's foreign ministers came to nothing. Pakistan stood by its claim that it could not order the withdrawal of the Kargil invaders because they were Mujahideen fighting for the independence of Kashmir, not Pakistani soldiers. Pakistan's foreign minister refused to acknowledge that the invaders had violated the LOC, maintaining that its delineation in the maps appended to the Simla Agreement had never been laid out on the ground. India was adamant that the LOC had been clearly defined by the Simla Agreement to which Pakistani was a signatory, that the Pakistani invaders had intruded into Indian territory, and that they should immediately withdraw. Such diametrically opposed stands left no room for compromise, and the two foreign ministers parted without a handshake and without setting a date for a subsequent meeting.

Following the failure of the June 12 meeting in Delhi, Pakistan's prime minister made a second attempt to elicit Chinese support by journeying to Beijing for a six day visit. To everyone's surprise, he cut short his stay and returned to Islamabad three days later. The reason why he had left Beijing three days early was revealed the next day when the Chinese foreign minister issued a press release that stated his country's position: "We seriously hope that both India and China can earnestly respect the Line of Control in Kashmir, resume negotiation as soon as possible and see a fair and reasonable settlement of all their differences." China's words were softer but they said exactly what the United States, Britain, Russia, and the G-8 nations had said earlier to the two combatants.

During the time that Pakistan's abortive diplomatic offensive was going on, its military position in the Kargil area was also under threat. As soon as the Indian military authorities realized that driving the Pakistani invading force from the Mashkoh Valley and from the Dras and Batalik sectors was going to require action by large infantry and artillery formations supported by a substantial number of aircraft, they hurriedly set in motion an extensive mobilization process. Three mountain divisions and an infantry division that had been stationed in Ladakh were rushed to the Kargil front, increasing from 5,000 to 25,000 the number of troops stationed there. The large quantities of cold weather clothing and sturdy mountain boots needed to equip this greatly augmented force were hurriedly procured. Bofors howitzers were moved to the Kargil area from other points along the LOC so that several hundred artillery pieces would be available to lay down concentrated fire on the Pakistani posts on India's side and the Pakistani supply bases on Pakistan's side. Kashmir's roads became clogged with trucks carrying thousands of soldiers to new positions and ammunition and supplies sufficient to support a major offensive.

To replace the army divisions that had been moved to the Kargil front, additional battalions of the Central Reserve Police, the Border Security Force, and the Rashtriya Rifles were brought into Kashmir and deployed in areas where army units had formerly provided protection against Kashmiri insurgent attacks. To enhance security along India's border with Pakistan in Rajasthan, Punjab, and Gujarat, army units stationed in Ahmedabad and Jodhpur were moved forward by road, followed by trains carrying their tanks and artillery to their new positions. India's air force and navy were placed on full alert, and all leave was canceled throughout the military establishment. Within a matter of a few weeks, India's armed forces had been placed on a war footing in order to recapture the mountain peaks lost in the Pakistani invasion of Kargil District and to prevent Pakistan from launching similar incursions into Indian territory outside Kashmir.

India's combined army/air force offensive against the Pakistani invaders, code named "Operation Vijay" (victory) reached full operational levels during the second week of June. By the middle of the month, the heights flanking the Jubar Ridge in the Batalik sector had been captured, and the flow of supplies to Pakistani bunkers occupied by approximately 300 Mujahideen and soldiers was curtailed. On June 18, the Pakistani position atop the Tololing Peak that dominated the Dras sector was taken, greatly reducing the Pakistani threat to traffic on the Srinagar-Leh road. On July 4, the second most important piece of high ground in the Dras sector, Tiger Hill, was occupied by Indian troops, making it possible to reopen the Srinagar-Leh road to civilian traffic for the first time in over two months. Two days later, Jubar Ridge itself was captured, after which it became impossible for the large Pakistani force in the Batalik sector to maintain its positions. At this point, the decisive phase of India's counteroffensive had come to a successful conclusion. All that remained was to carry out cleanup operations.

On July 7, after a flurry of diplomatic activity that resulted in Pakistan's being isolated in the world community except for an endorsement from the International Organization of Islamic States, Prime Minister Sharif announced that he would call upon the Mujahideen force to stop fighting, withdraw from its redoubts, and return to the Pakistani side of the LOC. Pakistan requested that the two countries' directors of general military operations (DGMOs) meet to work out arrangements for this withdrawal. The DGMOs met on July 11 and agreed that Pakistani forces should vacate all territory on India's side of the LOC by July 16. The Pakistani DGMO's acceptance of a deadline that required hundreds of Mujahideen to withdraw from dozens of dug-in positions high in the mountains within a week was further evidence that these so-called "freedom fighters" were directly under the command of Pakistan's army and were following its orders rather than their own strategy for freeing Kashmir from Indian rule. The very day that the withdrawal deadline was set, the first contingents of the Pakistani invading force began to retreat to Pakistan's side of the LOC. The day after he made his withdrawal appeal, Prime Minister Sharif turned his conciliatory face to India, the United States, and the rest of the world by proposing that Indo-Pakistani talks begin to address the issues raised by the Kargil "war." Six days later, India's prime minister responded by declaring "Operation Vijay" a success and informing Pakistan that no dialogue could take place unless Pakistan recognized the validity of the LOC and ceased its campaign to support the Kashmir insurgents by infiltrating Mujahideen fighters into Jammu and the Kashmir Valley.

While its successful military offensive was in progress, India was conducting a diplomatic offensive that was equally aggressive and equally effective. Its primary objective was to prevent Pakistan from "internationalizing" the Kashmir dispute, by convincing the world community that the fighting in Kargil was proof positive that outside intervention was needed if a major, possibly nuclear, Indo-Pakistani war was to be avoided. The second objective was to win support for India's handling of the Kargil crisis from the key external players in South Asian politics, particularly the United States and China. The initial step in India's diplomatic offensive was taken in pursuit of the first objective. Immediately after the fighting began in Kargil District, External Affairs Minister Jaswant Singh contacted the foreign ministers of four of the permanent members of the United Nations Security Council—the United States, Russia, the United Kingdom, and France—to obtain their assurance that they would make no moves to bring the Kargil problem before the Security Council. When Secretary General Kofi Annan responded on May 30 to Pakistan's request that the United Nations intervene to stop the fighting, offering to send an envoy to Delhi and Islamabad, Prime Minister Vajpayee flatly turned down his offer. According to Vajpayee, "Mr. Annan rang up last night to convey his proposal to send a special envoy to India and Pakistan to sort out the matter between the two countries. I firmly told him that if at all an envoy has to be sent, he should go to Pakistan and not to India."

Jaswant Singh also lost no time in pursuing the second diplomatic objective when American Secretary of State Albright and the British foreign secretary called him at the end of May to express their concern that fighting had erupted once again in Kashmir. He explained to them that the shooting that was taking place on the Indian side of the LOC had started because Pakistani forces had intruded into Indian territory. He assured them that, although it was necessary for India to drive out the invaders, India would not intensify the fighting by sending its forces into Pakistan's side of the LOC. When the June 12 meeting between Pakistan's and India's foreign ministers ended in failure, Prime Minister Vajpayee announced to the world that, while "India is fully prepared for war if it is thrust upon us," its forces were capable of countering the Pakistani invasion into Kargil District without extending the area in which fighting was taking place. Pakistan's prime minister followed the unsuccessful meeting by calling the Indian prime minister the next day to urge that India and Pakistan take steps to defuse tension and prevent "our region from descending into chaos and conflagration." Vajpayee replied by ruling out any further diplomatic discussions until Pakistan's infiltrators had completely withdrawn from Indian territory.

The day following the June 12 unproductive exchange between the Indian and Pakistani foreign ministers, President Clinton called Prime Minister Vajpayee to praise him for his restraint in refraining from sending Indian troops and aircraft across the LOC into Pakistani-held territory. The next day he telephoned Prime Minister Sharif, urging him to respect the LOC and pull his troops back from the positions that they had occupied on India's side. That same day, India's External Affairs Minister traveled to Beijing. Jaswant Singh's official purpose was to reestablish the political ties between India and China that had been broken when the May 1998 Pokhran nuclear bomb tests had been blamed on the threat to India's security coming from China. Although he did not go there to discuss the Kargil fighting, the fact that he had been invited by China and that he went as the first Indian foreign minister to travel there since 1991 augured well for the accomplishment of his hidden agenda, which was to increase the chances that China would refuse to support Pakistan's military action in Kashmir. This flurry of diplomatic activity continued on June 17 when India sent the prime minister's principal secretary to present its case to the meeting of the Group of Eight (G-8) industrialized nations that was being held in Cologne. His presentation produced exactly the response that India had desired. The G-8 representatives accused Pakistan of violating the LOC, characterized its effort to change the LOC by military means as "irresponsible," and called for an immediate end to the fighting in Kargil and a resumption of diplomatic efforts to end the Kashmir dispute.

Apparently thinking that Pakistan might take an American military voice more seriously, President Clinton followed up his June 15 call to Prime Minister Sharif by sending General Anthony Zinni, the commander-in-chief of the United States Central Command, accompanied by a deputy assistant secretary of state, to Islamabad "as part of our continuing close contacts with the Pakistani and Indian governments in pursuing our concerns about ending the fighting in Kargil." General Zinni reiterated what President Clinton had said on the telephone, but his message was characterized by Pakistan's foreign minister as "a narrow point of view which is not fair or balanced." It was dismissed in harsher terms by Pakistan's former army chief of staff: "We didn't give much importance to the visit. We are not an American colony. We cannot be dictated to by others and we will do what suits our national interests." All General Zinni could do was to inform Prime Minster Vajpayee of the total failure of his mission when he stopped in Delhi on his way back to Washington, where he reported to President Clinton that Pakistan had not taken the American message to heart even when it was spoken by a military voice.

On July 1, Jaswant Singh's trip to Beijing paid off when China endorsed the stand that had been taken by the G-8 countries, urging Pakistan to withdraw its forces that had intruded on the Indian side of the LOC and "return to the path of confidence building measures under the Lahore process." A spokeswoman of the Chinese Ministry of Foreign Affairs added: "We sincerely hope that both India and Pakistan can earnestly respect the Line of Control in Kashmir." At the same time, British Prime Minister Tony Blair was writing to Prime Minister Vajpayee to commend India's "measured response" to the Pakistani invasion by containing the fighting to India's side of the LOC. According to Blair's letter, India had earned thereby the "sympathy and support" of the international community. The letter which the British prime minister sent at the same time to Prime Minister Sharif was as negative in tone as the message sent to India was positive. Tony Blair wrote that Pakistan had created a "serious problem" by sending intruders across the LOC and could rectify it only by following the steps that had been urged by the G-8 countries at their meeting in Cologne.

Prime Minister Sharif's only hope on the diplomatic front now lay in using the collaboration that had gone on between Pakistan and the United States since the 1950s as a basis for a last ditch appeal to President Clinton to offer America's good offices to mediate the Kargil "war." The president called Vajpayee on July 3 to invite him to come to Washington to discuss the Kargil situation, but the prime minister declined the invitation, saying that the time was not "convenient." Sharif telephoned President Clinton the same day to request an urgent personal meeting. Although July 4 was a holiday in the United States, Clinton went out of his way to comply with the Pakistani prime minister's request, but only after ascertaining from Prime Minister Vajpayee that India had no objection to such a meeting. The White House meeting that followed, far from producing the outcome that Pakistan desired, ended with a joint statement that "concrete steps will be taken for the restoration of the Line of Control in accordance with the Simla Agreement." In plain terms, since Pakistan's intrusion into Kargil District was a violation of the sanctity of the LOC, its forces should be withdrawn to the Pakistani side. The only hopeful signs that could be seized upon by Pakistan were the portions of the statement expressing agreement that the Indo-Pakistani dialogue that had begun in Lahore in February "provides the best forum for resolving all issues dividing India and Pakistan, including Kashmir" and the assurance that the U.S. president "would take a personal interest in encouraging an expeditious resumption and intensification of continuing bilateral efforts once the sanctity of the Line of Control has been restored." Any comfort that Pakistan might have derived from President Clinton's "personal interest" was tempered when the White House official who elaborated on the meaning of the joint statement emphasized that the United States had no intention of offering to mediate in the conflict and that it believed the Kargil conflict had to be resolved through bilateral dialogue.

Having failed to persuade President Clinton to enter the fray to end the fighting in Kargil District on terms favorable to Pakistan, Sharif played his last diplomatic card by stopping on his way home to ask Prime Minister Blair to assume the role of mediator. He was rebuffed in London just as he had been rebuffed in Washington. By the time he arrived in Islamabad, he had become convinced that Pakistan had lost the Kargil "war" diplomatically as well as militarily. Maintaining to the bitter end that Pakistan could not order the Pakistani invading force to withdraw because it consisted of Mujahideen, not Pakistani soldiers, the Pakistani minister of state for foreign affairs and the army chief of staff announced on July 6 that they would appeal to the "freedom fighters" to withdraw to the Pakistani side of the LOC. The next day that message was repeated by Pakistan's prime minister.

Since the official Pakistani line was that the force that had crossed the LOC into Indian-held territory was made up entirely of "freedom fighters," the withdrawal announcement contained the proviso that the Mujahideen could take as much time as they needed to decide whether or not they would respond positively to the appeal. In fact, the Pakistani mixed force of regular troops and Mujahideen began to withdraw within five days. Indian troops and aircraft maintained their pressure on the retreating invaders in order to make sure that the withdrawal was completed by the July 16 deadline and refused to observe a cease-fire until the last Pakistani fighter had vacated Indian-held territory. It would be another two weeks before India would announce that there were no more Pakistani intruders in the Mashkoh Valley or in the Dras and Batalik sectors of Kargil District. By July 26 organized hostilities had ceased, and the seventy-five day Kargil "war," the first fought in uninhabited terrain where the mountains rose as high as 18,000 feet and night temperatures fell as low as -40°F, had come to an end.

13

Kargil "War" Repercussions

While India's army and air force were engaged in driving the Pakistani invaders back to their side of the LOC and India's diplomats were winning international support for the Indian cause, the Kargil "war" was having its impact on India's domestic front. The villages along the Indian side of the LOC in Kargil District were the first to feel the repercussions of the fighting. Heavy shelling coming from the Pakistani side of the LOC sought to disrupt the Indian army's mobilization and movement of men and supplies to the fighting front. Village homes and shops were hit, and villagers were killed and wounded. The result was that almost all of the civilian population, estimated at 50,000 men, women, and children, were forced to flee. Their flight was followed by the evacuation of almost 200 villages located at other points along the Indian side of the LOC, whose residents feared that the invasion in Kargil District was the prelude to a general Pakistani offensive in Kashmir. Civilian panic then spread to the Punjab, where almost 90% of the population living in border areas where fighting had gone on during the 1965 Indo-Pakistani war and the 1971 Bangladesh war, some 180,000 people, moved to other parts of the state where they would not have to fear the threat of Pakistani invaders. One of the Punjabi village leaders expressed the feeling that prompted them to move: "We are leaving the village due to war-like situation as the army has taken over and we cannot let our children die. Moreover, we still have not forgotten the previous two wars in which we were completely ruined. In this situation, how can we wait for the war to begin?"

Such panic reactions were limited to Kashmir and the Pakistani border areas in the Punjab. The Indian people as a whole remained relatively calm, and, for the most part, life continued to follow peacetime ways. Some signs began to appear of what might have become a general wartime fever if the Kargil fighting had lasted more than two and a half months. Pakistani TV channels were banned by the information and broadcasting minister. Web sites of Pakistani newspapers were closed. Demonstrators gathered outside the residence of a movie star calling upon him to return a Pakistani award that he had received. Thousands of young men volunteering for service in the armed forces overwhelmed recruiting offices. A crowd protested the Pakistani foreign minister's June 12 arrival in Delhi. Far from encouraging these public displays of animosity toward Pakistan, the authorities took steps to see to it that they did not get out of hand. Although there was a good deal of popular sentiment in favor of allowing Indian troops to cross the LOC and enter Pakistani-held territory, only the journal of the RSS urged Prime Minister Vajpayee to use nuclear weapons to destroy the Pakistani invaders.

A week after the Indian counteroffensive had begun, Prime Minister Vajpayee traveled to the Kargil front to visit India's fighting men. His courage in doing so was highlighted by the fact that during the week before his arrival Pakistani shells had fallen on the helipad where he landed and other shells had hit an Indian position located no more than two kilometers from the place where he was meeting with army personnel. After leaving Kargil, he flew to Srinagar where he talked with the wounded being treated in the 15th Corps's hospital. The only development which marred Vajpayee's efforts to encourage civilian support occurred in Srinagar, where a general strike was organized by the All Party Hurriyat Conference to protest India's military presence in Kashmir. Shops were closed and public transport was halted, but no protestors gathered to demonstrate because the police had stepped up security arrangements during the prime minister's visit and paramilitary troops were out in force on the streets to break up any gatherings that might take place.

Not only did Prime Minister Vajpayee's leadership style succeed in mobilizing the home front behind the "war" effort, but his words convinced the Indian people that it was a national rather than a partisan political enterprise. The "war" was being fought under a BJP-led caretaker government, and it could well have been seen as an effort to further the interests of the BJP rather than the interests of the nation. The result would have been a "war" that was supported by the BJP, the RSS, the Bajrang Dal, and the other Sangh Parivar organizations and opposed by the so-called "secular" parties. Vajpayee repeatedly denied that his BJP party sought to derive political mileage from the Kargil "war" and repeatedly "requested other political parties not to play politics with Kargil."

Vajpayee's campaign to "nationalize" the Kargil "war" by raising it above politics placed the Congress Indira Party and the other opposition parties in a position where they could not oppose the caretaker government's military and diplomatic operations without appearing to be unpatriotic. They were forced, Janus-like, to adopt a stance in which they faced in opposite directions. On the one hand, they backed the military effort to drive back the Pakistani invaders and the diplomatic effort to prevent the Kashmir effort from being "internationalized." On the other hand, they attacked the Vajpayee-led government by arguing that the failure of its military intelligence apparatus to detect the training and equipping of the Pakistani invading force that was going on during the months prior to the Lahore meeting and the failure of the army to discover the invading force's movement to India's side of the LOC until it was discovered in May by Kashmiri shepherds had placed India in a position where it had to fight a "war" that should not have needed to be fought.

Sonia Gandhi mirrored the Janus-like approach to the Kargil "war" effort that had been adopted by her party. While she made repeated public statements praising the bravery and sacrifice of the soldiers and airmen fighting in Kargil District, she was careful to absent herself from the first all-party meetings convened by Prime Minister Vajpayee to brief party leaders on how the "war" effort was going. To have attended the meetings as the Congress Indira Party president would have given the erroneous impression that her party endorsed the leadership that the BJP-led coalition government was providing. At the same time, she went out of her way to show her personal concern for the fighting men, particularly those who had been wounded. When the Congress Indira Party set up a blood bank to provide transfusions for the wounded, she was the first donor in line.

She proposed to pay a visit to the soldiers serving in the combat area but was turned down for security reasons. Forced to show her support for the troops in some other way, she visited the wounded in military hospitals and gave them gifts of candy and shawls. These visits displayed her support for India's fighting men, but they had a political downside because they revealed in a pointed way one of her weaknesses as a national political leader—her lack of fluency in Indian languages. Since the military authorities would not allow any of her entourage to enter the hospitals with her, no one from her staff was available to translate her words when she attempted to engage in conversation with the wounded soldiers. The result was that her distribution of gifts was carried on in silence, and the recuperating soldiers had to express their appreciation with smiles and gestures rather than words.

Prime Minister Vajpayee's pronouncement on July 26 that "Operation Vijay" had been a success and that the Pakistani invaders had been driven back across the LOC did not mean that the guns had fallen silent along the LOC and that there would be no more casualties in Kashmir. But it did mean that, with the cessation of concentrated firing and bombing in the Mashkoh Valley and the Dras and Batalik sectors, the Kargil "war" had come to an end, and that the time had come to assess its costs and benefits for the Indian nation. India's casualty figures were 410 killed, 593 wounded, and 4 missing in action. To this human cost was added the substantial monetary costs that had been incurred. No official figure was released, but unofficial estimates ranged from 1,000 to 1,500 crores of rupees ($250 million to $350 million) for the money that had been paid out to procure the ammunition and supplies that were used. If the figure was calculated on the basis of what it would cost to replace at current prices that ammunition and those supplies and to make good the combat damage done to artillery pieces, aircraft, and other equipment, the unofficial estimate rose to 5,000 crores of rupees ($1.16 billion).

These estimates included only costs incurred during the two and a half months of fighting. They went much higher when the cost of the military measures that would have to be taken in the aftermath of the Kargil "war" was taken into account. In the low key words of India's DGMO, "the Indian army will now maintain a presence in Kargil in greater measure." By that brief phrase, he conveyed the Indian army's realization that the mountain peaks in the Kargil District portion of the Line of Control could no longer be treated as a "no man's land" in which posts would be established in the summer and vacated in the winter. The experience of the Pakistani invasion had taught the Indian army that it would have to set up permanent bases on the Kargil District's peaks and at other vulnerable points along the LOC and man them throughout the year. That the Vajpayee government agreed with the army's reading of the Kargil "war's" tactical lesson was confirmed when Defense Minister Fernandes announced: "Of course, the LOC needs to be manned round the year. We must take quick steps to make the entire area secure as Pakistan has demonstrated its disloyal trust [sic]." He elaborated by saying that soldiers would be stationed in positions along the LOC throughout the year and that aerial and electronic surveillance would be maintained to prevent Pakistan from carrying out another Kargil-like invasion.

Implementing this new defense policy and carrying it out on a permanent basis would require a commitment of Indian manpower and resources on a large scale. Given the harsh environment in which soldiers manning the mountain posts would be operating, a rotation system would have to be followed, in which each contingent would serve a limited number of months before it was relieved. This rotation system would require more manpower than would be needed in a situation where the same troops remained on duty for an extended period of time. The commander of India's 15th Corps that had formerly been responsible for the Siachen Glacier front estimated that "the force required in Kargil will be twice as much. Probably more." He added the comment that holding Siachen was far easier because defending the LOC would require establishing as many as 250 posts compared with only 108 posts in the Siachen Glacier area. His comparison of the Kargil area with the Siachen Glacier was echoed by another Indian army officer who predicted that defending the former would require "three Siachens."

These two Indian army officers' estimates—"Twice as much. Probably more" and "three Siachens"—pointed to the necessity of maintaining at least 10,000 to 12,000 Indian troops on a permanent basis along the LOC in Kargil and adjacent districts. There were some 5,000 Indian soldiers stationed in the Kargil District before the Pakistani invasion. "Twice as much. Probably more" would bring this number up to 10,000–12,000. Indian manpower stationed in the Siachen Glacier area had fluctuated between 3,000 and 4,000. "Three Siachens" would raise the figure to 9,000–12,000. It might well turn out that maintaining a permanent defense line along the LOC at its most vulnerable points would force India to allocate for this task as many as one-half of the 25,000 personnel that had been engaged in the Kargil fighting. India would also be forced to strengthen the Border Security Force (BSF) and the Central Reserve Police (CRP) so that they could take over the internal security duties formerly handled by the army units that would be assigned to the LOC front. Home Minister Advani had already announced that the government intended to raise an additional fifty BSF and CRP battalions (40,000 men) and that a large number of them would be stationed in Jammu and Kashmir.

Maintaining this permanent defensive force in an extremely cold mountainous area where protecting its members from the climate as well as from hostile action would be exceedingly difficult and would cost much more than the 5 crores of rupees ($1.2 million) per day being paid out to hold the Siachen Glacier area. The daily cost of the LOC defense line could run as high as 12 crores of rupees ($3 million). This daily cost would include only expenditures for paying the troops and for procuring and transporting their ongoing requirements for ammunition, equipment, fuel, clothing, and food. It would not include the cost of establishing and winterizing some 250 defense posts and constructing new roads so that supplies could be moved by truck to points closer to the posts. Nor would it include the cost of providing the new LOC defense force with the special weapons, surveillance and communication equipment, and vehicles that it would need to do its job. This cost had been estimated to be of the order of 1,000 crores of rupees ($240 million). The first official numbers indicating the amount that would have to be spent to cover the immediate cost of the Kargil "war" were not revealed until October 30, when the minister of state for defense informed the press that the government proposed to request the new Lok Sabha to add a supplementary amount of 5,000 to 7,000 crores of rupees ($1.16 to $1.63 billion) to the defense appropriation for 1999–2000.

While Pakistan did not achieve its military objective of taking over mountain peaks from which it could impede and perhaps block traffic on the Srinagar-Leh road, it did succeed in using the fighting in Kargil as a cover for infiltrating reinforcements to join the Kashmir insurgency. During the two and a half months of the Kargil "war," approximately 1,500 Pakistani and Afghani Mujahideen had crossed the LOC into Indian-held territory from the Muzaffarabad region of Azad Kashmir, bringing the number of insurgent fighters to an estimated 3,500. According to Jammu and Kashmir's police chief, "The new ones are better armed and better trained. They're professionals with good radios and heavy explosives." The newcomers were also different in that they were foreigners. Before the Kargil "war," the overwhelming majority of the insurgents were Kashmiri natives. After the Kargil "war," 40% of the force was foreign-born, mostly from Pakistan and Afghanistan. Many of these foreigners were Islamic fundamentalists who saw the struggle against Indian rule as a holy war against infidels. As such, they were ready to fight more fanatically for Kashmiri independence than were the Kashmiris themselves.

That the Pakistani government would continue to provide solid backing for the insurgents fighting in Kashmir was stated by its foreign minister, who reiterated on July 17 Islamabad's "unequivocal and consistent" support for the Kashmir freedom struggle, which would go on until "the Kashmiris can access their right of self determination." According to the foreign minister, the Kargil "war" had injected Kashmir's "freedom struggle" with "new vigor and vitality. . . . Kargil will always be remembered as a glorious chapter in the history of resistance against alien occupation and tyranny." A commitment to carry on the insurgency campaign long after the Kargil "war" had ended was also voiced by the leader of the All Party Hurriyat Conference, the main Kashmiri insurgent organization. "Now Kargil is safe, but there are many headaches in store for India."

An August 16 assault by a force of sixty insurgents armed with rocket launchers and machine guns against a detachment of Rashtriya Rifles was a pointer to the kind of "headaches" that were in store for India. This was the first time that insurgents had attacked an army camp, and it signaled the beginning of a more aggressive phase of the war against India's security forces in Kashmir. That it was part of a broader strategy was seen the next day when an Indian colonel, a junior officer, and soldiers belonging to the Rashtriya Rifles were ambushed and killed by insurgent gunmen, and another encounter between insurgents and Indian troops resulted in the deaths of seven insurgents and two soldiers. A newspaper report from Kashmir described the more aggressive insurgency campaign that had begun to unfold by August 1999:

Police outposts have also been raided and a number of encounters have taken place between the militants and security forces. It has been observed that the militants do not employ hit and run tactics, like they used to do, when attacking the security forces but engage the troops in direct and prolonged exchanges of fire. Pitched battles involving the use of rocket launchers and other arms have taken place and it is a matter of serious concern that some of the militant camps from which the attacks were launched had been set up very near the armed forces' installations. This shows that the preparations for the attacks, which must have taken place over a period of time, went undetected by the intelligence agencies. It has also been observed that most of the militants captured or killed in the last few weeks during operations are trained foreign mercenaries. The changed nature of the attacks shows that they are a deliberate attempt to boost the morale of discontented elements, [to] create insecurity among the people and to draw the attention of the world.

Another newspaper article datelined August 9 laid out in some detail how the redeployment of Indian army units from counterinsurgency operations to the offensive operation against the Pakistani invaders of Kargil District had encouraged insurgent attacks against weakened internal security arrangements:

The most crucial change triggered by the Kargil conflict has been the redeployment of the Army in Jammu and Kashmir. Troops experienced in counter-insurgency have been sent to guard the Line of Control. For instance, the Eighth Mountain Division is now deployed north of the Zoji La pass. Though the shortfall in numbers has been partially made up with fresh inductions, the combat skills of this experienced Division are yet to be matched. Pakistan appears to be taking advantage of the relative inexperience of the new troops by stepping up insurgency. Pakistan may also be taking advantage of the dissonance in the new command and control setup for countering insurgents in the State. Now, the Rashtriya

Rifles (RR) comprising specialized counter-insurgency troops is totally in charge of operations. Headed by a Major General, the RR is now the decision-making hub on the ground in the valley. . . . The 15th Corps based in Srinagar has been completely freed from counter-insurgency tasks. Safeguarding the LOC is its sole objective.

India's immediate efforts to counter the higher level of insurgent violence that followed the end of the Kargil "war" were unlikely to restore Kashmir to the relatively quiet state that had prevailed before May 1999. The Home Ministry directed the paramilitary contingents and police to adopt a tougher stance in dealing with pro-independence militants and to increase the number of village defense committees (VDC's) by 1,000. (Village defense committees were groups of villagers, mainly Hindu, that were organized, trained, and armed by the Indian military to provide local defense against insurgent attacks.) Each VDC was to be provided with automatic weapons, and two police officers were to be assigned to direct its operations. While the number of Rashtriya Rifles and Border Security Force troops could not be increased, those that were available were to be redeployed to fill the security gaps that had been created when army units had moved to the Kargil front. The army and the paramilitary forces were charged to be on the alert for any members of the Pakistani invading force that might return to Indian-held territory. All of the invading force remained on Pakistan's side of the LOC, but insurgent operations continued with greater intensity on the Indian side despite the fact that by this time India had been forced to commit a total of 700,000 military and paramilitary troops in an effort to maintain its hold on its share of Jammu and Kashmir.

Pakistan's success in reinforcing the Kashmir insurgent force and reducing the effectiveness of India's counterinsurgency apparatus meant that it had not lost out completely on the military front. Neither had it lost out completely on the diplomatic front. It had not succeeded in getting the United Nations to take a hand in ending the Kargil fighting or in persuading the United States, Britain, China, and the G-8 countries to take its side against India, but it had achieved its objective of "internationalizing" the Kashmir dispute. However much India might claim that its diplomatic effort had convinced the international community that the Kashmir problem had to be settled between India and Pakistan and that third parties should not become involved, the very fact that India had sought to win, and to prevent Pakistan from winning, the support of the United States, Britain, China, and the G-8 industrialized nations was tantamount to admitting that these countries did have a say in what happened in Kashmir. All of these countries were encouraged by India to adopt public positions that condemned Pakistan's military and diplomatic actions and endorsed those of India. None of them responded by saying that Kashmir was none of their business. All of them made the policy pronouncements which India sought from them. And when they did, India did not criticize them for butting in but welcomed their statements supporting the Indian cause.

Although Indian officialdom would be the last to admit that Pakistan had succeeded in "internationalizing" the Kashmir problem, several Indian political commentators were candid enough to point out that India's Kargil "wartime" diplomacy had produced this unintended result. One of them was newspaperman Ashok Mitra: "The Indians had already blotted their copy book. Even as Pakistan envoys trotted from one foreign capital to another trying to drum up support for themselves over Kargil, the Ministry of Foreign Affairs in New Delhi chose to imitate the Islamabad strategy. If you want Americans and other foreigners to intercede so that the short term war might end in your favor, it would be irrational to stick to the view that these same foreigners have no business to press us to agree on a long term solution of the issue." His view was seconded in an article in the *Hindu*, dealing with the July 4 meeting between Prime Minister Sharif and President Clinton, which agreed that "Mr. Sharif appears to have succeeded in forcing an internationalization of the Kashmir issue. While the US has been careful to stress that 'the bilateral dialogue begun in Lahore provides the best forum for resolving all issues dividing India and Pakistan including Kashmir,' it is also noteworthy that the Joint US-Pakistan statement has emphasized that Mr. Clinton 'would take a personal interest in encouraging an expeditious resumption and intensification of those bilateral efforts once the sanctity of the LOC has been fully restored.'"

So the Pakistanis were not blowing smoke when the members of their Cabinet Defense Committee called Prime Minister Sharif's July 4 meeting with President Clinton "a significant development as this is the first time that the United States has agreed to play such a role for the final settlement of the Kashmir dispute." This view was repeated in words spoken by Pakistan's minister of state for foreign affairs: "The President of the United States stands committed to his personal involvement to expedite and intensify the process for resolving the Kashmir dispute. This is the first time that the United States . . . has agreed to play a direct role in the search for a final settlement of the Kashmir dispute. . . . The United States regards Kashmir as an unresolved dispute." Indian officialdom's response was that these Pakistani officials were wrong because their reading of the meaning of the White House meeting was distorted by their interest in bringing the United States into the Kashmir picture. A neutral observer would say that they were right to express some satisfaction when they assessed the significance of what had transpired when President Clinton met with Prime Minister Sharif on the July 4 holiday.

Fighting and winning the Kargil "war" on both the military and diplomatic fronts had strengthened India as a nation. For a country whose people were divided into hundreds of contentious groups—religious, linguistic, and ethnic— and whose polity had been that of a nation state for only a little over fifty years, the experience of turning back the Pakistani invasion of Kargil District produced a feeling of national solidarity and forged cohesive bonds that brought the nation closer together. Swapan Dasgupta, writing in *India Today*, described that experience with enthusiasm and eloquence:

There was a war in the barren and inhospitable climes of Kargil. The army fought this one valiantly and victoriously. The government chipped in with a diplomatic offensive that conclusively nailed the lie that post-Pokhran India was more isolated than ever before. But there was another battle that was being fought in the cities and villages—a battle to embrace Indian nationhood. The significance of the emotional churning shouldn't be underestimated. For the past few years, cosmopolitan intellectuals, leftists and gung-ho free marketers have inundated impressionable minds with the belief that India is just a geographical term, bereft of emotional relevance. . . . Now they will have to think again. The national awakening over Kargil wasn't concocted or orchestrated. It was real, spontaneous, and touched every corner of India. From the bride in Orissa who donated her wedding jewels to the Congress MP who donated satellite phones so that soldiers could call home, the popular response to the war effort was overwhelming. Those who contributed hadn't even seen Kargil. Nor are they likely to ever visit it. Yet, Tiger Hill and Mashkoh Valley became as much a symbol of India as India Gate. Call it nationalism, call it xenophobia, call it whatever you want, but the Kargil war demonstrates India lives in the soul of Indians.

Fighting and winning the Kargil "war" converted Prime Minister Vajpayee's public persona from loser to winner. A fortnight before the Pakistani intruders were discovered in Kargil District, his government had fallen by a single vote in the Lok Sabha. When he proclaimed "Operation Vijay" a success on July 26, he was seen as a triumphant figure not only at home but abroad. He had kept himself out of military operations but had restrained the generals from attacking Pakistan's side of the LOC. He had led the caretaker government and rallied the Indian people to back the war effort, but had turned a deaf ear to the RSS's proposal that nuclear weapons be used against Pakistan. He had orchestrated an effective diplomatic campaign that had won support for India's cause from the United States, Britain, China, and the G-8 industrialized nations and had isolated Pakistan within the international community. From the Hindu fundamentalist who had ordered the May 1998 nuclear bomb tests, he had become the responsible statesman who had prevented the fighting along Kashmir's LOC from developing into a general Indo-Pakistani war. Nowhere was this change in Vajpayee's persona on the international stage more clearly stated than in the words spoken by one of the United States's undersecretaries of state following the July 4 meeting between President Clinton and Pakistani Prime Minister Sharif: "We have gained new respect for the political courage and leadership of Prime Minister Vajpayee whose strict maintenance of discipline and restraint in the face of pressures for escalation enabled the crisis to be resolved."

On the other side of the domestic political fence, the role that Sonia Gandhi had played during the Kargil "war" had diminished her standing as a politician who could lead the nation in a time of crisis. She had adopted an equivocal position on the "war" effort, supporting the military campaign to drive back the invaders but blaming the BJP-led government for allowing India to be dragged into a war that, she maintained, it should not have needed to fight. Her "for and against" stand did not generally raise questions regarding her patriotism, but it allowed her political opponents to remind the Indian public about her foreign origin. Her inability to mix with and encourage the soldiers at the front highlighted her "femaleness," and her inability to converse with the wounded displayed the limitation of her "Indianness." While Vajpayee played a manly role by landing in the Dras sector when shells had been falling only two kilometers away and showed his Indian roots by addressing the troops in fluent and eloquent Hindi, Sonia Gandhi could only visit the wounded in military hospitals far from the front and communicate with them through looks and gestures as she handed them her gifts. She may well have appeared to them as an angel of mercy come down from heaven, but that was a far cry from being seen as a national leader in time of war.

So far as India's political institutions were concerned, the Kargil "war" had strengthened the BJP party and weakened the Congress Indira Party. From the party that had led the government that had fallen in April, the BJP had become the party that had led the caretaker government that had presided over India's defeat of Pakistan and given India a more respected place in the international community. In the words of a leading independent pollster: "Kargil has reversed the national mood and done a U turn for the BJP. Instead of being forced to fight the campaign to elect a 13th Lok Sabha on the basis of the spotty record of the coalition government which it had led for thirteen months, the BJP could go to the people as the party that had undergirded India's victory over Pakistan in the Kargil 'war.'" That this would be the campaign strategy that would be followed by the BJP was made clear when Prime Minister Vajpayee used the occasion of India's fifty-second Independence Day to prepare the way for that campaign. He asserted in his speech that Pakistan's defeat had not only proved the superiority of India's military might but vindicated his government's May 1998 decision to test nuclear weapons: "The world saw Pokhran as irresponsible, but today the world has seen what we risked for our national security. We showed that we do not bow down to pressure. Kargil showed that when our patriotism is challenged, every Indian stands together."

The Janus-like stance which the Congress Indira Party had taken during the Kargil "war" prevented it from sharing in the political spoils of victory over Pakistan. It had given only half-hearted support to the "war" effort, cheering the fighting forces but attacking the government when it attempted to mobilize the home front and gain the diplomatic support of the international community. Instead of joining with other parties and the Indian people to help generate an all-out "war" effort, the Congress Indira Party insisted upon castigating the Vajpayee regime for having allowed Pakistani forces to invade Kargil District and persisted in calling for a special session of the Rajya Sabha so that the government's intelligence failing could be debated. The party showed its weakness not only by its failure to undermine the caretaker government by making headway at either of these two points of attack but also by the way that it was forced to accept Prime Minister Vajpayee's maneuvers to defuse the issues that it had raised. Having played the major role in bringing the 12th Lok Sabha to an end, the Congress

Indira Party could hardly complain that it had no appropriate parliamentary forum in which to attack the BJP-led government role for allowing the Kargil "war" to break out.

Vajpayee deferred the airing of the "intelligence failure" issue by appointing a commission that would investigate the events preceding the outbreak of the Kargil "war" but would report to the new government after the 1999 General Election. He deferred consideration of the opposition parties' demand that a special Rajya Sabha session be held, by saying that a divisive debate on the merits of the Kargil "war" while the fighting was going on would undermine the morale of the armed services because the services' members would see it as a sign that India's political parties were not solidly behind them. He took the position that any parliamentary review of the Kargil "war" should be undertaken only after the fighting had been brought to a successful conclusion. Sonia Gandhi and the other leaders of the Congress Indira Party had good grounds for suspecting that Vajpayee's real reason for refusing to call a special session of the Rajya Sabha was that, since opposition parties held a large majority of the seats, any debate would inevitably go against the government. But with no sessions being held in either of the two houses of Parliament, all they could do was to drop the issue for the time being and attempt to raise it again during the course of the coming election campaign.

Another of India's institutions that had benefited from India's victory in the Kargil war was its military establishment. After they had recovered from the invasion's initial surprise, the armed forces had acquitted themselves with distinction and earned the wholehearted admiration of the Indian people. In addition, the difficult conditions under which they had fought had highlighted their need for additional equipment. Even though the Pakistani invaders had been driven back across the LOC, their success in establishing numerous posts on the Indian side showed that permanent defense emplacements would have to be established and maintained along a several hundred-kilometer stretch of mountainous terrain if future incursions were to be prevented. It was also clear when the fighting ended that the military establishment would require additional funding if it was to do its job of defending India against future Pakistani intrusions. It was also clear that the military establishment would get the additional funds that it needed.

President Narayanan, following his customary activist style, set the ball rolling in the address that he delivered on August 15 as India celebrated the fifty-second anniversary of its Independence. He warned India against being caught unaware by surprise attacks by Pakistan: "As we have been let down more than once in the past, it is prudent of us and it is our duty to our people to be prepared for any surprise attack on us." In order to be "prepared," he suggested that defense expenditures be increased so that the armed forces could be strengthened and equipped with "the latest weapons and force multiplyers." His was not a voice crying in the wilderness; Indian opinion as a whole agreed with him. The 1999–2000 budget had contained an 11% increase in defense expenditures, but, since this budget had been passed a month before the Kargil "war" began, the increase did not include the cost of fighting the "war," much less the anticipated cost of establishing a permanent defense line along a multi-district portion of the LOC. These costs would be substantial, would have to be paid during the months and years following the cessation of hostilities, and would push the percentage of India's Gross Domestic Product (GDP) allotted to national defense above its current 2.5%. If the fiscal deficit was to be maintained at the 1999–2000 budget's level, such substantial increases in defense expenditures would have to be accompanied by increased revenue or cuts in nondefense allocations. If the new government that emerged from the 1999 General Election did not pass a supplementary budget incorporating one or the other of these two ways of compensating for the costs of the Kargil "war," the result would be a substantial increase in the 1999–2000 budget deficit.

The economic bottom line of the Kargil "war" and its long-term consequences in real terms were that the Indian people, particularly the poor, would have to pay the cost in the form of a lower standard of living. If the additional expenditures that would be required to make good the Kargil "war" losses and to establish and maintain a permanent LOC defense line were met by increasing the revenue stream going to the government, the public would have to pay higher taxes and would have less money available for consumer goods. Cutting nondefense expenditures would mean that infrastructure development and social welfare programs would be curtailed. Allowing budgetary deficits to increase would cause inflationary pressures to increase, with the result that prices of consumer goods would rise and people's incomes would buy less in the market. Whatever fiscal form it took, providing the funds needed to give India a stronger defense against invasion by Pakistan in Kashmir or along India's international border would require a substantial shift of resources from consumption to investment. India would be more secure, but all Indians would be less well off than they would have been otherwise and the burden of the dispossessed would become even more onerous.

14

1999 General Election Campaign

As the 1999 General Election campaign developed, it began to look more like a presidential style election and less like a parliamentary style election. This trend had emerged during the 1998 General Election, when A. B. Vajpayee had been identified at the outset as the man who would become prime minister if the BJP and its allies succeeded in capturing a majority of the seats in the 12th Lok Sabha and Sonia Gandhi had campaigned as the Congress Indira Party's "star." But it had merely begun, because Sonia Gandhi's role had been restricted to that of the party's principal campaigner. She had not been presented to Indian voters as the party's candidate for the prime minister's post or even as a candidate for a Lok Sabha seat. The 1999 General Election saw the seeds of the presidential style that had been planted sixteen months earlier come to full flower. A. B. Vajpayee repeated his 1998 role as the BJP's prime ministerial candidate. Sonia Gandhi's political status was elevated to the point where she became his primary rival for the post. She was now the Congress Indira Party president, chairman of its Parliamentary Committee, the party's candidate for a Lok Sabha seat in two constituencies, and its candidate for prime minister. The election campaign became a two-candidate contest for the most powerful political office in the land, and a two party contest to decide which of the two would dominate the 13th Lok Sabha. The core of the struggle became "Atal versus Sonia" and "the BJP versus the Congress Indira Party."

A. B. Vajpayee campaigned as the man who had led India to victory in the Kargil "war," and his BJP party sought to be swept into power on a "Vajpayee wave." What he and the BJP needed was to launch a campaign based upon an accomplishment about which Indian voters were enthusiastic and which was not an object of controversy. The obvious drum to beat was victory in the Kargil "war," and the obvious drum beater was A. B. Vajpayee. According to the BJP minister of information and broadcasting, "everything has changed in the last 100 days. In spite of the bus, bomb, and Bihar, we did not register as a performing government. But after Kargil, when Vajpayee steered us to diplomatic and military victory, we acquired a larger than life image. Over night respect has turned to reverence." Writing in the news magazine *India Today*, Sabanaqui Bhaumik summarized the BJP's basic campaign strategy: "Vajpayee and Kargil will be the twin themes of the BJP campaign. [Combining] a victorious nation, a popular leader, and a patriotic party, the BJP believes that it has a potent cocktail for Election '99. . . . Leaders like L. K. Advani, M. M. Joshi, Lashma Sivery, Pramod Mahajan, Uma Bharati, and the various chief ministers will hit the campaign trail in their hired aircraft and helicopters. But this time round the party will not highlight a collective leadership. It will focus solely on Vajpayee's personality. 'Unfulfilled claims have to be fulfilled,' one of the ad lines which is being considered, gives a sense of the mood that Vajpayee would project." When public opinion polls conducted as the campaign got under way showed an 80–83% approval rating for Vajpayee's handling of the Kargil crisis while only 8% of the respondents expressed the view that Sonia Gandhi would have done a better job, the BJP had good reason to think that following this strategy would make it a winner.

A sampling of public opinion taken during the course of the campaign showed that the strategy was working. When opinion poll respondents were asked who they thought would make the best prime minister, 56% named Vajpayee. Only 23% opted for Sonia Gandhi. Commenting on the poll's returns, *India Today's* Swapan Dasgupta observed:

The unchallenged leader of the BJP and the hero of Kargil now enjoys a popularity rating comparable to Indira and Rajiv in their hey days. In a parliamentary election that bears the hallmark of a presidential contest, Vajpayee gives the impression of being the only candidate. From his detractors in the Sangh Parivar to the newly acquired allies in the Janata Dal (United), the Prime Minister has become the meal ticket for an amorphous umbrella coalition. The people haven't shed their distrust of a coalition, but they are overcome with the love affair with Vajpayee. Ours may be Vajpayee's last election but it's certainly going to be his election . . . Before Kargil Vajpayee was first among equals. After Kargil, he is the towering leader seeking votes on the strength of his record and leadership.

The leading role which Sonia Gandhi had played in the Congress Indira Party's abortive attempt to form a successor government to the Vajpayee regime had made it plain to political observers that she would be the prime minister if her partywon the 1999 General Election. Ten days after the president had ordered the dissolution of the 12th Lok Sabha, the Congress Indira Party's choice had been made more or less official when one of its senior leaders described her selection as "the most natural thing as she is the leader of the party." Not all of the party's leaders agreed that, because Sonia Gandhi was party president, she should automatically be its prime ministerial nominee. Sharad Pawar was first and foremost among those who did not see her nomination as "the most natural thing."

His unhappiness with Sonia Gandhi's leadership position stemmed from decisions taken by the party's leadership following the 1998 General Election. Largely due to his efforts, the Congress Indira Party candidates had won thirty-three of the Lok Sabha seats that had been contested in Maharashtra. Pawar had expected, because of this outstanding performance and because Sonia Gandhi had not been elected to the Lok Sabha, that he would be chosen as the chairman of the party's Parliamentary Committee. To his great disappointment he was passed over and Sonia Gandhi was given this post as well as that of the party president.

The smoldering intraparty conflict burst into public view on May 15 when Pawar, supported by two senior party leaders, addressed a letter to Sonia Gandhi questioning her suitability as the party's candidate for the prime minister's post. "It is not possible," these three members of the Congress Working Committee (CWC) wrote, "that a country of 980 million with a wealth of education, competence, and ability can have anyone other than an Indian, born of Indian soil, to head its government." Going further, they requested that the Congress Indira Party's campaign manifesto contain a commitment to support a constitutional amendment that would require that the posts of president, vice-president, and prime minister be held by "native-born Indian citizens." To the delight of the BJP's leadership, the question of Sonia Gandhi's "foreignness" had been raised openly for the first time by leaders of the Congress Indira Party itself. Earlier in May, Home Minister Advani had requested that the Congress Indira Party reconsider its selection of Sonia Gandhi as its prime ministerial candidate because, in his view, a foreign-born Indian should not occupy that post. Advani was echoing a position that had been taken originally by George Fernandes, India's outspoken defense minister (who had characterized China more than a year earlier as India's "public enemy Number One"). Vajpayee had reacted to their efforts to turn the spotlight on Sonia Gandhi's "foreignness" by advising his caretaker government's leaders to refrain from making it an issue in the campaign. Imagine their happiness when they were spared the task by the three "rebel" CWC members.

One day after the "rebels'" letter was made public, a special meeting of the Congress Working Committee was held to discuss the issue that they had raised. The three members who had written the letter did not attend. At the very beginning of the meeting and to the members' surprise, Sonia Gandhi presented her resignation as party president and immediately left the room. In her resignation letter, she stated that she was "pained by their lack of confidence in my ability to act in the best interests of the party and the country. Under the circumstances, my sense of loyalty to the party and duty to the country compel me to tender my resignation from the post of party President. Though born in a foreign land, I chose India as my country. I am Indian and I will remain so till my last breath. India is my motherland, dearer to me than my own life." The astonished committee members responded by passing a resolution refusing to accept her resignation and asking her to continue as party president. That resolution was followed by a resolution rejecting the "rebels'" proposal that the party's campaign manifesto include a statement of support for a constitutional amendment precluding foreign-born Indians from occupying the country's three highest political positions. While the members were unanimous in viewing the "rebel" letter to the party president as highly improper, they did not take any immediate action against the "rebels.".

The Congress Working Committee's urgent plea that Sonia Gandhi reconsider her resignation was followed by hundreds of Congress Indira Party members rushing to her well guarded bungalow. They unfurled banners and chanted slogans, urging her to resume her position as party president. A few threatened to commit suicide if she did not withdraw her resignation. The three "rebel" members of the CWC were castigated as traitors who were working for the BJP, and demands were shouted that they be expelled from the party. Sonia Gandhi ventured out of the bungalow from time to time and advised members of the crowd to desist from violent behavior, but she gave them no indication that she would change her mind about resigning. Party leaders backed up this noisy public demonstration by the party's rank and file. Four chief ministers of states controlled by the Congress Indira Party and a large number of party officials resigned their positions, saying that they were not willing to continue serving the party if Sonia Gandhi was not its president.

On May 20 the Congress Working Committee met again and by a majority vote expelled the three "rebels" for six years. Sonia Gandhi did not attend the meeting because, having resigned as party president, she was no longer a member. Not surprisingly, the three members who had signed the rebellious letter absented themselves. Four days later and only a day before the special session of the All-India Congress Committee (AICC) that had been called to persuade her to continue as party president, Sonia Gandhi withdrew her resignation. The May 25 meeting of the AICC, over which she presided, began with a twenty-five minute speech in which she warned that "those who question my Indianness will get the reply not from me but from the people of the country. It will be a crushing reply." She then went on to charge that "the very same people who came to me with folded hands urging me to save the Congress are now sowing seeds of doubt among the people about my patriotism. They are [*sic*] in glove with those forces to confront whom I entered politics. . . . Those who harbour doubts . . . can choose their own separate path. We are not bothered by them."

Sonia Gandhi emerged from the drama of her resignation and its retraction as the unchallenged leader of the Congress Indira Party and the party's unchallenged candidate for prime ministerial office. The Sharad Pawar faction, which had been the only voice raising questions within the party ranks, had been purged. Any thought that she might step aside and name another party leader like former Finance Minister Manmohan Singh as the party's choice for prime minister was silenced by her address at the AICC meeting. An editorial that appeared two days later in the *Hindu* analyzed her performance and what it said about her role in the coming election:

Rather than picking up the gauntlet and serving the rebels with summary expulsion orders —the way Indira Gandhi dealt with those who came to be known as the syndicate and Rajiv Gandhi with V. P. Singh—Mrs. Gandhi simply withdrew and watched the revolt being quelled by others. Her speech at the AICC session, declaring that only those with absolute loyalty to her remain in the party and anyone with "even the smallest doubt must travel separately on their own" clearly smacked of political arrogance. The message was clear and simple. That the Congress Indira should give her carte blanche to run the party on her own and the AICC simply gave this to her.

Sonia Gandhi had triumphed within the ranks of the Congress Indira Party, but the question remained as to whether or not she would triumph in the country. The course that had brought her control of her party had not been followed without damage to her chances of emerging from the election as India's next prime minister. When BJP leaders first began to argue that it would be a disgrace to choose anyone other than a native-born Indian for India's most powerful political post, Prime Minister Vajpayee had expressed a reluctance to make this a campaign issue. Now that it was clear that he would be standing against Sonia Gandhi, he changed his position and proposed that the National Democratic Alliance's election manifesto call for restricting holders of the president's, vice-president's, and prime minister's offices positions to native-born Indians. His position was seconded by Home Minister Advani, who told reporters that the BJP would back a constitutional amendment giving effect to the prime minister's proposal. The issue of Sonia Gandhi's "foreignness," first raised by leaders of her own party, had now been picked up by the BJP and injected into the forefront of the campaign.

Making it more difficult for the Congress Indira Party to emerge victorious from the 1999 General Election was the party split that produced the Nationalist Congress Party (NCP), that was created by Sharad Pawar and the other two "rebels" who had been purged. The NCP became official when it was registered with the Election Commission on May 25. According to Pawar, the new party would be committed to secularism and the welfare of India's minorities. Its ultimate goal would be to strengthen the "spirit and forces of nationalism and vigilantly preserve the Indian national identity." Its immediate goal would be to prevent Sonia Gandhi from becoming prime minister and to see to it that only native-born Indians occupied the highest political offices in the land. Party membership would be open to all, including those in the Congress Indira Party who, in Pawar's words "are with us in mind, heart, and soul, but reticent at the moment." While the NCP would stand equidistant from the BJP and the "Sonia Congress," it would seek "secular" allies with which to contest the 1999 election.

Although Pawar announced that the NCP would campaign throughout the country, it was clear that its power base would be in Maharashtra where Pawar had led the Congress Indira Party's 1998 campaign that had won thirty-three of the state's forty-eight seats. The strength of his personal following was such that he had good reason to expect his NCP to capture a significant number of those seats in 1999.

So far as the nationwide configuration of political parties was concerned, the 1999 General Election campaign took the general shape of a vast coalition of parties, led by the BJP, versus a single party—the Congress Indira Party. Except for the defection of Jayalalitha's eighteen Anna DMK MPs, Vajpayee's earlier coalition had held together despite the loss by one vote of the April confidence motion. With its solidarity having stood the test of defeat, it entered the election campaign in May as a stronger common front against the Congress Indira Party. The Anna DMK had gone over to Sonia Gandhi's side, but it had been replaced in the Vajpayee coalition by the DMK. The smaller Tamil parties that had earlier been Jayalalitha's allies had fallen out with her during the course of her needling of the Vajpayee regime and were now members of Vajpayee's coalition. Only a remnant of the Janata Dal had remained after Laloo Prasad Yadav had formed his Rashtriya Janata Dal and the party's ranks in Orissa and Karnataka had split. The Janata Dal remnant called itself the Janata Dal (United) and joined the Vajpayee forces. Including several other small parties, the coalition headed by Prime Minister Vajpayee now numbered twenty-four parties. Its prominent members were the BJP, the Shiva Sena, the Akali Dal, the Lok Sakthi, the Trinamool Congress, the DMK, the Marumalarchi Dravida Munnetra Kazhagam, the Patali Makkal Katchi, the Puttiya Tamizhagam, the Tamizhaga Ravi Congress, the Biju Janata Dal, the Janata Dal (United), the Arunachal Congress, the Lok Dal, the Himachal Vikas Party, and the Sikkim National Congress. (The Jammu and Kashmir National Conference did not campaign with this coalition but, following the voting, added the four seats which it had won to the coalition's majority in the 13th Lok Sabha.)

Thus enlarged, the Vajpayee-led coalition called itself the National Democratic Alliance (NDA) and campaigned with a manifesto that represented a program of action that all of its members could support. This meant that the three planks that comprised the BJP's Hindutva agenda—building a Hindu temple in Ayodhya, terminating Jammu and Kashmir's special constitutional status, and adopting a uniform civil code—were conspicuous by their absence. Under the title "National Agenda for Governance," the NDA's twenty page manifesto was released on August 16 with Vajpayee's picture prominent on its front cover and repeated nine more times on the inside. For the most part, it was a reprise of the March 1998 manifesto that had promised India a stable government and a strong national defense, but there were some significant additions. The NDA, if voted into power, would pass constitutional amendments that would mandate five year terms for future legislatures and would reserve the country's highest legislative, judicial, and legislative posts for native-born Indians. To address the fear felt by minority groups because of the attacks that had taken place against the Christian community during the BJP-led coalition's thirteen months in office, the manifesto promised that minorities' constitutional rights would be safeguarded. To address the national security concerns that had been aroused by the Kargil "war," it contained a commitment to make good the damage that the armed forces had suffered because of their neglect by the Central Governments that had ruled before the Vajpayee regime. While the campaign manifesto did provide the NDA with a certain amount of cohesion because it represented an agenda to which all members could subscribe, a much stronger cohesive force came from the common agreement that an NDA coalition government would be headed by the BJP's A. B. Vajpayee.

In sharp contrast to the approach followed by the enlarged BJP-led coalition, the Congress Indira Party decided to fight the 1999 election largely on its own. Promising to provide India with a stable government because it would be a single-party rather than a coalition government, the party continued the strategy that it had adopted in April when it had insisted upon forming a Congress Indira Party minority government. It was willing to cooperate with two regional parties— Jayalalitha's Anna DMK and Laloo Prasad Yadav's Rashtriya Janata Party—but it maintained that these relationships were "understandings" rather than alliances. Its cooperative association with the Rashtriya Janata Party had grown out of the leading role that the Congress Indira Party had played in frustrating the Vajpayee government's attempt to impose President's Rule in Bihar. Its seat-sharing arrangement with the Anna DMK was a continuation of the political friendship that had been born when Jayalalitha and Sonia Gandhi drank tea together at Subramaniam Swami's March reception.

The Congress Indira's sixty page campaign manifesto was released on August 13. Its principal commitments were to safeguard "secularism" and to provide a stable government and a secure defense. In releasing the manifesto, Sonia Gandhi engaged in a verbal charade that attempted to give the impression that someone other than herself might become prime minister if the election resulted in a Congress Indira Party victory. After taking a strong stand against coalition governments and refusing to commit her party to sharing ministerial power with any cooperating parties, she stated that "the [next] prime minister would be chosen and decided by the victorious MPs after the election." Keeping in mind the role that she had played in the party's April attempt to capture power from the Vajpayee regime and what had transpired at the May 25 meeting of the AICC, no one who heard her words had any doubt that she had already been selected as the person who would be "chosen and decided by the victorious MPs after the election."

Since fighting had broken out along the LOC shortly after a general election had been ordered by the president and had reached its height as the campaign was getting under way, it was inevitable that politics would become involved with the Kargil "war." A major component of the campaign took the form of a battle between A. B. Vajpayee as the leader of the "war" effort and Sonia Gandhi as the "war" effort's leading critic. It was clear from the outset that victory in the Kargil "war" would favor Vajpayee's NDA, and the tilt in its favor provided by the "war" persisted throughout the campaign, even after the fighting ceased in mid-July. A July 17 *Times of India* poll showed that, while respondents were split on whether or not an intelligence lapse had led to the "war," 78% were satisfied with the way that Vajpayee's caretaker government had responded to the military and diplomatic crisis. Capitalizing on this high level of support for the "war" effort, the BJP portrayed Vajpayee's leadership as a striking example of his mature statesmanship and the success of "Operation Vijay" as proof positive of his government's ability to counter any Pakistani threat to India's national security.

On August 15, India's fifty-second Independence Day, Prime Minister Vajpayee addressed the nation from the ramparts of the Red Fort in Delhi. He maintained that conducting the Pokhran nuclear bomb tests had been necessary for India's security and proclaimed that they had raised India's status among the nations of the world because all countries had seen that "we will protect our interests at all costs whether it is in developing atomic weapons or achieving missile capability." According to Vajpayee, his government's successful handling of the Kargil crisis had shown the world that India was capable of safeguarding its territory by "driving intruders from our land. . . . Our response was well thought out. It was so effective that it left the enemy stunned." He went on to take credit for the conduct of a "war" effort that had led to a diplomatic as well as a military victory. India's refusal to send its troops across the LOC into Pakistani-held territory had brought India international support for the first time since Independence in its dealings with Pakistan. Pakistan, on the other hand, had ended up isolated on the world stage.

Following its use of this national celebration to highlight the Vajpayee caretaker government's success in "Operation Vijay," the BJP's campaign strategy focused upon attacking Sonia Gandhi's foreign origin and political inexperience and attacking her party for its criticism of the way that India had responded to the Kargil invasion. Speaking at a press conference held a few days later, L. K. Advani, the chairman of the BJP's campaign committee, drew a sharp contrast between A. B. Vajpayee, whom he described as a leader who was "mature, seasoned and diffused with patriotism," and Sonia Gandhi, whom he character-ized as a politician who was "alien to the ethos and problems of India and also bereft of experience." Regarding the Kargil conflict, Advani charged that, while the Pakistani intruders had been evicted and India had scored a diplomatic victory under Vajpayee's leadership, Sonia Gandhi and the leaders of the Congress Indira Party had become "celebrities" in Pakistan because of their criticism of India's "war" effort. Based on Vajpayee's performance before as well as during the Kargil "war," Advani advanced the BJP's claim that Vajpayee "has proved to be a prime minister without peer" who had become the centerpiece around which an atmosphere of hope and confidence had been restored to the nation.

The NDA campaign's personal attacks on Sonia Gandhi continued during the weeks that followed. Advani focused on her membership in the Nehru dynasty, claiming that "dynasty is the disease that debilitates democracy" and proclaiming: "Gone are the days when a Sonia Gandhi or a daughter of a monarch ascended the throne as a matter of birthright." Defense Minister Fernandes asked with biting scorn at a BJP meeting in Bellary where Sonia Gandhi was contesting the Lok Sabha seat: "What is Sonia's contribution to the nation? Yes, there is one contribution—the two children she gave birth to. She contributed two people to the 100 crore [1 billion] population—Is there anything else?" Another BJP spokesman compared her to a Pakistani infiltrator. "Next we will have some Kargil intruder wanting to be prime minister." Bal Thackeray, the head of the Shiv Sena, ridiculed her lack of fluency in Indian languages: "Suppose someone replaced a single page of her written speech with a bazaar list. She will probably read it out word for word." Pramod Mahajan, the BJP minister of information and broadcasting, delivered "the unkindest cut of all" when he asked at a public meeting in Maharashtra, "If we are keen on having a foreigner as a prime minister, why not Tony Blair, or Bill Clinton, or Monica Lewinsky?" He coupled his slur against Sonia Gandhi with the charge that "when she says that she will die for her motherland, she means her mother-in-law's land," a remark that was tantamount to saying that members of the Nehru dynasty regarded India as their personal property.

Although the bulk of the verbal abuse that was inflicted during the campaign fell on Sonia Gandhi, the Congress Indira Party hit Vajpayee below the belt on several occasions. Sonia Gandhi called Vajpayee a "traitor." A Congress Indira Party spokesman accused him of being a "habitual liar." The AICC office distributed extracts from the memoirs of former Prime Minister Morarji Desai in which he referred to a rumor that Vajpayee spent more time drinking and flirting with women than administering his foreign affairs department. In a television interview, a Congress Indira Party general secretary implied that there was a hidden story behind Vajpayee's bachelor status: "We may have to ask even the prime minister how, without being married, he has a son-in-law. Whose son-in-law? Who is married to whom?"

Sonia Gandhi continued throughout the campaign to maintain that the Congress Indira Party's choice for prime minister would be determined by the MPs whom the party succeeded in electing to the 13th Lok Sabha, but the first speech that she had delivered after her failed attempt to head a successor government to the Vajpayee regime had revealed that she expected to be the victorious candidate for that post. At a June 10 public meeting in Andhra Pradesh, she had offered herself to the Indian people as the member of the Nehru dynasty who would be their next prime minister: "You have showered so much love and affection on my family. I stand in front of you in the hope that I might prove worthy of such love and affection. . . . As a member of that family, known for its sacrifice and concern for the poorest of the poor I am making this pledge on the banks of the Godavari that I will complete the unfulfilled mission of Indiramma and Rajivji [Honorific names for Indira and Rajiv Gandhi]. . . . I have seen my family work tirelessly in the service of the nation. I will walk in their footsteps."

It would be a month and a half before her party acted officially to take her up on her offer to assume the prime minister's post. On July 29, the AICC announced that Sonia Gandhi would stand for a seat in the 13th Lok Sabha. She followed this announcement by filing nomination papers in not one but two constituencies—Bellary in Karnataka and Amethi in Uttar Pradesh. These two constituencies were carefully chosen because neither she nor the Congress Indira

Party wanted to run the risk of her being defeated. Bellary was a constituency that had been won by a Congress candidate in every general election that had been held since India became independent. Amethi had been captured by a BJP candidate in the 1998 General Election, but the constituency had strong historical ties with the Nehru dynasty. Both Sanjay Gandhi and Rajiv Gandhi had been elected to the Lok Sabha from that constituency when Indira Gandhi was preparing them to become prime ministers. Sonia Gandhi and A. B. Vajpayee having emerged as the two candidates for the prime minister's post, the overriding characteristic of the 1999 General Election was its "presidential" style. Instead of attention being focused on the thousands of candidates contesting the 535 Lok Sabha seats, the campaign was centered on the two national parties' nominees for prime minister —A. B. Vajpayee leading the BJP and Sonia Gandhi leading the Congress Indira Party.

Another noteworthy characteristic of the campaign, lamented by one newspaper editorial writer among many others, was its "down and dirty" rhetoric:

An unfortunate feature of the electioneering for the 13th Lok Sabha is the frequent resort to verbal abuse of opponents by politicians in the last few weeks. In a campaign in which the real issues that concern the people and the country, which should be the stuff of politics and elections, have gone into the background, it is invectives, sly allusions and character assassination that [have] set the tone for the campaign rhetoric of many leaders. It may not always be possible to make a clear separation of the personal and the political in a country where personalized politics has held sway and gained strength through decades. In such a situation, the maturing of politics through the democratic process would demand a progressive shift away from personalities and an increasing orientation to issues. Instead, what is being seen is not just a deterioration in degree, but a qualitative change for the worse in political and electoral discourse. The shameful comments about opponents are too many to be quoted and cross the limits of decency and civility. Both sides have indulged in the scandalous game. There are charges that the Prime Minister was called a traitor by Ms. Sonia Gandhi. But the worst remarks have come from the leaders of the ruling coalition, with Mr. Mahajan, Mr. George Fernandes and Mr. Bal Thackeray trying to outdo one another in invoking the lowest expression of street culture. India cannot claim to be a democracy by holding elections periodically. The quality of democracy depends on the quality of public life, the terms of debate and the character and attitudes of persons in public life. The sinking into the viler and baser realms of human conduct marks a retrogression to barbarism, with its attendant intolerance and insensitivity based on the divisions of caste, race, gender etc. Respect for others and restraint in words and action are the cardinal norms of civilized conduct. Many of our politicians are yet to imbibe these values. It is easy to lower the standards of public life—a bad word and a wrong action will do the damage, but it is much more difficult to undo it. Politics is often called dirty; it should not be made dirtier.

15

1999 General Election Results

The first phase of polling took place on September 5, when balloting was held in 145 Lok Sabha constituencies located in sixteen states and union territories. Overall voter turnout exceeded 58% but varied considerably from state to state. Nor surprisingly, the lowest figure recorded was 25% in Jammu and Kashmir. While 81% of registered voters turned out in thinly populated and Buddhist Ladakh, the 12% vote registered in Muslim Srinagar, where the bulk of Kashmir's population was concentrated, lowered the state figure to the point where it was only half of the 1998 figure.

The reasons for this sharp decline in Kashmiri voter participation were not far to seek. The All Party Hurriyat Conference, which had led the Kashmir insurgency since its start in 1989, had called for a boycott of the election, and the army personnel who had succeeded in forcing large numbers of Kashmiris to defy a similar boycott in 1998 were now in short supply because of the army's deployment to the LOC that had taken place during the Kargil "war." Fifteen hundred Pakistani infiltrators had reinforced the Kashmiri militants during June and July, substantially increasing the number of armed enforcers of the election boycott. The limited paramilitary force that was available did its best to "get out the vote" but, shorthanded as it was, it encountered stiff resistance, not only from Pakistani infiltrators and Kashmiri insurgents but from Kashmiri Muslims who were emboldened to resist. The result was an increased level of violence that caused the deaths of some 300 civilians, militants, and security personnel during September alone and made it not only difficult but dangerous for many of the Kashmiris who wanted to vote to go to the polls.

On October 3, the curtain came down on what one newspaper called "the longest, dirtiest and most tiresome campaign" in free India's history when ballots were cast in 118 Lok Sabha constituencies scattered over eleven states. Prominent among these were the Lucknow constituency where A. B. Vajpayee was contesting the seat and the Amethi constituency where Sonia Gandhi was standing for election as an MP. When the final phase of voting had been completed, a spokesman for the Election Commission expressed his satisfaction that, despite a dearth of security personnel and a burst of monsoon weather, India had been able to conduct an orderly election in which a majority of eligible citizens had cast their votes. Although voter turnout was lower than the 62% in the 1998 election, the decline could be attributed as much to heavy rains as to voter fatigue.

Counting of ballots began on October 6, and the results were reported three days later. As predicted by exit polls conducted while the voting was under way, NDA candidates captured a comfortable majority of the 545 Lok Sabha seats. The NDA's election victories originally numbered 297, but when the National Conference and the Sikkim Democratic Front joined the coalition after ballots had been counted, the NDA total rose to 302. Maneka Gandhi, who had stood as an independent and had won her seat with the largest number of votes except for those cast for Sonia Gandhi in the Amethi constituency, announced that she would support the NDA, bringing its Lok Sabha holdings to 303 seats. The BJP had secured 182, two more than in the 1998 General Election. Its allies had added 115 seats. The allied parties that had gained more than one seat were the Telegu Desam Party with 29, the Janata Dal (United) with 20, the Marumalarchi Dravida Munnetra Kazhagam with 16, the Shiv Sena with 15, the Biju Janata Dal with 10, the Trinamool Congress with 8, the Lok Dal with 5, the Pattali Makkalkatchi with 5, the Akali Dal with 2, and the Loktantrik Congress with 2.

The number of NDA victories varied from state to state, from clean sweeps in Delhi, Harayana and Himachal Pradesh to poor performances in Assam, Jammu and Kashmir, Karnataka, Punjab, Uttar Pradesh, and West Bengal, to no victories at all in Kerala.

State	Total Seats	NDA Victories
Andhra Pradesh	42	36
Assam	14	3
Bihar	54	40
Delhi	7	7
Gujarat	26	20
Harayana	10	10
Hamachal Pradesh	4	4
Jammu and Kashmir	6	2
Karnataka	28	9
Kerala	20	0
Madhya Pradesh	40	29
Maharashtra	48	28
Orissa	21	19
Punjab	13	3
Rajasthan	25	16
Tamil Nadu	39	25
Uttar Pradesh	85	30
West Bengal	42	10

In the smaller states and territories, the NDA won two seats in Goa, one seat in Andaman and Nicobar, and one seat in Daman and Diu.

The positive results that the NDA achieved in Delhi, Madhya Pradesh, and Rajasthan stood in sharp contrast to the defeats that the BJP had suffered in the state elections held there in November 1998. Its poor showings in Assam, Karnataka, and the Punjab were the result of the Congress Indira Party's success in winning 9 seats, 19 seats, and 8 seats respectively in those three states. In Jammu and Kashmir, the NDA candidates were opposed by the National Conference which captured two-thirds of the state's seats. In Uttar Pradesh, where Vajpayee's old coalition had won 57 seats in 1998, his new coalition lost 26 seats to the Samajwadi Party, 14 seats to the Bahujan Samaj Party, and 8 seats to the Congress Indira Party. West Bengal continued its tradition of electing a preponderance of Communist Party (Marxist) candidates, with that party capturing 30 seats. The NDA's failure to win a single seat in Kerala was the result of the Congress Indira Party's winning 12 seats and the two Communist parties' scoring victories in the remaining 8 seats.

That the NDA won a comfortable majority of Lok Sabha seats, and A. B. Vajpayee became the first non-Congress prime minister to be reelected, was due, not to a substantial increase in the number of seats won by the BJP, but to the large number of scats captured by its allied parties. Even though the BJP succeeded in winning 55% of the seats that it contested compared with 48% in 1998, it added only 2 seats to its list of Lok Sabha successes. Measured by its share of the votes cast, it had achieved modestly improved results, increasing its percentage from 26 to 28. Its allies in the NDA added 121 seats to the BJP's total, 35 more than in 1998. But even if the BJP could not claim overwhelming credit for the NDA's comfortable Lok Sabha majority, its leader, A. B. Vajpayee, could. Not only had he held his old fourteen-party coalition together after his regime's fall in April but he had also made its twenty-four-party NDA successor coalition a united force supporting his candidacy for the prime minister's post. Its constituent parties were able to fight the election with a common manifesto because Vajpayee saw to it that the BJP's Hindutva agenda found no place in it. Whatever their ideological and programmatic differences, all the NDA's members agreed that A. B. Vajpayee, the man who had led India to victory in the Kargil "war," should continue to be India's prime minister.

Although Sonia Gandhi had won her Lok Sabha seats by wide margins—300,000 in Amathi and 60,000 in Bellary—her party had suffered its worst defeat in post-Independence history. The 113 seats which it captured were 27 fewer than in 1998. The only states where it did well were Assam, Karnataka, and Kerala. While it captured only 12 seats in Uttar Pradesh, this was a marked improvement over its 1998 performance in which it had won none. It also did comparatively well in the Punjab, where it captured 8 seats after winning none in 1998. Offsetting this gain was a substantial loss of seats in Maharashtra, where the party had won 33 in the previous general election. Its sharp fall to 10 seats there was directly attributable to the split in its ranks that had led to Sharad Pawar's formation of the NDC. Not only did NDC candidates who entered the field win 6 of the Maharashtra seats that had been held by the Congress Indira Party in the 12th Lok Sabha, but they deprived the Congress Party candidates of enough votes to cause them to lose to a number of Shiv Sena and BJP candidates.

Some of the reasons for the Congress Indira Party's dismal showing had to do with the party itself. As a grassroots political institution, the party had been for years "decrepit or non-existent," to use one newspaperman's pithy descriptive phrase. The program that had been announced, when Sonia Gandhi had become president, to resuscitate the party's organization never had gotten beyond the changes that she had made in the personnel and functioning of its top level committees. After the party's euphoric reaction to the favorable results of the November 1998 state elections, this "priority" party rebuilding effort was forgotten in the rush to take control of the Central Government. Portraying itself during the campaign as the party that would give India a "stable secular government" produced a cynical reaction rather than votes. India's citizenry was aware that the Congress Indira Party had ceased to be a truly secular party since the days of Indira Gandhi, and a party that had played the major role in bringing down India's last three Central Governments could hardly claim that its overriding aim was to provide the country with stable government. Its two-faced, for and against, attitude toward fighting the Kargil "war" had brought its patriotism into question, and its personal attacks on Prime Minister Vajpayee did not sit well with voters who saw him as the leader who had achieved a military and diplomatic victory over Pakistan.

While the party as an organization was responsible for a share of the nonfeasance and misfeasance that had led to its worst performance since Independence, Sonia Gandhi had to shoulder much of the blame for the Congress Indira Party's debacle. It was not altogether her fault that she was put in a position which she could not handle. She was not responsible for the fact that the leaders of the Congress Indira Party were determined to rely on the surviving member of the Nehru dynasty as their "ace in the hole" for arresting the party's decline. She was not responsible for the fact that she was a Roman Catholic who had been born in Italy and was new to the Indian political game. But she was responsible for the uncompromising, almost arrogant, way in which she had launched herself into the leading political role that had been thrust upon her. She was foreign-born, and she was inexperienced in politics, but she plunged into the campaign as though these handicaps did not exist, defying her NDA opponents by saying that she would "show them the kind of stuff she was made of." While her foreign origin did not prove to be a problem in the two constituencies in which she stood for election to the Lok Sabha, it did hurt her party nationwide. Voters knew that if the Congress Indira Party was given a parliamentary majority, she would become India's prime minister. While voters in Bellary and Amethi were quite willing to have a foreign-born Indian as their MP, most of India's voters did not relish the idea of having a foreign-born Indian as their prime minister.

A greater handicap than her foreign birth was her inexperience in Indian politics. It was her inexperience that led her to insist that the Congress Indira Party fight the campaign largely on its own rather than as part of an anti-NDA coalition. Her inability to understand and deal effectively with politicians, especially leaders of other parties, made her uncomfortable at the prospect of heading a coalition government. The only government that she could see herself heading was one that was controlled by the party that she controlled. Her inability to persuade those who disagreed with her also showed in the autocratic leadership style that she displayed within the Congress Indira Party. Relying on the advice of a small coterie of carefully selected advisors, she made all of the party's major decisions and would tolerate no dissent from within its ranks. When three "rebels" questioned the party's assumption that she would be its candidate for the prime minister's post, instead of allowing their question to be deliberated in the appropriate party forum, she had resigned the party presidency simply because they had raised the question and withdrew her letter of resignation only after they had been expelled from the party for six years.

In the absence of a record of governance of her own, Sonia Gandhi's only political recourse had been to project herself as the surviving member of the Nehru dynasty. Over and over in her campaign speeches, she had emphasized the contribution and sacrifice that had been made in the past by her mother-in-law and husband rather than what she herself had done for the country or what she would do in the future. To give the Nehru dynasty the look of having a future that went beyond her, she had put her son and daughter on display during the campaign. While these tactics did bring out the crowds and did help to produce victories in the Amethi and Bellary constituencies, they did not give her party the votes needed to win more than 113 Lok Sabha seats. Outside the Congress Indira Party, her appeal to the historical prestige of the Nehru dynasty had little relevance to Indian politics in 1999. Voters facing the coming millennium were interested in what Sonia Gandhi and her party would do to help solve the everyday problems that they faced, not what the party and its Nehru family leaders had done for them in the past.

Sonia Gandhi's responsibility for the Congress Indira Party's dismal showing was the major subject of postelection newspaper and magazine commentary. Swapan Dasgupta's piece in *India Today* put it this way: "Opinion polls—contemptuously dismissed by Congress leaders—clearly indicated there was popular indifference to Sonia's leadership claims. The 'Italian' question did play a role but more significant was the wariness over her lack of experience. Congress General Secretary Oscar Fernandes claimed Sonia encapsulated the 'experience of four generations' but this dynastic hype was greeted with mass incredulity. The scepticism increased as the Congress tried to confuse everyone with wild charges that did not even spare the army. The claim that being the possessor of the Nehru-Gandhi trademark automatically qualifies a person to hold the highest political office didn't sell."

Adding to the Congress Indira Party's woes was the relatively poor performance of the regional parties with which it had worked out "understandings"— Jayalalitha's Anna DMK in Tamil Nadu and Laloo Prasad Yadav's Rashtriya Janata Dal (RJD) in Bihar. The Anna DMK won 10 seats and the RJD 7, compared with 18 and 17 respectively in the 1998 election. While Jayalalitha had not stood for election, Laloo Prasad Yadav had lost by 30,000 votes the seat that he had won handily in 1998. As significant as the wide margin by which he lost was the fact that the winner was Sharad Yadev, his most bitter political rival. Laloo Prasad Yadav's and his party's collapse were the result not only of the merger that had been engineered by Defense Minister Fernandes between the Samatha Party and the Janata Dal (United) that had consolidated the anti-RJD vote in Bihar but also of the split that had taken place in the ranks of the state's Yadav population. Whereas all the Yadavs in the state had formerly been solidly behind Laloo Prasad Yadav, the miserable performance of his and his wife's government, particularly its failure to deal with a chaotic law and order situation and with the only negative rate of economic development in the nation, had motivated a large segment of the Yadav caste's members to shift their political loyalty to the state's other leading Yadav politician. Collaboration with the Anna DMK and the RJD had added 17 seats to the Congress Indira Party–led bloc in the 13th Lok Sabha, but the party's image could not help but be tarnished by its partnership with the country's two most corrupt politicians. Any further attempt by the Congress Indira Party to portray itself as a party dedicated to "clean" government would be laughed out of court.

The United Front, which had played a major role in the 1996 General Election but had faded during the 1998 General Election, had been conspicuous by its absence as a "third force" in the 1999 election. The two Communist parties, after campaigning cooperatively with the Congress Indira Party in support of Sonia Gandhi for the prime minister's post, had had a difficult time maintaining their traditional hold on Lok Sabha seats in West Bengal, Kerala, and Tripura. The DMK had joined the NDA. The Janata Dal had fractured three ways, with the result that only the remnant calling itself the Janata Dal (United) had played a significant role in determining the election's outcome and only in Bihar where it had joined forces with the Samatha Party to win seats for NDA candidates. The Samajwadi Party had prospered in Uttar Pradesh but after campaigning on its own rather than as a member of a "secular" front.

With the total demise of the "third force," Indian politics had continued the move that had begun in 1998 toward the evolution of a two-party system. Only two parties—the BJP and the Congress Indira Party—had campaigned on a national scale and had won more than 100 seats and more than 25% of the votes cast. But the 1999 General Election had seen one of these national parties decline to its smallest number of victories since Independence, and the other national party, while it had added only two seats to its holdings in the Lok Sabha, had led a coalition that had increased its majority in the Lok Sabha from 39 seats in 1998 to 71 seats in 1999. The result had been the emergence, not of two equally strong national parties, but of one national party that was considerably stronger than its rival. At the same time, the 1999 General Election had produced thirty-six regional parties that had managed to capture seats in the 13th Lok Sabha. Twenty-five of these regional parties had added 121 seats to the 182 won by the BJP, giving them "bragging rights" based on their contribution of almost 40% of the NDA's seats.

The 1999 General Election had also witnessed a continuation of the process that had been going on in Indian politics since the decline of the Congress Party and the rise of the BJP—consolidation at the national level and diffusion at the regional level. India had left behind the era of single-party Central Governments and had entered an era of coalition Central Governments. Neither of the national parties could win a majority of Lok Sabha seats on its own. Only with the help of a number of regional parties could one of the national parties muster enough "letters of support" to form a Central Government. The BJP had realized that this was the basic fact of political life in the India of 1999. It had succeeded in putting together a twenty-four-party coalition that had enabled the resulting NDA to form a new government under BJP leadership. The Congress Indira Party had turned a blind eye to this basic fact of political life, with the result that it had experienced an election disaster that had brought it to its lowest level of Lok Sabha strength since Independence.

16

NDA Government's First 100 Days

The decisive margin by which the NDA had won the general election and the key role that its leader in the campaign had played in its victory made it easy for President Narayanan to usher in India's millennial government. A. B. Vajpayee was the obvious choice to be offered the prime minister's post, and he was duly appointed on October 11 without being asked to prove that his government would enjoy majority support in the 13th Lok Sabha. Vajpayee's political muscle was strengthened within the next two days by the decision of the Telegu Desam Party to give "unconditional support" to his new regime, even though it would not be a member, and the decision of the DMK to join his government. With these two strong South Indian parties behind him, Prime Minister Vajpayee and his Council of Ministers were sworn in on October 13, 1999.

The Council was a two-tiered seventy person ministry made up of twenty-five members with cabinet rank and forty-five ministers of state. The four cabinet members who would preside over the major ministries were carryovers from the previous regime—L. K. Advani as home minister, Vashwant Singh as finance minister, Jaswant Singh as external affairs minister, and George Fernandes as defense minister. Fernandes was a member of the Janata Dal (United), but the other three were BJP members. Twelve of the other cabinet posts also went to the BJP, giving the prime minister's party over half of the cabinet slots. The rest of the cabinet was made up of four ministers chosen from the Janata Dal (United), two each from the DMK and the Shiv Sena, and one each from the Trinamool Congress and the Biju Janata Dal. Thirty-one of the forty-five ministers of state also came from the BJP. The remainder included two each from the Janata Dal (United), the DMK, and the Patali Makkal Katchi, one each from the National Congress, the Trinamool Congress, the Marumalarchi Dravida Kazagham, the Shiv Sena, the Biju Janata Dal, and the Manipur State Congress, and one independent.

Aside from the preponderance of BJP members, which was to be expected given the 182 seats that it held in the 13th Lok Sabha and its leader's occupation of the prime minister's post, the new ministry was broad based with respect to party affiliations, caste membership, and, except for the northeast, regional representation. The Janata Dal (United) received a generous share, four cabinet ministers and three ministers of state, even though the party had elected only twenty members to the Lok Sabha, but one of its most prominent leaders, Ramakrishna Hedge, who had been commerce minister in the previous Vajpayee government, did not find a place. So far as state representation was concerned, Bihar enjoyed the lion's share, eleven ministers, followed by Tamil Nadu, Maharashtra, and Madhya Pradesh with eight each, Uttar Pradesh with six, and Andhra Pradesh with four. The NDA's poor showing in Kerala and Karnataka accounted for these states' being provided with few places. The Punjab received none. Orissa was given only one ministerial position, but it was a cabinet post. Although the gender distribution showed only eight women with ministerial posts, this was double the number in Vajpayee's 1998 Council of Ministers and brought female representation to 11% of the total. Members of Scheduled Castes and Tribes accounted for the same number of ministerial offices and the same percentage of the total. Muslims were represented by two ministers of state.

The smooth transition to a new government augured well for the stability and durability of the second Vajpayee regime, but even before its Council of Ministers was sworn in, a dark cloud had arisen on India's border, foretelling that its future road would be a rocky one. Once again, the dark cloud was produced by India's troubled relations with Pakistan. On October 12, General Pervez Musharraf, who had been a leader in both the Pakistani campaign on the Siachen Glacier front and the invasion of Kargil District, had ousted Prime Minister Sharif's civilian government and had replaced it with military rule. Even before his coup took place, it had become clear that Pakistan was committed to continuing the fighting in Kashmir after the end of the Kargil "war," not only along the LOC but throughout the state. Pakistan's support for the insurgency, far from being reduced after its Kargil invading force had been withdrawn, had increased, with the result that attacks on India's security personnel and installations had intensified.

Indian authorities tried to curb the insurgents' higher level of effort by jailing the leaders of the All Party Hurriyat Conference except for its chairman who was the chief imam of Kashmir. Their preventive detention did not stem the increasing tide of militancy because the insurgent force was now spearheaded by the 1,500 fanatical Pakistani and Afghani Mujahideen who had slipped into Kashmir during the fighting along the LOC. These new arrivals, who brought the total number of non-Indians fighting in the insurgency to between 2,000 and 2,500, did not take their orders from the Conference but from more radical organizations like the Harkat-ul-Mujahideen. Reinforcements had strengthened insurgent manpower not only quantitatively but also qualitatively because the additions were men who saw the struggle with the Indian security forces as a "jihad" (holy war). The result was that, rather than abating after India's July declaration of victory in the Kargil war, the anti-India insurgent campaign reached its highest level of intensity three months later.

On November 3, a "suicide squad" of militants invaded the headquarters of the 15th Corps, which had been the center of gravity of the Kargil defense force, killing a Defense Ministry public relations officer and six other army personnel. A week later a sizable Pakistani contingent attacked an Indian army post sixty miles north of Srinagar. Seventeen of the attacking troops were killed, and the others were forced to withdraw. The Indian casualties were fewer, but, considering the fact that they occupied defensive positions, their number attested to the intensity of the fighting—one officer and three enlisted men killed and nine enlisted men wounded. These high profile military assaults against Indian army personnel were followed by the bombing of a train that was on its way to Delhi from Jammu. Twelve passengers were killed and 108 were injured, many of them members of India's Kashmir security force who were traveling home on leave, by a bomb that had been planted by Kashmiri militants. While these "front-page" incidents were taking place, ten insurgents, four security personnel, and six civilians died in small-scale fire fights which broke out during searches for Mujahideen hideouts and weapons storage sites.

These insurgent attacks were not part of a campaign initiated by General Musharraf's new military government. They had been planned and organized before he took charge of Pakistan's government, as a way of continuing the effort that had been going on for a decade to end India's hold on Kashmir. But the general's seizure of the reins of power from Prime Minister Sharif meant that the attacks would not stop. General Musharraf had felt the sting of Pakistan's defeats in the Siachen Glacier area and in Kargil District with special force. He was all the more determined to strengthen Pakistani military positions in Kashmir, and one of the immediate ways to accomplish this objective was to do whatever he could to step up the insurgency campaign. It was no surprise that one of his first acts as Pakistan's military ruler was to free from prison the leaders of the Lashkar-e-Taiba who had been jailed as fanatical extremists because they were difficult for Prime Minister Sharif's government to control. (It was this organization that had supplied many of the Mujahideen recruits for the Kargil invading force and had mounted the November attack on the 15th Corps' headquarters.) The next step that General Musharraf took to strengthen the Kashmir insurgency was to appoint one of the generals who had worked with him in organizing Pakistan's Kargil "war" effort as the new head of Pakistan's Inter-Service Intelligence Agency and assign him the task of providing support for insurgent forces.

Within a few days of taking command of Pakistani's government, General Musharraf tried to give the impression that he was holding out an olive branch to India by announcing that Pakistani troops would withdraw from areas bordering India. His announcement was later clarified when a Pakistani army spokesman pointed out that this withdrawal would not be carried out along Kashmir's Line of Control. This clarification prompted Prime Minister Vajpayee's top security advisor to remind the world that the "tensions were not on the international border. [They were] on the Line of Control." India's army commander played down the military significance of Musharraf's announcement and, rather than responding by ordering his troops to withdraw from Pakistan's international borders, instructed them to be more vigilant than ever to prevent cross-border invasions.

Not convinced that General Musharraf intended to make peace after Pakistan's defeat in the Kargil "war," the Vajpayee government responded to his seizure of Pakistan's government by expressing its "grave concern" and by placing its armed forces on full alert. The general commanding India's security force in Kashmir characterized the setting up of a military regime in Pakistani as "an internal matter of that country" but then went on to say that "any attempt aimed against India on the borders or inside will receive a befitting reply." Five days after his military coup, General Musharraf made his first televised address and announced that Pakistani would welcome an unconditional, equitable, and result-oriented dialogue with India. Stating that "it is our desire that the situation on our borders and on the Line of Control remain calm and peaceful," he asserted that Pakistan and India could relieve the tense atmosphere in South Asia by working to resolve their problems, especially the "core issue" of Kashmir. As a prerequisite for solving the Kashmir problem, he admonished India to terminate its "repressive rule" and honor the UN resolutions on Kashmir and its commitments to the Kashmiri people. India's national security advisor to the prime minister reacted to the general's offer by saying that India would not participate in negotiations until Pakistani ceased its campaign of cross-border terrorism. This response was repeated and raised to a higher level by President Narayanan when he addressed a joint session of Parliament to outline the program that would be implemented by the new NDA government.

During his first news conference, General Musharraf reiterated his offer of talks with India and said that it was up to India to determine the future course of Indo-Pakistani relations. On Pakistan's side, said the general, "hostility will be met with hostility and peace with peace." India reacted very negatively to what it called the general's "strident language" and reminded him of the Indian prime minister's trip to Lahore and Pakistan's betrayal of the Lahore Declaration by invading Kargil District. India's External Affairs Ministry spokesman then laid down the preconditions for resuming dialogue, namely, that "Pakistan must facilitate restoration of trust through actions [and] abandon its state-sponsored terrorism against India in Jammu and Kashmir and other parts of the country."

General Musharraf's response did not come for several weeks, but when it did come, during the course of an interview with the BBC, he made it clear that he had no intention of acceding to India's preconditions. After describing himself as a "man of peace who was ready to go ten steps ahead of India for peace," he turned belligerent: "If they [Indians] are trying to be clever and say 'We want peace, but we do not want to talk on the main issue of Kashmir,' I say, 'Sorry, I am not coming.' " In a newspaper interview some weeks later, Prime Minister Vajpayee elaborated India's prerequisites for resuming negotiations with Pakistan: "Let Pakistan first take steps to restore confidence and create the right atmosphere for meaningful dialogue. Even before the military coup in Pakistan, India had made it clear that Islamabad must stop cross-border terrorism and end its hostile propaganda against India. Pakistan also has to demonstrate its commitment to the Simla Agreement and the Lahore Declaration." With General Musharraf "not coming" and India insisting that Pakistan agree to preconditions that it refused to accept, the two Kashmiri adversaries remained at swords' points, and the new NDA government faced its first serious foreign policy problem.

The next dark cloud on the NDA government's horizon appeared on its domestic front, and it sprang from natural causes. On October 29, the worst cyclone in 100 years struck the most densely populated and most fertile districts of coastal Orissa. A storm packing winds that exceeded 190 miles per hour produced twenty-five foot high tidal surges that brought fifteen feet of sea water fifteen kilometers inland along an eighty-seven mile stretch of the coast line. Thousands of villages containing more than 1.8 million houses were destroyed, and as many as 15 million people were rendered homeless. One and a half million hectares of rice paddies were inundated, destroying one-third of Orissa's annual rice crop. Six million coconut palms and larger trees were toppled, and at least 500,000 head of cattle were destroyed. Eight thousand villages lost their electricity. Hundreds of miles of roadways and rail lines were washed out. The Orissa government estimated the monetary loss resulting from the almost total devastation within the storm-impacted area at 10,000 crores of rupees ($2.3 billion).

The exact loss in human lives will never be known. Bodies were hurriedly cremated or buried as soon as they were found, and careful records of the number of dead were not maintained. The Orissa government was at pains to minimize the human loss because it felt that a high number of dead would reflect badly on the effectiveness of its relief effort. Nine days after the cyclone had struck, the official figure was 1,715, but a few days later it was raised to 7,447, although an assurance was given that the total would not go above 10,000. On the same day, residents of the worst hit area where the official death toll had been set at 5,300, identified 8,000 of its people as having died. Foreign correspondents who visited the storm ravaged area estimated that the overall death toll would be as many as 20,000, and, according to a news magazine report, their figure was substantiated in a secret report that was submitted to Delhi by central government observers.

Since the state's police had been rendered inoperative, the forces of law and order were conspicuous by their absence, and food riots prevented food and relief supplies from reaching outlying villages that had been cut off by the storm's flood waters. Only when army troops moved in was some semblance of public security restored. The only relief that isolated villages received during the first week following the storm was provided by military personnel who were dispatched to the devastated area by the NDA government. An infantry division consisting of 10,000 men as well as units of the navy and air force were ordered to use their trucks, ships, and helicopters to rescue marooned villagers and to bring food, clean water, and medicine to inundated villages. They did yeoman service and prevented the death toll from climbing even higher as a result of rampant starvation and disease following the storm.

Despite Orissa Chief Minister Gamang's failure to encourage contributions from the Indian states and from national and international non-governmental organizations, the armed forces went ahead and rushed in hundreds of relief and medical personnel and thousands of tonnes of food, clothing, utensils, and other essential supplies. The immediate problem was not a shortage of the wherewithal to relieve the suffering but getting it to the places where it was desperately needed. Here the Orissa government proved to be inept or worse. Two weeks after the cyclone had struck, 13,000 tonnes of rice and 60,000 saris and dhotis had not been distributed to storm victims. Half of the storm-battered villages were still without electricity, and half of the telephone exchanges were still dead. The state government's failure to perform effectively in providing immediate relief was not due to a shortage of funds, because 52 crores of rupees ($12 million) of the Central Government's first installment of financial assistance remained unspent.

One month after the cyclone had struck, the state government's performance was still dismal. Aware that the Orissa government could not manage the relief effort on its own, and unhappy with the state government's efforts to phase out participation by the armed forces, the NDA government finally decided that it should play a more active role in the operation. While it continued to resist the Orissa chief minister's request to increase the Central Government's contribution to the relief effort above the 1,500 crores of rupees ($350 million) that had been allocated, the cabinet took action on November 10 to create a special task force to coordinate the relief efforts that had been undertaken by various central government ministries. The task force's commissioning made it possible to continue the armed forces' role in the face of state government pressure to bring it to an end and to guide national and international nongovernmental organizations to the villages that were most in need of assistance.

The result was an increase in the effectiveness of relief operations. But the Central Government was not of a mind to take ultimate responsibility for the management of relief despite the mounting evidence that the Orissa government was not up to the task. The cabinet's resolution establishing the central government task force stipulated that its relief activities would supplement but not supersede those of the state government. However poorly the relief effort was going and however much the victims of the cyclone were continuing to suffer as a result, the NDA government insisted upon playing the role of the junior partner and leaving overall management in the utterly inept hands of the state government. The Central Government's financial contribution to the relief effort was increased by 860 crores of rupees ($205 million) in January 2000, bringing the total to 2,360 crores of rupees ($555 million), but it still covered less than one-quarter of the state's estimate of the monetary loss caused by the storm. To make matters worse for Orissa, 450 crores of rupees (more than $100 million) would be deducted by the Central Government from the state's allocation of 1999–2000 "revenue sharing" funds. The result was that the NDA government's net financial assistance of 1,910 crores of rupees ($450 million) did not look impressive when compared with the estimated 2,000 crores of rupees (about $500 million) coming from other Indian states, domestic and foreign nongovernmental organizations, foreign governments, and Pope John Paul II.

The October 29 Orissa cyclone caused immediate damage that the state government estimated at 10,000 crores of rupees ($2.3 billion). Orissa's officials also estimated that the state's economic development had been set back by ten years and that it would cost 25,000 crores of rupees ($5.75 billion) to make its coastal area a livable and productive human habitat once again. When the NDA government refused to back a relief and rehabilitation program that would cost anything like this amount of money, the result was bound to be a sad ending for the 15 million residents of Orissa who had borne the brunt of the storm. That sad ending was best described by a news magazine reporter who had visited the devastated area a few days after the cyclone had struck and who had written: "Months from now, even weeks, Orissa will be an old story, forgotten with time. The concern, so silent and minimal as it is, like the sea will have receded from their homes. But hardship has no regular tides, it does not recede so easily. For these people the cliche that life will never be the same again fits perfectly."

Complicating the situation facing the NDA government as it decided how it should respond to the Orissa cyclone disaster was another problem that had emerged at the same time and, once again, from outside the country. Unlike the cyclone, which was a product of natural causes, this problem was man-made. Pope John Paul II had decided to visit India for three days beginning on November 4, five days after the cyclone struck. The NDA government looked forward to his coming with some apprehension. To the extent that he came as head of state of the Vatican, his would be a state visit, and it would be a simple matter for the NDA government to welcome him as a head of state. But he would also be coming as the head of the Roman Catholic Church, and Prime Minister Vajpayee and his lieutenants would have to find a way to handle his visit so that India's self-image as a country that tolerated religious diversity was not tarnished and the government's Hindu fundamentalist supporters, who saw Christianity as a religion that was subverting India's way of life, were not incensed. Complicating matters further was the timing of the pope's visit because he would be in India during the days when India would be celebrating *diwali*, India's most popular Hindu festival. Finding a middle way between these contrasting schools of thought regarding Pope John Paul II and his religion and making adequate security arrangements at a time when thousands of revelers would be abroad would turn out to be no easy task.

The trouble began a fortnight before the pope's arrival when the Vishwa Hindu Parishad (VHP), one of the Sangh Parivar group of Hindu fundamentalist organizations to which the BJP belonged, began to organize protests against the Roman Catholic Church's evangelistic activities that were producing converts to Christianity. The object of these protests, according to the VHP's president, was "to send a message to the Pope that during his visit here he must condemn religious conversions for there are many ways to find God." The VHP's demands were elaborated by one of its former general secretaries to include an apology for "the atrocities of the Church" that had been committed against Hindus in general and, specifically, those who had suffered from the operation of the Inquisition during the years of Portuguese rule in Goa. The VHP also demanded that the Roman Catholic Church announce whether the pope would be visiting as its head or as head of the Vatican state. "If he is coming to India as a religious head, he should not be given the reception due to a head of state. If he is coming as a head of state, he should not participate in religious functions." Following the burning in Delhi of an effigy of the pope by members of the Shiv Sena, the VHP launched a protest march that would begin in Goa and, after a 300-mile journey through Karnataka, Maharashtra, Gujarat, Rajasthan, and Madhya Pradesh, arrive in Delhi on the first day of the pope's visit.

Leaders of the Roman Catholic Church, accusing the members of the Sangh Parivar of engaging in "mischievous and systematic propaganda constructed on half truths, lies, and misrepresentations," requested Prime Minister Vajpayee to do everything necessary to prevent the Pope's visit from becoming an occasion for civil unrest. Following his usual "hands off" policy, the prime minister did not respond by putting a stop to the Goa to Delhi protest march, but the chief minister of Madhya Pradesh did refuse to allow the marchers to enter his state. Since Madhya Pradesh's government was controlled by the Congress Indira Party, the marchers accused the chief minister of putting a road block in their way in order to please his party's Christian president, Sonia Gandhi, and proceeded on their way by another route. While the NDA government was careful to take no comparable action that would give the impression that it was acceding to the Roman Catholic Church's request, it was willing that one of its leaders should speak some words condemning the Sangh Parivar's anti-pope campaign. Home Minister Advani, the cabinet member responsible for the pope's security while in the country, made a public pronouncement that "the Pope is a revered guest of the country and the government of India condemns any burning of his effigy and disapproves of any protest against his arrival." He clarified the status of the pope's visit by saying that the pontiff came in response to the government's "invitation" and that he would be accorded the honors due to a head of state.

Advani's pronouncement was followed by a statement from a spokesman for the BJP that his party and the BJP-led government would welcome the pope but that those organizations that wished to protest his visit had a democratic right to do so. The positions taken by the government and the party spokesman showed that the middle way which the Vajpayee regime would pursue would be to go forward with the ceremonies called for by a state visit and, at the same time, allow the protest demonstrations to continue provided that they did not get out of control. The government would treat the pope as a visiting head of state and leave the religious elements in his program in the hands of the Roman Catholic Church. A week before the pope's arrival, the External Affairs Ministry issued an official notice that "all courtesies and honors" would be extended to Pope John Paul II and that his program would be finalized in consultation with the Vatican's representative. When asked if the matter of religious conversions would be discussed during the pope's talk with Prime Minister Vajpayee, the External Affairs Ministry's spokesman replied that "it would not be normal for a religious issue to come up during talks between a head of state and a head of government."

The *New York Times* correspondent who covered the pope's visit did a good job of summarizing the apparently divergent directions of the pontiff's messages. "The Pope came to India with two agendas. He preached ardently for religious tolerance for all faiths, but also instructed his own to convert new followers. To even the mildest leaders of other religions, the two messages do not easily mix." The second message flew in the face of the Sangh Parivar's demands that the pope forswear future conversions and apologize for those that had occurred in the past. One would have expected that his refusal to give ground would produce further Hindu fundamentalist protests as he left India. Fortunately for the NDA government, this did not happen. The pope departed the country on November 7 with a warm send-off from government officials and leaders of the Roman Catholic Church. The tight security regime which the NDA government had instituted undoubtedly played a part in preventing violent protests against the firm Christian stand which the pope had taken when he addressed the bishops who had gathered to celebrate the end of Christianity's second millennium. Coupled with this display of police muscle was a factor which had nothing to do with fear of the heavy hand of the law. Before the pope arrived, many had thought that the negative reaction to his visit would be heightened by its coinciding with the celebration of India's most popular festival. This fear overlooked the fact that *diwali,* although it is a Hindu festival, is celebrated by Indians of various religious persuasions. So thousands of celebrating Hindus and non-Hindus were enjoying themselves on Delhi's streets during the pope's visit, too busy to allow themselves to be diverted by Hindu fundamentalists into taking part in protests against the pope's presence in the city. Very few among the celebrating crowds were of a mind to join forces with members of the Shiv Sena and the VHP.

There can be little doubt that the NDA government greeted the pope's departure with a sigh of relief. The pope's visit had gone off well because the government had managed to navigate safely between the Scylla of world opinion and the Charybdis of Hindu fundamentalism. On the one hand, world opinion had not been offended by anti-Christian disturbances marring the pope's visit. On the other hand, Hindu fundamentalist organizations had no occasion to vent their wrath on a government showing support for the pope's message by cracking down on those who protested his very coming to India. The Sangh Parivar's residual anger was directed, not against the DNA government for treating the pope with courtesy and respect, but against the pope for "misusing our hospitality and planning to convert India into a Christian country."

During the days immediately following its swearing in, the NDA government had had little trouble dealing with opposition parties. The United Front was no more. The leaders of the Communist Party Marxist had ended their electoral collaboration with the Congress Indira Party, blaming Sonia Gandhi for having acted as the architect of the NDA's victory because she had refused to campaign for a coalition government. The Congress Indira Party had broken with Laloo Prasad Yadav's Rashtriya Janata Dal on the ground that Prasad Yadav's record of corruption and poor governance was responsible for their alliance's dismal showing in Bihar. Except for its continuing "understanding" with Jayalalitha's Anna DMK, the fallout from the 1999 General Election had produced a situation in which the Congress Indira Party was isolated as the only significant opposition party with which the NDA government had to contend. In addition to being isolated, the party's strength in the Lok Sabha was at its lowest level since Independence.

Realizing that the weakness of its political position meant that fighting the NDA government head-on would be an exercise in futility, the Congress Indira Party laid out a strategy that called for opposing the government on those issues where there was disagreement and supporting the government where the party and the government agreed. Addressing a meeting of the Federation of Indian Chambers of Commerce, Sonia Gandhi pledged her party's backing for the economic liberalization steps which the NDA government was preparing to take: "I wish to state categorically that our approach will be constructive and responsible. Just because our opponents played politics when they were in the opposition and now they are in power and have suddenly discovered the virtue of pragmatism does not mean that we will behave similarly. . . . Unanimity may not be feasible or even desirable. But what is certainly possible is consensus. The onus for crafting such a consensus lies with the government of the day."

Sonia Gandhi's easy transition to her new role as a member of Parliament did not mean that her elevation to the post of leader of the opposition was a sure thing. The 1999 General Election had ended with the Congress Indira Party reeling from the worst defeat in its history and Sonia Gandhi under the gun for the leading role that she had played in bringing it about. Her future as party president was at stake because previous party presidents Narasimha Rao and Sitaram Kesri had been ousted after the party had failed to win the 1996 and 1998 General Elections. Not only had the party been defeated once again, but the number of Lok Sabha seats that it had secured had hit a new low. Questions were also being raised about the advisability of keeping Sonia Gandhi as chairman of the party's Parliamentary Committee. She could point out in her favor that she was now a member of the Lok Sabha, which she had not been when she was first elected chairman, but the fact remained that she had no experience leading her party's members in the halls of Parliament.

Sonia Gandhi avoided both of these potential pitfalls by playing the role of the humble penitent and throwing herself on the party's mercy. She admitted that she had made "some mistakes" and assumed personal responsibility for the disappointing election results. With her next breath, she made it clear that she had no intention of quitting her party posts: "Whatever position I hold or role I fulfill in the future, I will not at any time abandon my responsibility to our loyal workers and to the people of our country." Instead of rising up to punish her for her "mistakes," the party's leaders reelected her as the chairman of the party's Parliamentary Committee and selected her to become the leader of the opposition to the NDA government. Since no one raised a question about her continuing as party president, she also retained that post.

Having sidestepped any move that might have threatened her absolute hold on the party's helm and having made certain that she would become leader of the opposition, Sonia Gandhi shifted the party's attention from her own responsibility for the 1999 election defeat to the conditions within the party that had led to its poor showing in the election. She called for "honest introspection" into the reasons for its meager number of Lok Sabha victories and created an eleven member committee to undertake the task. In order to make sure that its findings did not highlight her "mistakes," she appointed her faithful retainer, Kerala's A. K. Anthony, as its chairman. As a further safeguard against the "honest introspection" producing any findings that would threaten her position as the party's supreme leader, the committee was given until November 30 to submit its report, by which time the questioning that had occurred during the weeks immediately following the miserable election results would have dissipated. Even before the committee began its work, the movement was under way to place responsibility on the shoulders of party underlings rather than upon the shoulders of the party president. Five AICC general secretaries and one member of the Working Committee identified themselves already as among those who were to blame and resigned their party posts.

When the Anthony Committee presented its 200 page report on November 30, the movement to protect Sonia Gandhi continued. A complete copy was given to Sonia Gandhi, who ordered that a thirty-three page executive summary containing the committee's "overall perspective" and recommendations be prepared for distribution to members of the Working Committee. The copy of the full report was kept at Sonia Gandhi's residence where any member who wished to peruse it could do so, although no one did. By orchestrating this strategy, Sonia Gandhi and her coterie made sure that the discussion of the report that took place a fortnight later at an "informal" meeting of the Working Committee was centered, not on the evidence that the committee had gathered regarding what had gone wrong, but on the recommendations that it had made for reorganizing the party's structure and changing its campaign procedures so that future election results would be better. No mention was made of the political "mistakes" that Sonia Gandhi had confessed she had made or of the impact that her foreign origin had had on the election results. So far as the party president's role in the 1999 election debacle was concerned, the bottom line of the "honest introspection" called for by Sonia Gandhi was that her advisers had been at fault. The "mistakes" that she had made were the result of bad advice, not lack of sound political judgment on her part. This "bottom line" was written, not in the report of the Anthony Committee or in the actions taken by the Congress Working Committee based upon it, but by the "honest introspection's" silence on all of the questions raised by the party president's performance since the fall in April of the previous Vajpayee government. The statement made to the Indian public by the Working Committee's decision to do nothing more than to adopt eighteen of the Anthony Committee's twenty recommendations for restructuring the party's organization and revising its election procedures was that it was weakness in the areas of party organization and operation rather than the president's "mistakes" that had caused its election defeat.

The short-lived era of relatively "good feeling" between the NDA government and the Congress Indira Party opposition ended abruptly on October 22 when the CBI filed with a Delhi court a charge sheet naming those involved in the Bofors gun scandal. The evidence that was submitted to back up its charges did not go beyond what the CBI had reported two years earlier. What was new was the inclusion of Rajiv Gandhi's name as one of the persons who, according to the CBI, had "entered into a criminal conspiracy with other persons in New Delhi, Sweden, Switzerland and other places during 1985–87 and thereafter with the object of getting the Indian government to award a contract in favor of A. B. Bofors for the purchase of 400 155 MM FH 77-B gun systems by abuse of official parties by the aforesaid public servants and for causing wrongful gain to private persons and corresponding wrongful loss to the government of India in the deal." According to the charge sheet, in which his name was mentioned twenty times, Rajiv Gandhi had been the major player in ensuring that the contract was given to Bofors and in attempting to prevent any investigation of the charge that Bofors had paid substantial sums to persons in India as compensation for the help they had given in closing the deal. Even though he could not be tried because he had been assassinated in 1991, the CBI had included his name on the charge sheet so that the court could judge whether or not he had violated the Prevention of Corruption Act.

The initial reaction of the Congress Indira Party's spokesman was to dismiss the charge sheet as a "thirteen year old legal and political joke." Later, in a more serious vein, he said that the party would study it and make a formal statement after its contents had been evaluated. That statement came in the form of action taken during the course of a Working Committee meeting that had been called to identify the causes of its humiliating defeat in the 1999 General Election. The Working Committee condemned the NDA government for allowing the charge sheet to be filed "with the sole purpose of denigrating Rajiv Gandhi" and warned that the Congress Indira Party would not tolerate "this act of maligning and vilifying Rajiv Gandhi and the Congress Indira Party." Sonia Gandhi followed the Working Committee's denunciation by labeling the inclusion of Rajiv Gandhi's name on the charge sheet a "political vendetta" and calling upon Congress Indira Party MPs to organize protest demonstrations in their constituencies.

Party workers responded by staging a disturbance in front of the main gate of Parliament House, shouting slogans demanding that Rajiv Gandhi's name be removed from the charge sheet. When the Congress Indira Party MPs walked out of the Lok Sabha's chambers shouting the same slogans, the only other MPs accompanying them were the ten members of the Anna DMK. MPs representing the Communist parties, the Samajwadi Party, and the Bahujan Samaj Party did not join the parliamentary protest. Their position on the issue was stated publicly by one of the Communist leaders who labeled it a legal rather than a political matter and expressed his party's willingness to let the law take its course. The political complexion of the parade from Parliament House showed that it was only the Congress Indira Party that was vexed by the inclusion of Rajiv Gandhi's name on the charge sheet, and the shouts of the protesting MPs showed that the Congress Indira Party was vexed because he was the late husband of its president and supreme commander.

Prime Minister Vajpayee led the government's defense of its action with respect to the filing of the charge sheet. He denied that his government intended to denigrate Rajiv Gandhi's name. "The Bofors issue has been hanging fire for so many years. Complaints have been made against us that we are delaying the matter and that we have not been handling the issue honestly. Now we are being charged with the contrary." So far as the government was concerned, the matter now rested with the court, which would make the decision as to whether or not the CBI had acted properly in including Rajiv Gandhi's name on the charge sheet. Since the Congress Indira Party felt that it was an aggrieved party, Vajpayee advised its leaders to seek redress in the courts rather than in the streets. Home Minister Advani then joined the defense against the Congress Indira Party charge that the NDA government was playing politics. He revealed that the charge sheet had been ready for submission to the court in August 1999, but the prime minister had requested the CBI to delay action until after the election so that it would have no impact on the election results. According to Advani, the charge sheet's submission was "motivated by our commitment to battle corruption in high places," and, rather than being condemned as a "political and legal joke," it should be praised as a "political and legal triumph."

The Congress Indira Party then shifted from political maneuvering to direct action by taking to the streets with a noisy public demonstration. A mass rally of party workers was organized in Delhi, at which party leaders warned that "if Rajiv's name is not deleted, we will organize country wide demonstrations and not cooperate with the government." The Delhi demonstration was well attended and made a great deal of noise, but the "country wide" demonstrations did not materialize. The only Indians who cared whether Rajiv Gandhi's name was included or deleted were Sonia Gandhi and her supporters within the Congress Indira Party, and they did not constitute a force that was strong enough to rouse the nation to action. The final nail was driven into the Congress Indira Party's coffin when Home Minister Advani produced a definitive legal opinion on the issue written by the country's attorney general. He stated that, under Indian law, the government could not act to delete Rajiv Gandhi's name because, having been assassinated, Rajiv Gandhi was not threatened with prosecution under the Prevention of Corruption Act. Only a person so threatened had the legal right to request that his name be deleted from a CBI charge sheet. If the government were to act to delete Rajiv Gandhi's name, it would be interfering in the work of an investigating agency. The attorney general's opinion made it clear that the Congress Indira Party had no legal case for making its demand, and the country's refusal to support it with nationwide demonstrations showed that the party did not have the political clout to make its point in the streets.

In his first address to the nation following the NDA's victory over the Congress Indira Party in the dispute over Rajiv Gandhi's name having been included on the CBI charge sheet, Prime Minister Vajpayee had promised "good governance" and redeployment of resources to provide safe drinking water, primary health services, primary education, and rural roads and housing. His government would have "zero tolerance for terrorism and corruption," and measures for economic reforms would be put on the fast track. Adopting a cooperative stance toward opposition parties, the prime minister had appealed to them to "put the acrimony and bitterness of the last couple of months behind us and get down to the task of nation building. . . . Constructive criticism is an essential input for good policies and programs. Consensus on national issues is necessary for effective action. . . . We may have been sent to parliament under the banner of different parties, but we all have a common commitment to give India a stable and good government." As his speech neared its end, it had become more euphoric. He had pledged that his government would bring about the emergence of a "new India in a new century." Under its governance, and "with the help of a billion people proud of being Indian, there is nothing we cannot achieve, no problem we cannot tackle, no challenge we cannot face, and no opportunity we cannot seize."

The first important piece of legislation that the NDA government introduced to give effect to this ambitious agenda was the Insurance Regulatory Development Authority (IRDA) Bill. Because the NDA had a comfortable majority in the Lok Sabha, the bill would pass with no difficulty in the lower house of Parliament, provided that the MPs representing the coalition parties gave it solid backing. Prime Minister Vajpayee moved to strengthen the support of the government parties by calling a dinner meeting of the NDA's coordinating committee, at which a unanimous pledge was given to vote for the IRDA legislation. Now he had to shift his attention to the Congress Indira Party and do whatever he could to persuade its leaders to join forces with his government to pass the bill in the Rajya Sabha. That its support might not be forthcoming had been revealed in a press release issued by the All India Congress Committee's secretariat, warning the government that the Congress Indira Party would find it difficult to perform as a "constructive opposition" if personal attacks on its president and her deceased husband did not cease. Three days after the prime minister's dinner, the stand that the Congress Indira Party would take began to emerge; it was one of "constructive opposition." The secretary of the All India Congress Committee's economic cell announced that the party would support the bill provided the government agreed to four amendments that would protect the interests of the poorer sections of society. He revealed that an intense debate had taken place among Congress Indira Party leaders, but "while there was no unanimity, there was consensus."

The tide had been turned in the bill's favor by Sonia Gandhi herself. She had not only exerted her authority as party president but had sent an emissary to the prime minister and the finance minister to obtain their agreement to adopt the four amendments that were the price of her party's support. Although neither of the ministers felt that adopting the amendments would improve the bill, they readily agreed to accept them in order to assure its passage in both houses of Parliament. Sonia Gandhi's argument for playing the role of the leader of a "constructive opposition" with respect to the IRDA Bill was that it was another step in realizing the goals of the economic reform movement that had begun under Narasimha Rao's Congress Indira Party government and that it had been included in the party's campaign manifesto as a piece of legislation that the Congress Indira Party would enact if it became India's new Central Government. With Congress Indira Party support, the NDA government succeeded in passing its first major piece of legislation, one that would open India's insurance industry, until now a government monopoly, to private companies, including those headquartered in foreign countries.

The successful passage of the IRDA Bill stood in sharp contrast to the Lok Sabha's reception of the much disputed Women's Reservation Bill which sought to reserve 33% of all legislative seats for female candidates. The bill had been introduced by three previous governments—the Deve Gowda government in 1996, the Gujral government in 1997, and the first Vajpayee government in 1998. Each time it had received a stormy reception and each time the Lok Sabha had been dissolved before it could be debated. The NDA's 1999 campaign manifesto had called for its passage, and the second Vajpayee regime had been committed thereby to giving it a fourth try. Once again, its introduction caused scenes that violated most of the rules of parliamentary decorum. Once again it was the same MPs and the same parties that caused the worst of the uproar. Once again it was the same objection that fired their protests.

Mulayam Singh Yadav and his Samajwadi Party and Laloo Prasad Yadav and his Rashtriya Janata Dal insisted with great heat that the bill must include within the general 33% quota a special quota for Muslim women and women belonging to Other Backward Classes. Since Prime Minister Vajpayee had refused to grant this concession, they and their parties' MPs objected strenuously to the bill's being introduced without the special quotas. This time they were supported by Mayawati's Bahujan Samaj Party and the Muslim League. When the parliamentary affairs minister stated that the bill would be introduced in its original form, MPs belonging to the Samajwadi Party and the Rashtriya Janata Party shouted "No" and occupied the well of the Lok Sabha's chamber for almost two hours, bringing proceedings to a halt.

This disruptive occurrence had been preceded by another unusual event in the 13th Lok Sabha. Angered by the late date of the government's proposed submission of the Women's Reservation Bill which her party supported, Sonia

Gandhi had been moved to deliver her maiden speech as leader of the opposition. Pointing out that only three days remained before the end of the winter session, she had accused the Vajpayee regime of deliberately delaying the introduction of the bill so that it could not be debated before the winter session ended. "We want to know from the government whether it intends to pass this bill before the house rises for the new millennium. This is our demand." Failing to hear the answer that she had demanded, she had led the other Congress Indira Party MPs in a procession from the Lok Sabha's chambers. They had been followed by MPs belonging to the two Communist parties and the Anna DMK. Faced with this high degree of disruption and the large-scale walkout, Prime Minister Vajpayee could only lament the unseemly happenings and ask the question: "With what faces shall we go outside and face the people after the unprecedented incidents in the house?" Then he had announced that he would meet the next day with the floor leaders of all parties to discuss the issues that were in dispute.

Vajpayee tried to use this meeting to arrive at a consensus on the form in which the Women's Reservation Bill should be introduced. While no party opposed the 33% reservation, the issue of whether or not it should include a special quota for Muslim women and women belonging to Other Backward Classes remained unresolved. The NDA coalition parties and the Congress Indira Party took the position that the bill should be introduced without the special quotas and that the question of whether or not to include them should be decided when the bill was debated. The Samajwadi Party and the Rashtriya Janata Dal continued to insist that the quotas be included in the bill when it was first presented to the Lok Sabha. Despite the lack of a consensus, it was decided to introduce the bill in its original form on the last day of the winter session and to take the political consequences.

The first of these political consequences came the day after the bill had been introduced in the form of an address which Sonia Gandhi gave to the members of the Congress Working Committee. She called the government's action, in introducing the Women's Reservation Bill at a time when it was too late to debate it before the winter session had ended, a "ruse to buy time to cover up widening cracks in the ruling coalition. . . . We all know that mere introduction is not even a statement of intent. Indeed, it might be quite the opposite, a technique for disguising the real intent." According to the Congress Indira Party's president, the Vajpayee regime's "real" intent was to postpone a debate that would have revealed the increasing dissension within the NDA coalition on the issue of women's reservation. The NDA government's parliamentary affairs minister responded to Sonia Gandhi's attack by assuring members of the Lok Sabha that the government was "serious" about passing the bill and would be bringing it up for debate during the budget session that would begin during the third week of February 2000.

These words, coming from a government source, gave the impression that the Vajpayee regime would continue to press for passage of the Women's Reservation Bill and that the regime would be flexible enough to make it possible to work out the compromises that would enable the bill to receive Lok Sabha approval. But the political realities of the opening years of the 21st century supported Sonia Gandhi's scepticism regarding the NDA government's willingness to give the Women's Reservation Bill the priority status that it would need to become law. It was certain that the Samajwadi Party and the Rashtriya Janata Dal would continue to agitate by every means for the inclusion of the special quotas for Muslim women and women belonging to Other Backward Classes. A few cabinet ministers and some of the MPs who belonged to four parties that were members of the NDA coalition—the Janata Dal (United), the Shiv Sena, the Akali Dal, and the National Conference—were either opposed to or had reservations about the 33% general quota. To overcome these political obstacles and secure the bill's passage would require the Vajpayee regime to expend a good amount of political capital that could otherwise be used to accomplish higher priority objectives. Faced with security concerns that he viewed as more important for the country than reserving 33% of legislative seats for women, it seemed unlikely that Prime Minister Vajpayee would be willing to lead his government during the opening months of the new millennium to spend the political capital and devote the political energy that would be required to convert the Women's Reservation Bill into law. This was all the more certain because all he would have to do to get off the political hook would be to say to the nation that he had tried his best to carry out the NDA election manifesto's commitment to introduce the legislation but had been unable to obtain its passage because of the intransigence of certain opposition parties.

If there was anything that the NDA government did not want to happen during its first 100 days in office, it was to be presented with a surprise event, initiated from outside the country, that involved India's continuing struggle with Pakistan over control of Kashmir. That was what had happened to the first Vajpayee regime in May 1999 when a combined force of Pakistani regulars and Mujahideen had crossed the Line of Control and invaded Kargil District. Much to the NDA government's discomfort, another surprise came on the afternoon of December 24, 1999, when five masked gunmen hijacked Indian Airlines Flight 814 which was to have carried 178 passengers and eleven crew members from Kathmandu, Nepal, to Delhi. The gunmen spoke to each other and to the passengers in a mixture of three languages—Urdu, Hindi, and English. The charge sheet which the CBI subsequently issued identified all of the hijackers as Pakistani nationals who were members of the Harkat-ul-Mujahideen, one of the twenty-eight organizations on the American State Department's most recent terrorist list.

When the hijackers finally ordered the pilot to land at Kandahar in Afghanistan, the negotiating process could begin. Since India did not recognize the Taliban as the legitimate rulers of Afghanistan and had no diplomatic relations with the Taliban government, a special team had to be sent from Delhi to begin the process. They were not able to reach Kandahar until December 29, but, when they did come, they came as a force of fifty-two diplomats, doctors, engineers, and standby crew members. The diplomats were presented with the demands that the hijackers had given to the Taliban upon the plane's arrival in Kandahar. The hijackers would leave the plane's passengers unharmed and vacate the aircraft if Maulana Masood Azhar, who was a leader of the Harkat-ul-Mujahideen and the brother of one of the hijackers, and three other leaders of the Kashmiri insurgency were released from Indian jails. Although the Taliban had set no deadline for the plane's departure, it was clear that they wanted the hijacking incident ended as soon as possible. India's seven man negotiating team faced a difficult task not only because of the time pressure being applied by the Taliban but because of the uncompromising stand that Prime Minister Vajpayee had taken when he had declared on Christmas Day that "My government will not bend before such a show of terror" and exhorted the Indian nation to face the challenge of terrorism with determination and self-confidence.

The negotiating team's task became even more difficult when the hijackers stepped up their demands by raising the number of Kashmiri militants to be released from Indian jails to thirty-six, by adding the requirement that the body of another militant buried in India be returned to his homeland, and by tacking on a cash payment of $200 million. At this point, the Taliban leaders deviated from their earlier position that they would not become players in the negotiating process, persuading the hijackers that it was "un-Islamic" to demand money and the exhumation of a corpse and that the Indian authorities should not be forced to make the two additional concessions. This left the Indian negotiators with the simpler but still difficult task of whittling down the number of jailed militants that they would have to free in order to obtain the release of the Indian Airlines passengers. Despite Prime Minister Vajpayee's declaration that "My government will not bend to such a show of force," it was finally agreed that militants originally named would be released.

The negotiations with the hijackers were played out against the background of a maze of diplomatic discussions. The initial round of negotiations had not been made public at the time, and it was not until Prime Minister Vajpayee made his New Year's Day television broadcast announcing the release of the hostages that he was willing to admit that India had been anxious to prevent the hijacking incident from "internationalizing" the situation in Kashmir. India had taken immediate steps to avoid intervention by the United Nations and to enlist the help of a number of individual nations in freeing the hostages. The United Nations had agreed with India's position that it should not become involved in attempting to work out an agreement with the hijackers, even though the Taliban's foreign affairs spokesman had asked it to do so. One of the United Nations' senior officials made this plain when he responded to a reporter's question by saying, "An invitation from the Taliban isn't enough. Without an invitation from India we could not enter into negotiations."

Jaswant Singh had extended India's diplomatic web ever wider by seeking the support of the United States, the United Kingdom, France, Canada, Russia, Australia, Japan, Nepal, Iran, Bangladesh, and several other countries in bringing the hijacking to a peaceful end. He had requested each of the countries whose nationals were aboard the plane to send a representative to Kandahar in order that these might constitute a presence that would encourage the Taliban authorities to act in a responsible manner. One result had been that the diplomatic corps in Kandahar had increased manyfold and that by December 29 the countries that had diplomats there included Switzerland, Spain, Italy, Belgium, France, Canada, and Australia. The only country with a national on the plane that did not send a representative was the United States.

The United States had responded promptly not with a diplomat but with harsh words directed toward the hijackers. The promptness of the American response could have been due to President Clinton's estimate of the seriousness of any incident that involved the dispute between India and Pakistan over who should control Kashmir. Two days before the hijacking took place, he had stated in a television interview that "the Kashmiri issue is perhaps the most dangerous one in the world today, because you've got two nuclear powers who are somewhat uncertain about each other . . . ." Whether or not the president's remark had any bearing on it, the United States's response had been to condemn the hijacking. Calling it an "inhuman terrorist act," the White House had demanded the immediate release of the hostages and had urged the Taliban authorities to cooperate with India's negotiating team. The White House's words had been followed by a State Department spokesman's statement that "the United States condemns in the strongest terms the hijacking of Indian Airlines Flight 814."

This complicated and extensive set of political interactions had provided the international background for the December 31 arrival in Kandahar of an Indian plane carrying External Affairs Minister Jaswant Singh and the three Muslim militants whose release had been the price that India had been forced to pay for the release of the Flight 814 hostages. The three militants were Maulana Masood Azhar, Mushtak Ahmed Zargar, and Umar Saeed Sheikh, all of whom had played leading roles in the Kashmiri insurgency. The most important of the three was Masood Azhar, who was the chief fund raiser and propagandist of the Harkat-ul-Mujahideen and a principal recruiter of Kashmir insurgents. Umar Saeed Sheikh was a Pakistani-born British national who had been recruited by the Harkat-ul-Mujahideen to kidnap foreigners visiting Kashmir and use them as pawns in attempting to secure the release of Kashmiri insurgents who had been arrested by Indian security forces. Mushtak Ahmed Zargar was one of the first Kashmiri militants to have been trained in Pakistan. He had compiled a bloody record of killing Border Security Force personnel and had become the head of an insurgent organization called Al Umar.

Since the Taliban leaders had stated publicly that they would not allow the released militants or the hijackers to remain in Afghanistan, all eight were placed in a four-wheel drive vehicle and given ten hours to cross the border into another country. Accompanied by a Taliban official, they drove out of Kandahar to undisclosed destinations. The freed hostages were placed aboard two Indian aircraft and flown to Delhi where they were greeted by Prime Minister Vajpayee. Upon his return to Delhi, Jaswant Singh thanked the Taliban for their "constructive cooperation throughout this trying period" but denied that there had been any change in the "fundamentals" of India's Afghan policy.

On January 5 the first of the freed militants surfaced in Pakistan. Maulana Masood Azhar addressed a crowd of 10,000 Muslims gathered at a mosque in Karachi and, after telling his listeners that they "should not rest in peace until America and India are destroyed," pledged himself to continuing the "separatist fight in Kashmir." His words were fiery: "I have only come here because I need colleagues. I will not be at peace until Muslims get liberated. So marry for jihad, give birth for jihad and earn money only for jihad till the cruelty of America and India ends. But India first. . . . The struggle to rid Kashmir of Indian authorities will continue. Tell Indians and those who have suppressed Muslims that my children are a force of Allah and will raise the flag of Islam in this world soon." For the next several weeks, Masood Azhar remained in Pakistan, making incendiary speeches and recruiting Mujahideen for service in Kashmir. As late as a month after the release of the hijacked passengers and crew, nothing had become known regarding the post-Afghanistan whereabouts of Mushtak Ahmed Zargar, Umar Saeed Sheikh, and the five hijackers.

Although the hijacking episode had ended on December 31, its diplomatic repercussions continued to reverberate. On January 1, Jaswant Singh accused Pakistan of having played a major role in the carrying out of the hijacking and having given the hijackers asylum. Home Minister Advani later sharpened Jaswant Singh's attack by announcing that evidence had been gathered proving that all five of the hijackers were Pakistanis and that they had taken their orders from Pakistan. On January 4, Prime Minister Vajpayee characterized the hijacking as "an integral part of the Pakistani-backed campaign of terrorism and vowed that his government would seek to have Pakistan branded as a terrorist state: "[Pakistan's] active and sustained role in fomenting terrorism in India is now too obvious to be overlooked by the international community. India, therefore, strongly urges major nations of the world to declare Pakistan a terrorist state. Our government will work systematically towards this objective."

Pakistan responded to the charges levied by India's prime minister, external affairs minister, and home minister by denying that it had been involved in any way in orchestrating the hijacking or providing a haven for the hijackers. Commenting on Vajpayee's statement that Pakistani should be declared a terrorist state, General Musharraf declared that "it is sad that Mr. Vajpayee has made this statement because we have right through the incident played a very positive role. . . . I would ask Mr. Vajpayee to play cool and not get involved in building up this hype against Pakistan because this is not the requirement of a peaceful future for this region. . . . At the outset, I had a suspicion that the hijacking could be a big drama, and the statement of the Indian Prime Minister confirms that India has staged the drama to give Pakistan a bad name." One of the general's aides followed up his remarks by expressing amazement at India's charges. "What kind of absurd objective would Pakistan achieve by supporting such an incident? Are we bereft of reason? Why would we give something to India that they could use to distort Pakistan's image, disinform the world about what we are as a nation and damage us?"

Despite Pakistan's denial that the hijackers had taken refuge in Pakistan, India's foreign secretary informed Pakistan's high commissioner on January 15 that India expected Pakistan to apprehend the hijackers and send them to India for prosecution. He told the high commissioner that, since the hijackers and the three released militants had made appearances in Pakistan and "Pakistan-occupied" territory in Kashmir, Pakistan was responsible for arresting the hijackers and turning them over to Indian authorities, thus fulfilling its obligations under the international anti-hijacking agreement which Pakistan had signed. General Musharraf gave Pakistan's negative response during the course of an interview with an Indian newspaper: "They are not in Pakistan. I categorically deny this statement. And if they are in Pakistan, we will surely proceed against them according to the law. . . . We do not support hijacking at all. We are against all forms of terrorism and hijacking is one form of terrorism. . . . We abhor it and we will not let the hijackers come to Pakistan." These would not be the final charges and countercharges emanating from Delhi and Islamabad as a consequence of the hijacking of Indian Airlines Flight 814.

Knowing that his government would come under attack for having agreed to the release of the three jailed militants, Prime Minister Vajpayee began his defense when he greeted some of the hostages and crew members who had been flown back to Delhi. He made much of the fact that India's negotiators had whittled down the hijackers' demands from thirty-six to three militants and maintained that the hijackers had failed to achieve their goal of "internationalizing" the Kashmir issue. Their failure, according to Vajpayee, "has vastly furthered India's long term interests" because it had shown the world community that Pakistan's claim in Kashmir "is not only baseless, but is being pursued by recourse to terrorism, which constitutes a patent threat to global security." Pointing to the support of India's Muslim community during the hijacking crisis, the prime minister characterized the incident as having strengthened India's sense of national unity. The prime minister's opening defense was bolstered by External Affairs Minister Jaswant Singh, who explained that the hijackers' December 30 threat to blow up the A-300 Airbus had forced India's negotiators to examine the issue in totality and come up with the decision to release the three militants. He denied that India's honor and security had "been diminished by saving the lives of 150 people."

According to the *Times of India*, "the mood in the BJP and its alliance partners was of resigned acceptance of the deal. Despite being unhappy with the government's handling of the crisis, senior functionaries of the parties grudgingly admitted that the government had had very limited choices. As was to be expected, the leaders of the opposition parties were not inclined to follow the leaders of the coalition partners by reacting with "resigned acceptance." While the hijacking negotiations were going on, they had remained silent except to express their view that the government was the best judge of what steps should to be taken to bring the hijacking to a peaceful end. But when Prime Minister Vajpayee called an all-party meeting to review the hijacking crisis after it had ended, they abandoned their silence and condemned the way in which it had been handled. The Congress Indira Party's spokesman expressed his fears that India's security regime in Kashmir would become a "lame duck" and argued that "national interest does not mean surrendering to the demands of terrorists." Ten days later, the Congress Indira Party raised its critical voice higher by charging that the manner in which the government had managed the hijacking crisis had made the country appear "weak, hesitant and faltering." Its spokesman said that his party was "baffled and shocked" by Jaswant Singh's "regrettable and deplorable" action in accompanying the released militants to Kandahar. Sarcastically remarking that Jaswant Singh had gone there when "garlanding the hijackers was the only job left," the spokesman maintained that the NDA government had accorded "respectability and encouragement" to terrorism.

The Congress Indira Party's criticism of the government and of Jaswant Singh was echoed by the Nationalist Congress Party, the Janata Dal (Secular), and the Communist Party Marxist. The Nationalist Congress Party's spokesman called the government's performance "ham handed." Former Prime Minister Gujral, speaking on behalf of the Janata Dal (Secular) characterized Jaswant Singh's accompanying the militants as "most disgusting and humiliating. . . . This kind of dignified passage to known terrorists is a rare phenomenon which really brought down the honour and the reputation of the nation in the eyes of the international community. I am wondering why a farewell party was not arranged in honor of the terrorists before handing them over to the Taliban authorities." These attacks on the Vajpayee regime by opposition parties came as no surprise. What was surprising was the criticism which came from the BJP's supporters in the Sangh Parivar. The RSS described the handing over of the three militants as a display of cowardice. "The RSS has always believed that terrorists should never be released in exchange for hostages. The decision has brought to light how cowardly Hindu society has become. The Hindu community needs to rise to the occasion and national interest should be above everything else."

Nitish Chakravarty, in his newspaper comments on the hijacking, agreed with the views of opposition party leaders who predicted that the release of the three militants would give a boost to the Kashmir insurgency:

Observers see in the striking upswing in terrorist attacks since the hijacking of the Indian Airlines plane on Christmas Eve a pattern in militant operations. They think the derring-do of the hijackers and the hostages-for-militants deal have boosted the terrorists' morale. The terrorists have realized that high risks fetch higher rewards. Many army and police officials based in Kashmir are worried that the release of the three leading militants under the hijackers' pressure will fan terrorism in the Srinagar valley and demoralize the security forces. A senior army officer has expressed this fear in a talk with journalists. Even as the government' s argument that exchanging three militants for 155 passengers aboard the Indian Airlines plane was the best option is well taken, it can hardly be denied that the deal has not only given a fresh lease of life to militancy but shaken the faith of the common people in the government's ability to root out violence in Kashmir.

An article in the of the news magazine *India Today* analyzed in some detail the impact of the hijacking episode on the current and future security situation in Jammu and Kashmir:

In the Valley, where the public mood has increasingly become sullen and disenchanted with the Farooq regime, the outcome of the hostage crisis could well mark yet another phase of heightened pro-secession sentiments. Intelligence reports delineate the movement to Pakistan Occupied Kashmir of several Kashmiri youth for training in the coming summer—which was negligible in the past three years—as a pointer. Militants are bound to exploit their so-called victory in the hostage crisis. Especially in the light of the overtures by the military regime in Pakistan to extend "renewed moral" support to the anti-India movement in Kashmir. Security agencies reckon that the deal to let off the dreaded troika of terrorists would deal a body blow to the sagging morale of security forces currently the target of mounting militant offensive in the post-Kargil phase. Security forces, despite a high kill rate against militants, are yet to reestablish their post-Kargil ascendancy. "Militants are taking the security forces head on," says DGP Gurbachan Jagat. Adds an army official in Srinagar: "The militant attacks against security forces are getting more and more amplified."

Militants have been released in the past too but this is the first time that foreign mercenaries have been flown and delivered at a place where they get their training to begin with. This can only spell danger. One of the major aims of the renewed militant violence is to tie down security forces in securing their own protection. Militants' tactics are succeeding to the extent that fewer security forces are available for anti-insurgency operations. The Border Security Force authorities' recent decision not to have a deployment less than a company at any place in the Valley is a pointer to the siege complex that is setting in among security forces. Kashmir has been the biggest loser in the Kandahar bargain and the state apparatus knows it already.

Kashmir may well have been "the biggest loser" in the Kandahar bargain, but the NDA government also sustained losses. Its handling of the hijacking crisis was flawed, and the result was that India had to settle for a bargain that not only damaged its position in Kashmir but made the government look weak. Such negative political repercussions were particularly hurtful because, during both the 1998 and 1999 elections, the NDA had portrayed itself as the coalition that would provide India with a strong government. It had translated this portrait into action by conducting nuclear bomb and missile tests and by winning the Kargil "war" with Pakistan. The spectacle of the Vajpayee regime's being forced to release Muslim extremists who belonged to a militant anti-Indian organization, after the prime minister had vowed that India would never give in to the hijackers' demands, presented a picture of a government that looked weak rather than strong. The Vajpayee regime was also hurt because the BJP, which provided its leadership, was also tarnished by the deal struck in Kandahar. A defense specialist at the Center for Policy Studies in Delhi described to an American journalist the damage the BJP had suffered: "One of the calling cards of the BJP was its supposed great nationalist outlook and its firm stand on national security. That's precisely what is being eroded at the edges at the moment and it's going to get at their reputation and standing amongst the people." None other than L. K. Advani, the leader of the party's hard-line wing, agreed with this assessment when he admitted that the BJP's image had been "damaged."

Last but not least, the hijacking episode produced another setback in India's ongoing effort to prevent the Kashmir issue from being "internationalized." The Vajpayee regime had struggled to limit the diplomatic dimension of the Kargil "war" to a conflict that involved only India and Pakistan but had been forced to seek the help of the United States and other countries to put Pakistan in a position where it had to withdraw its invading force. In like manner, India's external affairs minister had persuaded the United Nations to turn a deaf ear to the Taliban's request that it negotiate a settlement of the hijacking crisis but had found that he needed to solicit the support of a dozen countries to put pressure on the Taliban and Pakistan to protect the hostages and help free them from the hijackers' grip. The hijackers said that they were fighting for the independence of Kashmir, and all three of the Muslim militants who were freed had played leading roles in the insurgency that was going on there. Faced with these elements of "internationalization," India could not make a convincing case that the hijacking of Flight 814 was nothing more than a random episode of terrorism and that only India and Pakistan had a stake in the way in which it was handled. Informed and impartial observers both inside and outside India saw that it was one of the continuing by-products of the Indo-Pakistani dispute over Kashmir that had been on the international community's list of problems since the 1950s.

Although the hijackers had seen the freeing of insurgent leaders as their objective and had not aimed at "internationalizing" the Indo-Pakistani dispute over Kashmir, this did become an unintended consequence of their hijacking operation. Prime Minister Vajpayee had maintained that "internationalization" had not developed, but his words had been contradicted by the way in which India had involved numerous countries in helping to bring the hijacking episode to a peaceful end. India's release of Muslim militants who had played and would play leadership roles in the ongoing struggle for control over Kashmir had contributed to the continuation of a conflict situation that constituted a potential threat to world peace. Nowhere was the "internationalization" of the Kashmir dispute that had been fostered by the hijacking incident more clearly evident than in a statement made by President Clinton. In a report to the U.S. Congress, he revealed that one of his administration's priorities during his last year in office would be to resolve Indo-Pakistani problems, the most serious of which was their dispute over Kashmir. Indian authorities ended 1999 expressing their hopes that President Clinton would visit India during March 2000, but they were worried that one of his aims in coming would be to attempt to broker a settlement of the Kashmir issue just as he had helped to negotiate a deal in Northern Ireland and was attempting to bring peace between Israel and the Palestinians and Syrians.

When a newly elected democratic government comes into office with a comfortable legislative majority, its first 100 days in office are often a "honeymoon" period during which it gets off to a good start and accomplishes a significant portion of what it intends to do. This is especially likely when the government faces an opposition that has been weakened during the election campaign that has just ended. Such was the situation when the NDA government took office in October 1999. It had a thirty seat margin in the Lok Sabha, and the Congress Indira Party had suffered the worst general election defeat in its history. In the event, the NDA's first 100 days in office were far from a "honeymoon," and the NDA accomplished little of the agenda that it had set forth in its campaign manifesto. Its record during this period was spotty and, on the whole, far from impressive. On the home front, it gave the impression of being a strong government when it refused to delete Rajiv Gandhi's name from the CBI charge sheet. It appeared to be weak when it failed to produce the strategy and means to bring under control the intensified phase of the Kashmir insurgency that followed the end of the Kargil "war" and when it brought the Flight 814 hijacking to an end by agreeing to release from jail three Muslim militants who had played leading insurgent roles.

The NDA government handled with finesse the delicate problems that arose with the visit of Pope John Paul II. Except for its military arm, it showed a high degree of hesitancy and a limited degree of commitment in dealing with the consequences of the Orissa cyclone. Its legislative production was meager. The only important bills which it managed to enact into law were those that opened the insurance business to private parties and eased the onerous foreign exchange regulations that were discouraging foreign investment. A third economic liberalization bill, this one to authorize and manage electronic financial transactions, was introduced but not brought to a vote during the winter session. Legislation that would have reserved 33% of all legislative seats for female candidates was presented to the Lok Sabha, but it encountered a storm of opposition and could not be debated before Parliament's winter session had come to an end.

The NDA government's "first 100 days" performance on the foreign front was also a mixed bag. The government continued to improve India's relations with the United States, China, and Japan and succeeded in bringing about the lifting of some of the economic sanctions that the United States had imposed following the Pokhran nuclear bomb tests. Relations with Pakistan worsened to an all-time low. The diplomatic struggle with Pakistan over Kashmir became more bitter as a result of the Kargil "war" and the Flight 814 hijacking incident. The two countries were not talking except to hurl insults at each other. To make matters worse, each side had set preconditions for beginning discussions that the other side was unwilling to meet. India insisted that it would not begin talks until Pakistan brought cross-border infiltration of "terrorists" to a halt. Pakistan insisted that it would not talk until India agreed that discussions should center on the Kashmiri dispute and showed signs of a willingness to negotiate a settlement that went beyond maintaining the status quo.   As the NDA government's first 100 days of diplomacy came to an end, it looked as though the Indo-Pakistani impasse would continue indefinitely and that the armed struggle in Kashmir would remain a flash point posing the continuing risk of hostilities' escalating from a border war into general hostilities.

17

Taking Stock in January 2000

During the sixteen months that had elapsed since the end of the Golden Jubilee Year in August 1998, India's political situation had undergone a marked improvement. Its NDA government had become the most stable of any that had held office since the Narasimha Rao regime of 1991–96 and had prospects of lasting the full five years of its constitutional term. With a Lok Sabha majority of thirty plus votes, the BJP prime minister who led its coalition was no longer vulnerable to a pullout by one of the BJP's junior partners with enough Lok Sabha votes to ensure that his government would lose a vote of confidence. Since the BJP, which led the NDA coalition, was supported by a number of regional parties with agendas that differed from its traditional party platform, the Hindutva elements that were opposed by most of its junior partners had been eliminated from the NDA plan of governance. With a moderate and shrewd BJP politician like Vajpayee at its helm, it was unlikely that these programmatic differences would be allowed to threaten the NDA coalition's unity. The only substantial opposition facing the NDA government was the Congress Indira Party, whose Lok Sabha strength had fallen to the lowest level in its history. Adding to its weakness was the inexperienced politician at its head and an organization that was held together only by its leaders' devotion to the surviving member by marriage of the Nehru dynasty, Sonia Gandhi.

Prime Minister Vajpayee's image had risen during the sixteen months since the end of the Jubilee Year from that of a potentially dangerous Hindu fundamentalist who might subject India and all of South Asia to the threat of destruction in a nuclear war to that of a responsible statesman who would maintain India's security without rattling its nuclear bombs. For India, Vajpayee had led the military and diplomatic effort that had won the Kargil "war." For the world, he had done so while keeping India's armed forces on their own side of the LOC in Kashmir and he had prevented the outbreak of a multi-front general war with Pakistan. Prior to the Kargil "war," he had attempted to begin a peace process with Pakistan by traveling to Lahore and initiating discussions with the Pakistani prime minister aimed at settling the issues that divided the two countries. After the Kargil "war," he had led the NDA coalition to a resounding victory in a general election that had produced the stable government India needed if it was to begin solving its domestic and foreign problems. He had accomplished this political feat as the candidate backed by all members of the NDA coalition for the prime minister's post and, in the process, had made the coalition the beneficiary of a unity that was based on common acceptance of his leadership. Whatever might be the regional programmatic differences that separated its constituent parties, the coalition that had emerged from the election was held together by the man all parties had agreed should be at the helm of their new government.

Vajpayee had not only come to occupy a position of preeminence within the NDA coalition, but he had managed to disengage his party from the tentacles of the Sangh Parivar, without turning its members against him. The radical elements in the Sangh Parivar—members of the Vishwa Hindu Parishad, the Bajrang Dal, and the RSS—were still committed to making India a Hindu country, and the BJP needed their political support if it was to do well in general elections and maintain its leadership position in the Central Government. Vajpayee had succeeded in convincing the BJP that, so far as the Central Government was concerned and for the foreseeable future, the party must content itself with working with other parties that did not share its Hindu fundamentalist goals. Rather than pursuing a strategy of going all out during the years that the NDA government was in power to clear the way for a BJP government to take over when the coalition left office, Vajpayee had persuaded the BJP leadership that they must seek to maintain the support of regional party allies and that the only way to do so was to follow a national agenda that their allies could endorse. The political truth he had managed to get across to the BJP was that the country had entered an era in which the regional political parties that held almost half of the seats in the 13th Lok Sabha were becoming more involved in national issues and that it behooved a national party like the BJP to accord them a voice in national affairs even though some of the elements in their agendas differed from BJP positions.

Vajpayee's triumph was made official when the BJP's 1,400 member Executive Council met in Chennai in late December 1999 during the height of the crisis caused by the hijacking of Indian Airlines Flight 814. Even though the prime minister was not able to attend the party session because he had to remain in Delhi to oversee India's handling of the hijacking incident, his position that governance rather than ideology must be the BJP's guiding light for the future was written into a declaration which was described as a blueprint for "a march toward making the 21st century India's century." In a message which he sent to the party delegates from Delhi, Vajpayee called for a "transformation of attitudes, approaches, and articulation" that would change the party from one of former opposition to one of responsible governance. Home Minister Advani, who broke away briefly from the hijacking's Crisis Management Group to deliver the speech that Prime Minister

Vajpayee would have delivered had he been able to attend the gathering, told his audience that, while they should "never be apologetic about ideology," the party's future tactics must be "based on a proper assessment of the changing circumstances of the country" and that the BJP could not wait for the time when it had its own majority and could implement its own agenda. According to Advani, the BJP's success in leading coalition governments was attributable to its honesty, to its willingness to accommodate regional aspirations, and to Prime Minister Vajpayee's leadership.

The BJP's Chennai Declaration "expressed the confidence that every BJP worker understands that our agenda for governance is the national agenda for good governance." The party recognized that "the onset of the coalition era in Indian politics is a national phenomenon, fully in consonance with the democratic will of the people and rich diversity of our society." As a result, "one of the biggest achievements of the BJP during its two decades of existence has been its success in winning the support and confidence of a large number of political parties in all parts of the country, and in forming the National Democratic Alliance." In the opinion of a *Times of India* reporter, "the declaration clearly is a recommendation for making the BJP subservient to the coalition. The leadership seems to be telling the supporters to forget the party as they have known it and develop an attitude of accommodation in keeping with the demands of the common culture. . . . The leadership is clearly keen to reassure the allies and consolidate the coalition, knowing this is the only route to power."

But it was clear to informed observers that the conciliatory tone of the Chennai Declaration did not indicate that the BJP had become "secularized." Rather, it had been issued as part of the BJP strategy to practice "coalition'" politics until such time that it had the Lok Sabha votes to implement its Hindutva agenda. A newspaper editorial written as the year 2000 dawned summarized its unchanged ideological position: "What emerges from all these developments is that the BJP, for all its perceived anxiety to project itself as having evolved into a 'liberal' organization, deems political power and the apparatus of the state as effective instruments for promoting its basic philosophy of 'one country, one culture, and one nation,' and it would also be unrealistic to expect the party to delink itself from other organizations of the Sangh Parivar." The editorial writer's warning that, for all its talk about adjusting to an era of "coalition" politics, the BJP had not given up its original goal of making India a Hindu state, was borne out when the Chennai Declaration was issued in its final form. Included in it was a statement that the party had the opportunity to give "a new direction to politics and governance in India" but that it could do so only if it remained "committed to the ideals and ideology that brought [it] into existence as a political party."

The leader of the opposition, Sonia Gandhi, had also emerged in a position of unchallenged leadership within her party, holding all three of its top posts. But, whereas Vajpayee was an unqualified asset to his party, Sonia Gandhi was a liability as well as an asset. As one political writer put it in commenting on her postelection status, the Congress Indira Party "cannot do with her and also without her. She is the center where the divergent elements within the Congress meet. Without her, the party may split into two or three elements. At the same time, the party is going down under her leadership. It appears the people still accept her as Congress president. When it comes to her heading the government, they seem to be dragging their feet. She does not sell well beyond a point. The Congress leaders know this. But they are afraid to say so to her face. It was not dynastic politics which scared the electorate at the polls. It was her foreign origin. There is no questioning of her devotion or dedication to India. But the voters are not yet ready to make her Prime Minister. The longer she takes in appreciating this point, the less the chances of the Congress making any headway."

The writer might well have added the observation that the longer she took to appreciate the fact that her party did not have the political strength to enable it to form a Central Government on its own or to persuade other parties to provide outside support for a Congress Indira Party minority government, "the less the chances of the Congress making any headway [were]." Not only had Sonia Gandhi entered the new millennium clinging to her dream of becoming prime minister; she had also refused to give up the notion that her party should not enter into coalition arrangements but campaign with the goal of forming its own government or, if it could not obtain a majority in the Lok Sabha, of persuading other parties to support a government made up exclusively of Congress Indira Party ministers. It appeared that Sonia Gandhi had learned nothing from the fiasco she had engineered when she had attempted to form an alternative to the previous Vajpayee government and learned nothing from the disastrous results of the 1999 General Election. It also appeared that she had turned a blind eye to the Congress Indira Party's primary membership roll which showed a precipitous drop from 45 million to 22 million between 1997 and 2000.

Just as India's political situation had improved at home since August 1998, so had its political situation improved abroad. Prime Minister Vajpayee's restraint in preventing the Kargil "war" from widening into a general war and his willingness to carry on talks with the United States on nuclear proliferation issues had increased his stature in the eyes of political leaders throughout the world. Shortly after the end of the Kargil "war," Secretary of State Albright had met with External Affairs Minister Jaswant Singh and had expressed the view that "India-US ties should be taken to qualitatively new levels." According to Jaswant Singh, Albright had told him that President Clinton frequently expressed his desire to visit India, reflecting a growing American commitment to move closer to India in the conduct of its foreign policy. Although no date had been set during the NDA government's first 100 days for the president's arrival in Delhi, the Indian ambassador to the United States and the United States ambassador to India had both predicted that it would occur in March 2000. (President Clinton did visit India for five days during that month.)

Increasing support for India in the U.S. Congress had resulted in the insertion of a rider in the Fiscal Year 2000 Defense Appropriation Act that gave the U.S. President the authority to waive some of the economic sanctions that had been imposed on India following its nuclear bomb tests. Support for India had reached its zenith on November 17, 1999, when 396 of the 434 members of the House of Representatives voted for a resolution congratulating Prime Minister Vajpayee on his reelection and calling for a presidential visit to India as the first step in the establishment of a strategic partnership between the two countries. Commenting upon the reasons behind the resolution's passage, Congressman Gary Ackerman expressed the view that "no country reflects our own values more in that part of the world than does India. It is high time that we seriously begin recognizing that fact and graduate from mere platitudes to some tangible policy changes towards India."

Although he had not done so in response to the prompting of a Republican congressman, President Clinton had taken action to make "some tangible policy changes toward India" by using the waiver authority granted in the Defense Appropriation Act to lift the restrictions that had been imposed on export-import and commercial bank loans and to resume Indo-American military training and educational programs. A further easing of the sanctions regime had occurred in December 1999 when the U.S. Commerce Department announced that it was removing the names of 51 Indian companies from the list of 200 that had been denied access to American trade and technology because they had been involved in the development of India's nuclear weapons program. Since the ban on Agriculture Department credits and credit guarantees and on financial contributions and commercial bank loans to underwrite India's purchase of American agricultural products had been lifted some months earlier, the only significant sanction that remained in force was the stipulation that the United States use its dominant voting power to block most World Bank loans to India. Members of both the Senate and the House of Representatives had urged President Clinton to call a halt to this policy, but he had refused. He had not stated his reasons for keeping this sanction in force, but it was easy to see that his effort to persuade India to sign the CTBT and to take other nuclear nonproliferation steps would be less likely to succeed if he were no longer in the position where he could offer to support India's requests for World Bank loans if India agreed to call a halt to its nuclear weaponization program.

India's relations with China had also taken a turn for the better. The June 1999 meeting in Beijing between External Affairs Minister Jaswant Singh and China's foreign minister had broken the ice that had frozen constructive negotiations between the two countries since May 1998 when India had conducted its nuclear bomb tests. China had been concerned about the tests themselves because of their implications that its large neighbor to the south was becoming a nuclear weapons state, but concern had escalated to outrage because Defense Minister Fernandes had branded China as India's "public enemy Number One" and Prime Minister Vajpayee had written to President Clinton that India had been forced to conduct the nuclear bomb tests because of the threat to its national security posed by China.

The two ministers had agreed during their June meeting that neither country should regard the other as a threat and that their relations should be guided by the five "panch shila" principles that had been adopted by Jawaharlal Nehru and Chou En-lai as the basis for the era of good feeling that had characterized Indo-Chinese relations during the 1950s. This "about-face" on China's part prompted External Affairs Minister Jaswant Singh to announce when he returned to Delhi that "the Pakistan chapter is behind us," meaning that the era when China had favored Pakistan over India had come to an end. The two ministers had met again the following month at the Asian Regional Forum meeting in Singapore. They had agreed that a number of concrete steps should be taken to put their countries' dealings with each other on a positive track. Diplomats and military officials would resume discussions to strengthen the truce arrangements that had been worked out for the Zone of Actual Control in the disputed border areas. Talks would be conducted on ways of enhancing mutual national security and developing common positions in the deliberations of international organizations. Efforts would be made to raise the level of economic, academic, and cultural cooperation between the two countries.

These diplomatic statements had been translated into concrete diplomatic action in November 1999 when Chinese and Indian delegates had met in Delhi to discuss the truce arrangements along the Line of Actual Control in Ladakh and Manipur that would be recommended for adoption by the Joint Working Group that had been constituted in 1993 following Rajiv Gandhi's visit to Beijing five years earlier. The Joint Working Group, which had ceased to function after India's nuclear bomb tests, was to meet in January 2000 to resume its efforts to frame mutually acceptable proposals that would end the Sino-Indian border disputes. But, despite these steps that would be taken to help free Indo-Chinese relations from the deep chill produced by India's blaming China for being forced to conduct the Pokhran nuclear bomb tests, relations between the two countries would continue to manifest an air of mistrust.

The year 2000 was only a few days old when an unexpected foreign policy problem involving China landed in the Vajpayee regime's lap. A traveler had crossed the Indian border into Himachal Pradesh bringing with him the possibility that Indo-Chinese relations would once again turn sour. He was Ugyen Trinley Dorji, the fourteen year old 17th Karmapa and leader of the Kogyu sect of Tibetan Buddhism. Accompanied by his sister and five Tibetan monks, he had trekked for eight days from his monastery near Lhasa and had arrived, unannounced and uninvited, at the northeast India town of Dharamsala, the site of the Tibetan government in exile. He had been welcomed by the Dalai Lama and then lodged in a Tibetan monastery. He had not followed his arrival by applying for a permit to remain in India and had not asked for political asylum.

His silence had been matched by the official silence of the Indian government regarding what it intended to do with him. No steps had been taken to send him back to Tibet as a foreigner arriving in India without an entry visa. It was obvious that the Indian government had been taken by surprise by his arrival and had been moving slowly to deal with a situation that needed to be handled with great delicacy. The 17th Karmapa was the third highest ranking monk in the Tibetan hierarchy, and the Chinese government had been grooming him since 1992 to become a religious leader who would help to strengthen its control over Tibet. Embarrassed by his surreptitious departure, Beijing had stated that he had traveled to India to recover certain relics, highly prized by members of his sect, and that he would return to his monastery when he had taken possession of them. At the same time, China had warned India not to repeat the action that it had taken in 1959 when it granted political asylum to the Dalai Lama. According to the Chinese government, to do likewise with the 17th Karmapa would constitute a violation of the 1954 Indo-Chinese agreement in which India recognized Chinese sovereignty over Tibet.

As had been the case when it had been forced to deal with the highjacking of Indian Airlines Flight 814, the Vajpayee government found itself caught between a rock and a hard place. If it gave the 17th Karmapa political asylum, it would incur China's wrath just as when it had given the Dalai Lama political asylum. This would cause a serious foreign policy setback, for two reasons. First, it would counteract the progress that had been made since Jaswant Singh's June 1999 visit to Beijing in assuaging China's anger over Prime Minister Vajpayee's letter to President Clinton explaining India's reasons for conducting the Pokhran nuclear bomb tests. It would have induced China to take steps to make good the setback which occurred in its cooperative relationship with Pakistan when it scolded its ally for invading Kargil District. India's foreign office had been reminded of the latter danger a fortnight after the 17th Karmapa's arrival by the red carpet treatment accorded to General Musharraf during a two-day visit to Beijing. Premier Zhu Rongji had greeted the general as China's "first important guest of the new millennium" and had assured him that the "cooperative partnership" between China and Pakistan would endure whatever changes had taken place in Pakistan's domestic or foreign situation.

Second, if India decided to avoid these foreign policy pitfalls by forcing the 17th Karmapa to leave India, it would incur the wrath of the 130,000 Tibetans living in India, the disapproval of the Dalai Lama, a Nobel peace prize winner respected throughout the world, and the scorn of those Western countries that had condemned the way in which the Chinese had used force to assert its sovereignty over Tibet. Pressure had been put upon India's Foreign Office to end its silence when a representative of the Tibetan government in exile filed a petition requesting that the 17th Karmapa be given political asylum, but no response had been forthcoming, favorable or unfavorable. Several of India's leading newspapers had advised the government to act cautiously in deciding his status, one of them suggesting that he be treated as a refugee and allowed to remain in India without granting him political asylum. A month after the 17th Karmapa's arrival, the Foreign Office remained closemouthed about his status. All it would say was that he had not applied for political asylum and that Indian and Chinese authorities had been sharing information about why and how he had come to India and how he had been treated since his arrival. In the meantime, India's failure to deport him indicated that the Vajpayee government had no intention of sending him back to Tibet and would permit him to stay in India for an indefinite period of time. The Chinese government had issued no statements condemning India for allowing the 17th Karmapa to enter India without a visa and had confined its dealings with the Indian government to seeking assurances that he would be adequately cared for until his return to Tibet. If many more months were to go by and he did not return, these condemnatory statements could well come forth. But India appeared to be hoping that China would decide that the 17th Karmapa's joining the Dalai Lama in India was not worth a return to another ice age in Indo-Chinese relations. If India persuaded him to keep a low political profile and China turned its attention to grooming for religious leadership in Tibet two-year-old Soinam Puncog, who had been ordained on January 16 to become the 7th incarnation of the Reting Lama, Indo-Chinese relations could continue in the positive direction they had taken during the months between the Golden Jubilee and the millennium.

A third country, whose earlier dealings with India had had an important impact on its economic development, had also begun to show a more friendly face during the period between the Golden Jubilee and the millennium. Japan, which had been the largest donor of governmental funds and among the four largest investors in India's economy, had reacted harshly to the Pokhran tests. Because of its experience as the victim of nuclear bombing in Hiroshima and Nagasaki, it had displayed strong sensitivity to India's contribution to nuclear proliferation and had cut off all grants and other forms of economic assistance, totaling almost $1 billion. This economic freeze had been accompanied by a freeze in diplomatic relations. Taking the initiative to end this impasse, External Affairs Minister Jaswant Singh had journeyed to Tokyo in November 1999 and had met with Japan's foreign minister. In addition to inviting the Japanese emperor to visit India, Jaswant Singh had proposed that an Indo-Japanese parliamentary association and other bilateral consultative forums be revived and that an official dialogue be started to address disarmament and Asian security concerns.

Japan's vice-minister for foreign affairs had responded publicly and positively by saying that India is "too big and too important a country to be pressured into doing what it does not want to do." Going further, he had conceded that Japan's recognition that India had national security reasons for conducting nuclear bomb tests could lead to "some adjustments," to ease the economic sanctions which had been imposed. He had also announced that a Japanese delegation would be sent to India to carry on sustained discussions to explore that possibility and that Japan's prime minister would visit India in February 2000, accompanied by a commission from the Ministry of International Trade and Industry that would identify areas where new Japanese investments might be made. The vice-minister had made it clear that, while Japan would not make India's signing the CTBT a precondition for instituting talks aimed at restoring productive economic relations, any indication that India was leaning in that direction would receive a favorable Japanese response.

While the representative of its foreign affairs ministry had spoken words of accommodation, Japan's prime minister had reiterated his stance that his government's economic assistance would not be resumed until India signed the CTBT. "Relations between Japan and India are basically good," he had told Jaswant Singh, "but the nuclear issue remains a thorn in the throat. India's signing the CTBT would remove the thorn." When Jaswant Singh invited him to visit India, he replied that India needed "to make efforts so that a proper climate for that could be prepared," saying in so many words that India could ensure that his visit would go well if India preceded it with a commitment to sign the CTBT. Even though Japan's prime minister had refused to budge on the precondition that India sign the CTBT, his country had moved a considerable distance from the hard line that it had taken immediately following India's nuclear bomb tests when it had insisted that India should not only sign the CTBT but also refrain from deploying nuclear weapons and curtail its missile development program.

Although India's political situation had improved both at home and abroad during the sixteen months that preceded the start of the new millennium, it was still beset with problems. At home, Prime Minister Vajpayee faced the difficult political task of steering a safe course between the more "secular" tendencies of the non-BJP members of his coalition and the Hindu fundamentalism of the BJP and its fellow members of the Sangh Parivar. If he veered too far in the "secular" direction, he ran the risk of losing the hard core political support that came from BJP extremists and members of the RSS, the Vishwa Hindu Parishad, and the Bajrang Dal. If he veered too far in the Hindu fundamentalist direction, he ran the risk of losing the support of the parties in his coalition who stood for a more "secular" brand of government. Given that the opposition was fragmented and led by a party that had been badly wounded in the 1999 General Election, the serious threat to the stability of Vajpayee's regime came from the possibility that he would not be able to steer a safe course between the "secularism" and the communalism that separated the parties making up his coalition rather than from attacks by parties that opposed the government he led.

Even before Parliament had begun to meet for its winter session, Prime Minister Vajpayee had been at work for some time setting his government's course between "secularism" and Hindu fundamentalism. He had begun when he constituted his Council of Ministers. Since the BJP held only 60% of the seats in the Lok Sabha, he had given almost one-third of the places to members of its allied parties in order to satisfy the more "secular" contingent in his coalition. Not losing sight of the need to capitalize upon the support of the Hindu fundamentalist organizations that constituted the political base for his regime, he had chosen the remaining two-thirds plus from the ranks of the BJP. To further tighten the BJP's grip on the NDA government, every ministry that had been placed in the hands of a non-BJP party member had been given a BJP member as second in command. The net result was that Vajpayee's Hindu fundamentalist party members were either in direct charge of ministries or were in positions from which they could exert substantial influence on the actions of ministers who came from the "secular" parties.

Prime Minister Vajpayee had faced troubled political waters while getting his regime under way not only at home but in one crucially important segment of his foreign front. Relations with the United States, China, and Japan had improved during the second half of 1999 but relations with Pakistan had gone downhill at a rapid pace. The promising détente of the Lahore meeting between Prime Minister Sharif and Prime Minister Vajpayee had been shattered by the Kargil "war." The prospect for an improvement in Indo-Pakistani relations after the fighting had ceased had been darkened by the military coup that had put General Musharraf, one of the principal sponsors of Pakistan's invasion of Kargil District, in power. Musharraf had made it clear that he was determined to continue Pakistan's military effort to free Kashmir from Indian rule. India's director of military intelligence had summarized the general's intentions by saying that "Pakistan wants to keep the pot boiling in Kashmir for all time." General Musharraf had ordered the Pakistani troops who had moved closer to India's international borders during the Kargil "war" to return to their regular encampments, but the forces occupying positions along the Line of Control in Kashmir had remained in place. Pakistani support for the insurgency against India's security forces in Kashmir had been stepped up during and immediately following the Kargil "war" and was sure to be increased further once the Musharraf regime was firmly established.

India's counterinsurgency program had proved unable to stem the increased number and intensity of insurgent attacks. But instead of moving toward a political settlement of the Kashmir problem that would involve negotiations with Pakistan and the All Party Hurriyat Conference that represented the Kashmiri people, the Vajpayee regime had continued to follow the military route by attempting to strengthen its martial law regime within the two-thirds of Jammu and Kashmir that it treated as part of India. The inevitable result was that the Kashmir wound was kept open, and more dead bodies were added to the number that had been counted variously by the parties who faced each other in the insurgency struggle. The situation on the ground in Kashmir as the new millennium dawned was well described by a correspondent for *Time International*:

Ten years after the uprising that turned Kashmir from a tourist paradise into a killing field, there's little sign of dawn; if anything the outlook is darker than ever. . . . Having declared itself the victor of that [Kargil] conflict, Delhi is in no mood to talk of compromise. Humiliated by their defeat, the Pakistani military—whose leader, General Pervez Musharraf, seized the government in a bloodless Oct. 12 coup—is in no mood for parleys, either. The Hurriyat Conference continues to issue pox-on-both-your-houses broadsides. As the three parties to the dispute paint themselves into the farthest corners, ordinary Kashmiris are left stranded, their lives stuck in a decade-long limbo.

Time International's somber description of the situation in Kashmir as the year 2000 dawned was repeated by an op-ed piece that appeared in *The Hindu* on January 2:

Even after ten years of militancy and at the end of the century, there is no message of peace in sight as Kashmir seems to be stepping into the new millennium with a "disgusting note" of a plane hijacking directly connected with the problem of Kashmir. The senseless violence not only continues unabated but has taken new dimensions. While the entire world is witnessing rapid changes in almost every sphere of life, a commoner in Kashmir is as dejected as he was a decade ago. Having seen many ups and downs, not necessarily since 1989 when the Kalashnikov arrived to change everything in their life but when India was partitioned 52 years ago and this part of the subcontinent plunged into an era of uncertainty, the Valley along with parts of Doda, Rajouri and Poonch in Jammu had to go through the pain of bullets, bombs and mines taking a heavy toll. Notwithstanding the fact that a "popularly" elected Government is in power which replaced the tiring seven years of gubernatorial rule in 1996, the things are changing from bad to worse with the security forces losing grip over the situation. Though those at the helm of affairs are reluctant to accept the ground reality, it is evident that the dawning of the new century holds no message which could give a sense of comfort.

More than ever following the hijacking of Indian Airlines Flight 814 to Kandahar, Pakistan remained the dark spot on India's foreign relations front, and Kashmir remained the political flash point where large-scale armed conflict might once again begin. Relations with China had improved, but they were still beset by problems. The border dispute remained unsettled, and China stuck to its hard line on India's joining the nuclear club by insisting that India must comply with the Security Council resolution which demanded that India halt its nuclear weaponization program and sign both the Comprehensive Test Ban Treaty and the Non Proliferation Treaty. The Chinese Liberation Army's newspaper had stated the Chinese government's position when it attacked India's draft nuclear doctrine statement: "India had earlier promised that it would sign the CTBT in September 1999 but has not done so. India now claims that this would be done by the new government. The announcement at this time of the draft nuclear doctrine indicates that India's attitude on the nuclear disarmament issue was fundamentally without sincerity. As a result, it could cause a chain reaction which would further obstruct the international arms control effort." The red carpet reception that General Musharraf received on his first visit to Beijing showed that China was not going to adopt a more friendly posture toward India by terminating its long-standing policy of assisting Pakistan's nuclear and missile development program.

India's "draft nuclear doctrine," to which the Chinese Liberation Army's newspaper referred, was a thorn in the flesh of harmonious relations not only between China and India but also between India and the United States. President Clinton's senior advisor on arms control policy had gone out of his way to disabuse Indian newspapermen of the idea that the Strobe Talbot–Jaswant Singh talks had led to the United States's acceptance of the idea that India was justified in developing a minimum credible nuclear deterrent. "I don't want to speak for Strobe Talbott on the content of his discussions. But I do not believe it's the case, and I don't think you've seen a US person say we accept the idea that India should have a nuclear capability. . . . We think that from our perspective, India's security requirements are best served without a nuclear capability." Commenting upon India's failure thus far to sign the CTBT, he expressed the view that it would not be difficult for India to give in to American pressure. "It seems to me that the CTBT is consistent with India's own policy of not conducting further nuclear tests, of continuing a testing moratorium. Therefore, I don't think that it would be a giant step. It should be a fairly easy step."

The American Arms Control advisor's description of India's signing the CTBT as a "fairly easy step" had revealed that the Clinton administration expected India to sign the treaty even though the Senate had refused to ratify the United States's own signature. The United States's unhappiness that India had not yet signed had been expressed at a higher level when President Clinton had shared with Congress his disappointment that nine rounds of Strobe Talbott–Jaswant Singh talks had "yielded little progress" toward the United States's nuclear nonproliferation goals. His assessment echoed the statement that had been issued by the participants after the last round of talks had concluded on November 17. Both Strobe Talbott and Jaswant Singh had admitted that India and the United States remained far apart on the nonproliferation issues that had been discussed and that there was a need to make "tangible progress" in the next round, scheduled for January 2000.

As that date approached, there appeared to be no chance that India would be in a position to produce "tangible progress" by announcing that it would sign the CTBT. Prime Minister Vajpayee had begun a series of consultations with opposition parties in an effort to develop a "national consensus" in favor of signing the treaty. But the Congress Indira Party had been noncommittal, requesting more time to study the issue, and the Communist parties had raised bitter objections to India's becoming a signatory to a treaty that had been forced upon it by the capitalist and hegemonic United States. It is doubtful that Vajpayee had ever thought that forging a "national consensus" supporting India's acceptance of the provisions of the CTBT in their present form would be a "fairly easy step" but, if he had, the opposition parties' reactions to his attempt to develop that "national consensus" showed him that President Clinton's arms control advisor was mistaken.

President Clinton's concerns about the direction that India had taken as it had gone down the nuclear weaponization road had been shared by the chairman of the House International Relations Committee on Asia and the Pacific, who had spoken out against the Indian National Security Advisory Board's white paper on nuclear arms policy. According to his estimate, the nuclear triad of air, sea, and ground launched missiles that the white paper recommended would give India a total of 500 strategic nuclear weapons, a nuclear force greater than that of any country except the United States and Russia. "If India would actively pursue such a nuclear force, it would surely trigger an arms race with both Pakistan and China and would certainly leave that entire sub-continent at far greater risk of nuclear war."

The nuclear arms policy that had been outlined in that white paper and had produced concern on the part of both China and the United States had been made public in draft form by the Indian National Security Advisory Board on August 17 in the midst of the 1999 General Election campaign. It opened with a statement that India would not launch a "first strike" against a nuclear weapons state and would not use its nuclear weapons to attack any state that did not possess nuclear weapons or was not allied with a nuclear weapons state. Its nuclear force would not be maintained in a state of alert but would be ready to become operational in the shortest possible time. A triad of land, sea, and air delivered strategic nuclear weapons would be developed with "maximum credibility" as to their effectiveness. The number of such strategic weapons was not specified, but they would be sufficient to give India the credible level of deterrence that would guarantee India's security and make it possible to fight a nuclear war. In the words of the draft white paper, "India's strategic interests require effective, credible nuclear deterrence" and "adequate retaliatory capability should deterrence fail." The draft was silent on the question of whether or not India needed to acquire battlefield nuclear weapons and also on what it would cost India to develop and control its strategic nuclear force. It did make it clear that this force would not take the place of but would supplement India's present conventional military establishment. This meant that the cost of developing and controlling the new nuclear force would have to be added to the cost of maintaining India's conventional armed forces.

As the new millennium dawned, the United States was still waiting for a definitive answer to the question of what India meant by "minimum deterrence," as well as to the question of whether India would sign the CTBT. It was India's reluctance to provide these answers that had delayed the finalizing of arrangements for President Clinton's much anticipated visit to India. Clinton had stated on numerous occasions that he wanted to be the first president in many years to journey to Delhi, and Indian officials had indicated on numerous occasions that they would be very happy if he were to do so. When asked during the waning days of 1999 about the date of his visit, a White House spokesman informed the press that "a number of things" needed to happen, including progress on nuclear nonproliferation issues, before the president would journey to South Asia. Despite the fact no progress was made on these nuclear nonproliferation issues during the month that followed, it was announced in February that he would arrive in India on March 20.

(It was not until almost eight months after President Clinton had returned from India that the first public statement was made as to what the Indian government meant by its use of the term "minimum nuclear deterrence." The convener of the National Security Advisory Board, during the course of a television interview, expressed the position that India should develop about 150 nuclear warheads and the missiles and bombers to deliver them. With "high value targets" within

India's military reach, he predicted that a nuclear arsenal of this magnitude would enable India to meet any Pakistani "first strike" with a "devastating" response that Pakistan could not afford to endure.)

Just as the political situation in India had improved during the months between the Golden Jubilee and the millennium, so too had the economic situation. Bumper crops had yielded a record 203 million tonnes of food grains during the 1998–99 growing season, and stocks in storage had reached 42 million tonnes. Prices of food grains had fallen because of this increase in supply, and, since the cost of fruits and vegetables had also come down, the rate of inflation had dropped to 3.31% by January 2000, less than half the rate at the same time during the previous year. Increased demand for manufactured goods had led to a 6.3% boost in production during the first half of 1999, compared with an increase of only 4% during the whole of 1998. These increases in agricultural and industrial production had caused the 1998–99 rate of increase in the Gross Domestic Product to climb to 6.8%, one percentage point higher than the rate for 1997–98. Exports during 1999 had increased in dollar terms by 10% in August, 11% in September, and 22% in October, after climbing only 7.4% during the first half of the year, pointing to the possibility of an annual increase of 10%. The value of the rupee, after falling steadily during the early months of 1999, had stabilized at 43 to the dollar.

Despite the continuing negative impact of the economic sanctions imposed by the United States and other industrialized countries following the Pokhran nuclear bomb tests, foreign exchange reserves had continued to climb and had reached $34 billion by the end of 1999. This favorable development had occurred in spite of the fact that foreign direct investment had fallen to $2.2 billion during the year. This fall had continued a downward trend that had started from the high point of $3.5 billion that had been reached in 1997. It was accounted for by the reluctance of foreign investors to put their money into India after its government had decided that it was going to become a nuclear weapons state. This diminution in private investment had been accompanied by the shortfall of more than $300 million in expected foreign governmental assistance that resulted from the post-Pokhran economic sanctions, putting the 1998–99 figure far below the $1.1 billion that had been received during 1997–98.

(One reason why foreign exchange reserves continued to climb despite these losses was that the Indian government implemented a Millennium Deposit scheme in which Indians resident abroad were sold high interest bearing certificates of deposit. The initial response was favorable, and over $5 billion dollars were collected during the first year. But it was clear that non-resident Indians would not be able to maintain such a high level of deposits for years to come. It was also clear that the Indian finance ministry would be paying out large sums for years to come as the high interest on the certificates became due.)

Given the overwhelming evidence that the economic reforms initiated by the Narasimha Rao regime during the early 1990s had been at the root of much of the improvement in the Indian economy during 1998 and 1999, the fact that both the

NDA government and the Congress Indira Party had committed themselves to supporting the continuation of the process augured well for India's future economic development. Unfortunately, the work of undertaking the second round of reforms had gotten off to a slow start under the NDA government. The only pieces of new legislation of major consequence that had been passed by the time 1999 came to a close had been a bill opening up the insurance business to the private sector, both foreign and domestic, and a bill easing the onerous foreign exchange regulations that had made it difficult for foreign investors to participate in the Indian economy. A bill to authorize the handling of financial transactions by electronic means had been introduced in the Lok Sabha but had not reached the debating stage. The NDA cabinet had approved a telecommunications policy that would enable private companies to participate in India's communications network and had agreed to the leasing of five national airports to private operators and the sale of a 51% interest in Indian Airlines to private parties, but none of these cabinet decisions had received parliamentary approval. No steps had been taken to privatize the 240 government-owned industries, despite the fact that one hundred of them had been operating at a loss and, taken together, they had been returning only 1.5% to 3% on the vast funds invested in them.

Turning from the problems that dampened the prospects for long-term economic growth to the economic problems of the moment, the matter of immediate concern at the beginning of the year 2000 was the growing fiscal deficits that were being generated by both central and state governments. During the 1999–2000 fiscal year, their combined fiscal deficits had crossed the 6% line and had climbed to more than 9% of the Gross Domestic Product. The Central Government's 1999–2000 budget, despite a revenue shortfall during 1998–99 that was 61% higher than the previous year, had called for a 20% increase in revenue collections and deficit spending of $18.6 billion, 4% of the Gross Domestic Product. With revenue collections falling $1.5 billion below the level of the previous fiscal year, rather than increasing by 20%, and the additional expenditure caused by the Kargil "war," the Orissa cyclone, and the 1999 General Election, it was estimated that the 1999–2000 budget deficit would increase 24% to $23.3 billion, 5.6% of the Gross Domestic Product. Of this $4.9 billion increase, $1.7 billion would be attributable to defense expenditures that had outrun the budgetary allocation of $10.7 billion. Central Government borrowing had increased 21% above the 1998–99 level during the first nine months of 1999–2000, bringing its indebtedness to the point where almost half of its revenues had to be used to meet interest payments.

The substantial increases in defense expenditures have made the problem of growing fiscal deficits more serious. Although the finance minister indicated that even more of the Central Government's resources might have to be allocated to national defense, the 2000–2001 budget that he introduced called for an increase of 13,000 crores of rupees ($3 billion), making defense expenditure 28.5% higher than the 1999–2000 budget figure. This increase, twice the size of the increase incorporated in the 1999–2000 budget, would bring the defense share to 17.5 %

of total budgetary expenditures. Keeping in mind the cost of upgrading the capabilities of the armed forces to make good the deficiencies in India's national defense that had come to light during the Kargil "war" and the substantial expenditures that would be required to make India's nuclear weaponization program operational, Defense Minister Fernandez had called several months earlier for an increase of 10,000 crores of rupees ($2.3 billion) in defense expenditures, increasing their share of the Gross National Product from 2.4% to 3%. His call had been endorsed by Prime Minister Vajpayee, and the figure that was finally presented to the Lok Sabha by the finance minister was even higher than the defense minister's original estimate and pushed defense costs to 3.3% of the Gross National Product, the highest figure since 1987–88.

Regardless of whether an increase of .9% in the share of the Gross National Product devoted to defense would be enough to cover the escalating expense of upgrading India's conventional forces and, at the same time, initiating a nuclear force, it was certain that the share of the Central Government's budget going to national defense would increase by a substantial amount as the 21st century got under way. This increase in expenditure could be met by an increase in tax revenues substantial enough to prevent a corresponding increase in the budget deficit. The NDA government had taken no action to implement tax increases during the 1999–2000 fiscal year despite its having had to request Parliament to approve a supplementary allocation of $698 million to cover the immediate cost of the Kargil "war." It had not given any firm indication that it would include tax increases in its budget for 2000–2001. Given the NDA government's obvious reluctance to levy additional taxes sufficient to cover the cost of implementing its stepped-up national defense program, it appeared likely that the country's fiscal deficit would continue to increase. The inevitable result would be a strengthening of inflationary pressure and an increase in the cost of living that would make it more difficult for the Indian people, especially the poor, to make ends meet. Whether they paid the price in the form of increased taxes or in a diminished supply of consumer goods, one way or the other they would have to compensate for the increased resources devoted to national defense.

While changes of historic proportions had taken place on India's political and economic fronts during the months between the beginning of the Golden Jubilee Year and the coming of the new millennium, a status quo situation had prevailed on the social front. In contrast to the Devi Gowda and Gujral governments, which had granted priority status to programs for improving the life of India's depressed classes, the NDA government had done nothing more than pay lip service to a similar commitment, making clear by its actions that its priorities were to speed up economic development and strengthen national defense. Given the BJP's middle- and upper-class "Brahmin-Bania" constituency, it had come as no surprise that the NDA government which it led would relegate the uplift of India's poor to the lower reaches of its priority list. The government had taken a few minor steps that could lead to benefits for members of the lower orders of society, but these had been limited in scope and had been taken for political purposes rather than out of a commitment to social reform. During December 1999, Prime Minister Vajpayee had announced that his cabinet would propose a constitutional amendment establishing quotas to expedite promotions for the members of Scheduled Castes and Tribes who held government jobs. Although this benefit, if it became a constitutional reality, would be a substantial boon for the minority of Dalits who had become government employees, it would not help the majority of their fellows who had not been able to take this road as a way to improve their lives.

A study conducted jointly by the National Council for Applied Economic Research and the International Development Research Center of Canada and published in December 1999 documented what was plain to see on India's streets and in its villages. The economic growth that had taken place during the era of liberalization had not "trickled down" to the lowest levels of Indian society. There was evidence that the percentage of people living below India's official poverty line as the new millennium approached had actually increased slightly during 1998 and 1999. Using data drawn from the National Planning Survey, a member of the Planning Commission had produced estimates that were more reliable than government statistics, which painted a brighter picture than was warranted. The Planning Commission member's estimates showed that, while the percentage of people living below India's poverty line had fallen from 44% in 1983 to 35% in 1991, the incidence of poverty had risen to 37% by 1997. There was no reason to think that this upward trend would not continue during 1998 and 1999, producing an officially defined poverty percentage that approached 40% by the time that the new century dawned.

It was unlikely that the opening years of the 21st century would see a change in the direction of the betterment of India's poor. Continued growth in the Gross National Product would provide additional resources that could be used to underwrite the educational and social welfare initiatives that would be required to move a substantial number of India's poor to higher rungs on the socioeconomic ladder, but it had become clear by January 2000 that a large share of these additional resources would have to be allocated to national defense if the Vajpayee government was to produce the enhanced conventional military establishment and the nuclear weaponization program that it had convinced the nation was necessary for its defense. The Vajpayee government had announced that it would revamp the Public Distribution System (PDS) that had been established, supposedly, to provide the poor with food at subsidized prices and to function as a nutritional safety net to ensure that the poorest of the poor received enough sustenance to keep body and soul together. It remained to be seen whether the government would have the political guts to institute the radical reforms that would be necessary to make it possible for the PDS to achieve its stated purpose.

The PDS that the NDA government had inherited was a national scandal. Misdirected coverage and administrative irregularities had combined to put subsidized food and kerosene in the hands of ineligible recipients and the commercial market, with the result that as much as 35% of the 10,000 crores of rupees ($2.3 billion) spent on the system during 1998–99 had gone astray. The minister of food and civil supplies admitted that 35% of the PDS's food grain distribution ended up for sale in merchants' shops. Only 30% of families living below the poverty line had been beneficiaries, but 37% of families living just above and 31% of families living far above the poverty line had also received subsidized food and kerosene.

Adding to the wastage caused by benefits going to families that were not poor by Indian standards, gross inefficiencies in the transport and storage of subsidized commodities ate up substantial PDS funds that were supposed to provide food and kerosene. Much of the estimated 35 million tonnes of food grains that had spoiled in government hands up to 1999 had been procured for the PDS program. The net result of these various forms of wastage, according to the director of the Indira Gandhi Institute for Development Research, had been that only 12% of the money spent on the PDS put food in the mouths and fueled the lamps of the poorest of India's poor. To raise that percentage to the level required for the PDS to achieve its stated objective would require revolutionary changes in its *modus operandi.* Given the administrative inertia that would have to be overcome and the political clout of the millions of "non-poor" who would be deprived of benefits as a result, it was unlikely that the kind of revamping that the NDA government might carry out would result in a major improvement in the system's effectiveness in delivering food to the poorest of India's poor.

In addition to the "human rights" problem of poverty, the "human rights" problem of restricted religious freedom was unlikely to be ameliorated during the opening years of the 21st century. Hindu-Muslim conflicts had been conspicuous by their absence during the months between the Golden Jubilee and the millennium, but attacks against the Christian community had reached record proportions. Although the Vajpayee governments had not condoned these attacks, they had refrained for political reasons from taking steps to bring the attacks to a halt. Core support for the BJP which led those governments came from some of the Hindu fundamentalist organizations that were behind the attacks. A government crackdown on those organizations would have risked a backlash against BJP leaders that would have eroded the government's stability. To avoid that kind of political damage, both BJP-led regimes had followed a policy of verbally condemning attacks on Christian institutions and persons but doing nothing to prevent them or to punish their instigators. Given the BJP's continued dependence on the backing of members of Sangh Parivar organizations, there was little reason to think that this "hands off" policy would change during the remaining years of the NDA government's tenure.

Casting a shadow over these immediate problems were two large and threatening clouds on India's longer-term horizon—a steadily deteriorating environment and a rapidly increasing population. Ignoring these two ominous clouds, India had taken no steps during the months between the Golden Jubilee and the millennium to arrest the steady decline in its environmental and demographic state. Nothing had been done by either of the Vajpayee regimes to slow down the pace at which India's water and air resources were becoming polluted or to reduce the solid waste stream that was producing bigger and bigger piles of rubbish along its roadsides and in its open spaces. Nothing had been done to make good the environmental damage that had already occurred. Governmental inaction had allowed the 1999 level of environmental damage to reach an estimated cost of $10 billion. Nothing that the NDA government had said or done since it had taken office indicated that it intended to shift from inaction to action on the environmental front during the years ahead.

The two Vajpayee regimes had compiled a similar record of inaction with respect to India's increasingly serious population problem. India's population had continued to grow at a rate approaching 18 million per year and, according to a United Nations report, had reached 1 billion by August 1999. At an annual rate of increase of just under 2% and with an expanding demographic base, India would pass China in fifty years, becoming the most populous nation in the world with 1.5 billion mouths to feed. Before the population figure had risen to that level, the depletion of India's natural resources of fresh water, land, and forests would have reached the point where they would be unable to support the country's population at the year 2000 standard of living. Despite the handwriting on India's demographic wall, the NDA government had given no sign that it was committed to reinvigorating and extending the family planning program that had been put on the Central Government's back burner ever since it had become discredited during the 1975–77 Emergency.

On January 26, India observed the fiftieth anniversary of the adoption of its Constitution. Since this was a golden anniversary Republic Day, it was a time when its political leaders were expected to reflect upon the state of the nation fifty years after its Constitution had come into force. The prime minister had little to say. After affirming that "at this historic moment, India looks at its past with pride and to her future with confidence," he went on to urge the Indian people to remain vigilant about threats to the country's unity and integrity and to rededicate themselves to "justice, liberty, equality, and fraternity." President Narayanan had much to say. He characterized the continuing oppression of women and Dalits as "our greatest national shame" and warned that the "fury of patient and long suffering poor people" would explode into violence if economic development did not improve their lot. He highlighted the contradictions in contemporary Indian society by pointing out that "we have the largest reservoir of technical personnel and also the largest number of illiterates, the largest middle class but the largest number of people below the poverty line and the largest number of children suffering from malnutrition." He pointed out that more than half of India's population had no access to clean water and that Indian society was rife with violence and social inequalities. He called for national movements to protect the environment and promote literacy and population control.

Those who heard these speeches could not help but notice the difference in the picture of the January 2000 state of the nation that they presented. According to Prime Minister Vajpayee, India's glass was more than half full. According to President Narayanan, India's glass was more than half empty. Vajpayee said that

India should take pride in what it had accomplished. Narayanan said that India should be ashamed of what it had not accomplished. Vajpayee called for the defense and improvement of the status quo. Narayanan called for a radical reform movement that would deal decisively with the nation's ills. Those who heard their speeches could not help but remind themselves that Prime Minister Vajpayee was the head of government who had the power to make good the country's shortcomings and that President Narayanan was the head of state who could do little more than act as the nation's conscience. With that in mind, listeners could not help but conclude that it was Vajpayee's speech rather than Narayanan's that pointed in the direction public policy would take during the years immediately ahead.

The major thrust of this near-term public policy emerged when the 2000–2001 budget was presented to the Lok Sabha. It was to be "guns over butter." In the words of an *Indian Express* editorial: "The NDA has turned its back on the poor." Whereas spending for social service and development programs was to increase by 3,600 crores of rupees ($860 million), defense expenditures would total 13,000 crores of rupees ($3 billion), 28% more than during the previous fiscal year, the biggest increase in a single fiscal year since India had become independent. The poor would also be hurt by the provision calling for an increase of almost 70% in the price of wheat and rice supplied under the Public Distribution System to families living below India's poverty line. Even though the amount of food grains that they could purchase at subsidized prices would increase from twenty-two to forty-four pounds per month, the substantial price increase would prevent the poorest of the poor from enjoying the benefit of the higher allotment. The amount of Gross Domestic Product devoted to social sector spending during 2000–2001 would decline below the 1999–2000 figure of 1.7%, while the percentage allocated to defense would increase to 3.3%. Commenting critically on the NDA government's "guns over butter" approach to solving India's problems, an editorial in the *Hindu* observed: "It is a strange feature of public discourse that military spending is considered a sacred cow but expenditure intended to improve the lives of ordinary citizens is not afforded the same protection. It is a truism that security cannot be measured merely by defense of the country's borders. Security must just as much mean a decent standard of living for the majority of Indians."

18

Golden Jubilee to Millennium in Historical Perspective

Only twenty-eight months had passed between the beginning of India's Golden Jubilee Year and the coming of the third millennium, but during that relatively short period of time a number of events transpired whose significance went far beyond the time frame in which they were set. A coalition government headed by the Hindu fundamentalist BJP party took control of the nation. Within a month of its installation, it ordered a series of nuclear bomb tests that were the first steps toward making India a nuclear weapons state. A border war of limited duration was fought in Kashmir when a Pakistani invading force crossed the LOC into Indian-held territory. The result was a higher level of conflict with Pakistan and an intensification of the insurgents' campaign that was being waged to end India's hold over two-thirds of pre-Partition Kashmir.

These developments took on crucial importance when viewed from the perspective of the first half century of India's life as a free nation, because they set the nation on a radically different course from the one that had been set at the time of its birth. That radically different course can be graphically defined by recalling a memorable biblical passage in which God addresses the ancient Israelites and tells them that he has set before them two roads. One road leads to life, and the other road leads to death. God advises the ancient Israelites to follow the road that leads to life. In a political rather than a religious sense and several millennia later, these two roads also lay before the Indian nation when Independence dawned on August 15, 1947. In the speech that he delivered at midnight from the ramparts of the Red Fort in Delhi, Prime Minister Jawaharlal Nehru, inspired by his collaboration with Mahatma Gandhi, admonished the citizens of free India to take the road that would lead them to life as a nation. Nehru set forth a vision of a new India that would be dedicated to providing all of its people with a good life and acting as a force for peace in the world:

At the stroke of the midnight hour, when the world sleeps, India will awake to life and freedom. A moment comes that comes but rarely in history when we step out from the old to the new, when an age ends, and when the soul of a nation long suppressed finds utterance. It is fitting that at this solemn moment we take the pledge of dedication to India and her people and to the still larger cause of humanity. . . . the past is over and it is the future that beckons us now. That future is not one of ease, of resting, but of incessant striving so that we might fulfill the pledges that we have so often taken and the one that we shall take today. The service of India means the service of the millions who suffer. It means the ending of poverty and ignorance and disease and inequality of opportunity. The ambition of the greatest man of our generation has been to wipe away every tear from every eye. That may be beyond us but as long as there are tears and suffering, so long our work will not be over. And so we have to labor and to work to give reality to our dreams. Those dreams are for India but they are also for the world, for all the nations and people are too closely put together today for any one of them to imagine that it can live apart. Peace has been said to be indivisible, so is freedom. So is prosperity now, and so also is disaster in this one world that can no longer be split into isolated fragments. . . . This is no time for petty and destructive criticism, no time for ill-will or blaming others. We have to build the noble mansion of free India where all her children may dwell.

In Nehru's mind, the "noble mansion of free India where all her children may dwell" would be a secular state in which followers of all of India's various religions would be equally at home. When Nehru spoke of the "disaster" that was "indivisible," he was thinking of the threat of the atomic bombs that had been dropped two years earlier on Hiroshima and Nagasaki. He was aware of their threat on a personal as well as a political level because he was a friend of J. Robert Oppenheimer, who had been the scientific director of the Manhattan Project that had built the first nuclear weapons. Oppenheimer linked India to the atomic bomb in a literary way at the time of its successful test in 1945. As his eyes were recovering from the tremendous flash of the first nuclear explosion, the words that came to his mind were some of those that had been written in the *Bhagavad Gita* to describe the god Vishnu:

> Of a thousands suns in the sky
>   If suddenly should burst forth
> The light, it would be like
>   Unto the light of the exalted one.

The words which followed were those which Vishnu used to describe one of his attributes:

> I am Death, cause of destruction of the worlds, matured
>   And set out together in the worlds here.
> Even without you, all shall cease to exist . . .

These mental images expressed Oppenheimer's awe as he contemplated the power of the atomic bomb and his realization that it could be used to destroy the nations of the world. Sharing this realization, his friend Jawaharlal Nehru not only refused to enter India in the race to match America's ability to build atom bombs but took the lead in attempting to curb nuclear proliferation by persuading other countries to sign a treaty that would commit them to refrain from further testing of nuclear weapons.

To be sure, Nehru, scientifically minded as he was and anxious as he was to develop India's energy resources, supported India's inaugurating an indigenous atomic energy program which he knew had the potential to be turned in a non-peaceful direction. Speaking in 1946, he observed that "as long as the world is constituted as it is, every country will have to devise and use the latest scientific devices for its protection. I have no doubt that India will develop her scientific researchers, and I hope that they will use the atomic force for constructive purposes. . . . I hope that India in common with other countries will prevent the use of atomic bombs." Eleven years later, in a speech delivered to the Lok Sabha, he translated his "hope" into an official policy that his government had adopted. "We have decided quite clearly that we are not interested in and will not make the bomb, even if we have the capacity to do so."

Even though the post-Partition conflict with Pakistan over Kashmir flared up into fighting shortly after he gave his "Tryst with Destiny" speech, Nehru did not demonize Pakistan or refuse to allow India's Muslim neighbor to have a say in deciding the country to which Kashmir belonged. He acknowledged that Kashmir was a "disputed" territory rather than an integral part of India, by taking part in the UN deliberations that led to the unfulfilled proposal that the people of Kashmir should decide their national allegiance in a plebiscite. He did not see Pakistan as the enemy at India's gates, whose threats had to be countered no matter what the cost, but as a breakaway state that would one day return to India. Rather than building up India's defenses so that they would prevail against neighboring states which had become part of a bipolar world dominated by power politics, Nehru took the lead in organizing a network of "nonaligned" states that were dedicated to settling international disputes by peaceful means.

For Nehru, India's dangerous enemies lay within rather than outside its gates—they were communalism and the centrifugal force of linguistic regionalism on its political front, poverty and malnutrition on its economic front, and illiteracy and caste discrimination on its social front. It was against these enemies that he concentrated India's resources in state-directed programs to industrialize the economy, build up the country's infrastructure, expand educational facilities, and improve health services, including family planning. His attack on caste discrimination took the form of an "affirmative action" program that provided legislative seats, government jobs, and scholarships for members of "Scheduled Castes and Tribes."

On May 11, 1998, the Indian people heard a speech that was radically different from Nehru's, a speech that set India on the other road, the road that leads to the death of the nation envisaged by Jawaharlal Nehru. Prime Minister Vajpayee announced that a series of tests of nuclear weapons had begun, the first step in "inducting" them into the nation's defense arsenal: "The [nuclear] tests have established that India has a proven capability for a weaponized nuclear program. . . . they provide assurance [to the Indian people] that their security interests are paramount and will be promoted and protected." Although he publicly identified China as the principal enemy at India's gates, Vajpayee's government had taken this step in response to the threat posed by Pakistan's acquisition of nuclear weapons and the missiles to deliver them to Indian targets.

This threat was considered to be acute, not only because India and Pakistan had been in conflict for fifty years over the disposition of Kashmir, but because the Indian and Pakistani armies were fighting in the Siachen Glacier area and shelling each other along the Line of Control in Kashmir. These limited military operations might at any time escalate into another Indo-Pakistani war to follow the three that had already been fought. While India's conventional forces were superior to those of Pakistan, nuclear weapons in Pakistan's hands could tip the military balance in its favor if India was not in a position to counter them with nuclear weapons of its own. According to Prime Minister Vajpayee, it was essential that India "go nuclear" to protect its people and its territory from attack, and, whether they liked it or not, the nations of the world would have to acknowledge India's right to do so. When the United Nations reacted to the nuclear bomb tests by passing a resolution deploring India's action, he responded: "We are conducting them for our national security. We want our borders secure. We want to live in our house safely." Although he did not go on to say so, his words implied that he could not see that other nations had any grounds for objecting when India was doing nothing more than looking after its own interests.

The conflict with Pakistan was farther than it had ever been from a peaceful settlement because Prime Minister Vajpayee spoke as the head of the Hindu fundamentalist Bharatya Janata Party (BJP) which defined India as "Bharat," the subcontinent as it existed in the 7th century before the Muslim invasions and European occupations. The "Bharat" of that day included not only Kashmir but all of Pakistan, and that portion of Kashmir that had been ceded to China by Pakistan. In the eyes of the BJP, Pakistan not only had no right to hold any portion of Kashmir, but it had no right to a voice in discussions aimed at settling the Kashmir conflict. It was no surprise that when the Huzbul Mujahideen, the principal Kashmir insurgent organization, declared a unilateral cease-fire in July 2000, proposed that talks begin to end the insurgency, and laid down the condition that Pakistan should be a party to the discussions, the BJP-led government refused to accept that condition. As a result, the cease-fire was terminated, and the talks never got under way. Looking within India, the BJP saw a state which should be a Hindu state because the Hindu way of life was followed by over 80% of the population. Hinduism was the dominant religion. In such a Hindu state, although minority religious groups might be allowed to live in the "noble mansion" of which Nehru spoke, only Hindus would be at home there.

Nehru's voice speaking for the new India had been replaced by Vajpayee's voice speaking for the old India. Nehru thought the old India had died when the British flag was lowered and the Indian flag was raised over Delhi's Red Fort. But he was wrong. The old India was still alive, and during the fifty years that followed his speech, it had reasserted itself. In May 1998, its triumph was made public. When that happened, it was clear that Nehru had to be placed among those postcolonial leaders who, in the words of Samuel Huntington, writing for a world audience, were "imbued with the hubris that they can fundamentally reshape the culture of their societies." According to Huntington, "They are destined to fail. While they can introduce elements of Western culture, they are unable permanently to suppress or to eliminate the core elements of their indigenous culture." Veteran commentator on Indian affairs, Kuldip Nayar, writing for Indian newspaper readers, made the same point using a different language: "Impressed by the industrial growth of the West, Nehru tried to duplicate a society which had no renaissance, no reformation, and no revolution. In fact, the situation was the opposite. The society was ridden with superstition, caste, and religious divisions."

Following upon Prime Minister Vajpayee's May 11 announcement and India's success in the 1999 Indo-Pakistani Kargil "war," India embarked upon a program to develop nuclear weapons and the missiles that could deliver them to Pakistani targets and, at the same time, to make it possible for its conventional forces to provide a year-round defense of the Line of Control in Kashmir. The inevitable result would be a substantial diversion of the nation's resources from programs that would have attacked the enemies within India's gates that had been targeted by Jawaharlal Nehru and still threatened the well-being of the nation. Henceforth, thousands of crores of rupees that could have been used to alleviate poverty, malnutrition, disease, illiteracy, infrastructural deterioration, and environmental decay would be spent to provide nuclear and conventional weapons to defend India from the enemy without.

But can one go so far as to say that going down this different road would take India in a direction that would lead to its death as the kind of nation that Nehru had in mind ? The answer to that question depends upon the time frame within which it is asked and upon how the death of a nation is defined. If one means death in a nuclear conflagration within the next decade, one would have to change the word "would" to "could."   India's embarking upon a nuclear arms race with Pakistan could lead to its death as a nation before 2010 if the current military conflict with Pakistan over Kashmir escalated into another general war, one in which the two countries ended up by using strategic nuclear weapons against each other.   Such a catastrophe may or may not become a reality depending upon the shape that the fighting takes in Kashmir and along the Indo-Pakistani border during the coming years and the restraint that is used on both sides to restrict its scope and limit its weapons to conventional arms.

But the word "would" has to be retained if the time frame is extended to include the next half century and the death of a nation is defined as a state in which its people can no longer lead a decent life as human beings. Here, one has to remember the closing lines of T. S. Eliot's poem, *The Hollow Men*, in which he tells us that the world ends in a "whimper" rather than a "bang." Just as a world may end with a "whimper" rather than a "bang," a nation can also end with a "whimper." The Indian nation may be able to avoid a death that takes the form of the "bang" of a nuclear conflagration but, if it continues on the nuclear weapons road for the next fifty years, it cannot avoid a death that takes the form of the "whimper" that was voiced by a famous Indian movie actor whom V. S. Naipaul met in Calcutta during the early 1990s: "Everybody is *suffering* here." India's "whimper" would take the form of a national chorus consisting of people from all walks of life who were, in varying ways and to varying degrees depending on their socioeconomic status, suffering. Even members of the urban elite like the movie star whom Naipaul met in Calcutta, living in their fine bungalows and high rise apartments, would take part in the chorus, although their voices would be more subdued because they would be suffering less than the poverty-stricken residents of nearby slums. Their wealth would make it possible for them to reduce to an appreciable degree the impact of the decayed natural and human environment that pervaded the city, but they would not be able to escape it entirely. They too would have to breathe the polluted air, smell and see the sewage-ridden waters, and make their way around the growing piles of rubbish in the streets and open spaces.

Urban residents would suffer the most from an almost uninhabitable environment, but the country as a whole would share their plight, albeit to a lesser degree. An indication of what lies in store over the next half century for the India that has joined the nuclear club was provided by a report issued by the Washington-based World Watch Institute following the May 1998 nuclear bomb tests. The report painted a picture of the state of India's natural resources, as it entered the third millennium, that raised serious questions regarding its ability to sustain a 1 billion plus population:

As the '90s unfold, the rise in grain productivity is slowing, as it is in many other countries. Against this backdrop, the continuing shrinkage of crop land per person now threatens India's food security. In 1960, each Indian had an average of 0.21 hectares of grain land. By 1999, the average had dropped to 0.10 hectares per person, or less than half as much. And by 2050, it is projected to shrink to a meager 0.07 hectares per person. At this point, an Indian family of five will have to produce their wheat or rice on 0.35 hectares of land or less than one acre—the size of a building lot in a middle-class US suburb.

Falling water tables are also threatening India's food production. The International Water Management Institute estimates that withdrawals of underground water are double the rate of aquifer recharge. As a result, water tables are falling almost everywhere. If pumping of water is double the recharge of an aquifer, then depletion of the aquifer will eventually reduce water pumped by half. In a country where irrigated land accounts for 55% of the grain harvest and where the lion's share of irrigation water comes from underground, falling water tables are generating concern. The Water Management Institute estimates that aquifer depletion could reduce India's grain harvest one-fourth. Falling water tables will likely lead to rising grain prices on a scale that could destabilize not only grain markets, but possibly the government itself. With 53 percent of all children undernour-ished and underweight, any drop in food supply can quickly become life-threatening. India's population is projected to reach 1.5 billion by 2050, but there are doubts as to whether the natural resource base will support such growth. These projections will not materialize only if India accelerates the shift to smaller families, alleviating stress on the resource base by reducing births, or, it fails to do so, deteriorating conditions will push up death rates.

In some ways, India today is paying the price for its earlier indiscretions, when, despite its impoverished state, it invested in a costly effort to design and produce nuclear weapons and succeeded in becoming a member of the nuclear club. As a result, it has a nuclear arsenal capable of protecting the largest concentration of impoverished citizens on earth. Even today, India spends 2.5 percent of its GNP for military purposes but only 0.7 percent on health, which includes family planning. Unless India can quickly reorder priorities, it risks falling into a demographic dark hole, one where population will begin to slow because death rates are rising.   It may be time for India to redefine security. The principal threat now may not be military aggression from without, but population growth from within.

During the 1950s, the danger threatening the country's viability was that India would explode into a mélange of independent states based upon language differences. A century later, after fifty years of nuclear weaponization and failure to come to grips with the country's domestic problems, India would implode rather than explode. Under the burden of an overwhelming population, weak Hindu fundamentalist-led coalition governments or repressive Hindu fundamentalist governments, deepening economic and social disparities, a seriously degraded infrastructure, and an environment that was verging on the intolerable, the country, figuratively speaking, would fall in on itself, would become saturated, stagnated, gridlocked.

"Death" is not too strong a word to use in describing India's state at the end of the next half century if the country diverts vast amounts of its resources from programs that are needed to deal with its domestic problems so that it can build a substantial arsenal of nuclear weapons and the missiles to deliver them and, at the same time maintain the third largest conventional military establishment in the world. The result will be that the country as a whole will become 1990s Calcutta writ large. Two of the most perceptive commentators on the India of the 1990s, V.S. Naipaul and Ved Mehta, both speak of death in their descriptions of Calcutta:

Naipaul: For years and years, and even during the time of my first visit in 1968, it had been said that Calcutta was dying, that its port was silting up, its antiquated industry dying. But Calcutta hadn't died. It hadn't done much but it had gone on; and it occurred to me that the prophecy was excessive. Now it occurred to me that this was what happened when cities died. They didn't die with a bang, they didn't die when they were absorbed. Perhaps they died like this; when everybody was suffering, when transport was so bad that people gave up jobs they needed because they feared the suffering of the travel; when no one had clean water or air and no one could go walking. Perhaps cities died when they lost the amenities that cities provided, the visual excitement, the heightened sense of human possibilities, and became places where there were too many people, and people suffered. *India: A Million Mutinies Now*, 1990.

Mehta: . . . I know I cannot accept Calcutta. . . . The perception that Calcutta forces upon me is not the fact of death—which perhaps I can accept—but of the process of dying, possibly the dying of an entire population, for Calcutta's spreading poverty, like the slow strangulation of the Hooghly River, foreshadows something more frightening than personal death: it forebodes social extinction. . . . I ask myself how the species could have reached such a point of degradation and yet have adapted itself to that degradation, for the adaptation seems to show only how the will to survive bends us downward. *Portrait of India*, 1970.

Both Naipaul and Mehta characterize Calcutta's state as a kind of "living death." Even if the state of the nuclear weapons India of the year 2047 is Calcutta writ large, it may sound too extreme—too gloomy, too bleak—to characterize it as a living death. But one has to remember that history provides numerous examples of cities and countries that died because they were no longer places where the inhabitants could lead a decent life—cities and countries that were overwhelmed by their demographic, political, economic, social, and environmental problems to the point where they became uninhabitable as human settlements. In some cases, they ceased to be, but, in other cases, they continued in existence because their inhabitants remained even though they were subjected to conditions that forced them to live as survivors rather than decent citizens. A century after its birth as a free nation, the India of 2047 with its arsenal of nuclear weapons would fall into the latter category, and its citizens would be enduring a "living death."

A report issued by the Carnegie Endowment for International Peace a few weeks before free India celebrated its fifty-third anniversary on August 15, 2000, pointed out that India has just begun its journey down the road toward becoming a full-fledged nuclear weapons state. According to this report, India has acquired some nuclear bombs, but it has not developed the missiles to deliver them or the command and control mechanisms to guide their flight. It went on to say that India could decide that it had gone far enough by proving its capability of producing nuclear weapons and could refrain from making the vast commitment of resources that would be required to increase their number and make them operational. But nothing had come out of Delhi by August 15, 2000, to indicate that Prime Minister Vajpayee and his BJP-led government were considering a halt to their nuclear armament program.

Nor had there been any suggestion that India was willing to soften the hard-line position that it had taken with Pakistan with respect to the Kashmiri conflict which posed the danger that the Indo-Pakistani nuclear arms race might end in a nuclear conflagration. In his fifty-third anniversary speech to the nation, Prime Minister Vajpayee accused Pakistan of waging an undeclared war against India and proclaimed that Kashmir was and would remain an integral part of India. No amount of pressure from the United States in the West and China in the East could force India to soften its hostile stance vis à vis Pakistan and curtail its drive to become a nuclear weapons state. India would have to make those decisions on its own, and the present Indian scene does not contain the slightest hint that it will do so. One month after he delivered his Anniversary Day speech, Vajpayee traveled to the United States to meet with President Clinton and address a joint session of Congress. He did not tell the president or the members of Congress that India had any intention of cutting short the nuclear weaponization program upon which it had embarked. Nor had any suggestion come forth during his American stay that he and his BJP party had given up on its goal of making India a Hindu state. Quite the opposite, in the speech which he delivered to a large gathering of New York area residents of Indian descent, organized by those among them who supported the BJP, he proclaimed that he had been a *swayamsevak* (RSS volunteer) all of his adult life and would always remain one. He assured his audience that the BJP party had put its Hindutva agenda on the back burner for the time being only because it headed a coalition government that included parties that did not share its Hindu fundamentalist ideology. But the party's long term aim remained, and that was to achieve a two-thirds majority in the Lok Sabha, at which time it would be in a position to make the Hindu state a reality.

In the minds of the leaders and followers of the BJP, India's strongest political party, India's nuclear weaponization program is driven by religious considerations as well as by national security concerns. It is directed toward Pakistan, a country inhabited by Muslims who, centuries ago, invaded the ancient Hindu land of Bharat, and, in the 1940s, seized the Indus Valley when British India was partitioned. In the 21st century, they are attempting to wrest Jammu and Kashmir from Indian hands and threatening Indian territory in other border areas. India's anti-Pakistani political sentiments intermingle with its anti-Muslim religious sentiments to produce a powerful combination of antagonistic feelings. In that sense, it would not be an exaggeration to say that India's nuclear bombs are seen by BJP supporters and their Hindu fundamentalist allies as Hindu bombs designed to counter the threat of Pakistan's Muslim bombs.

Adding to the powerful support that religion gives to India's continuing down the nuclear weapons road whatever the cost is the sense of national pride that Indians feel now that their country has become a member of the nuclear club. As George Perkovich points out in *India's Nuclear Bomb*: "Nuclear capability symbolizes India's achievement of scientific and technical prowess and established India's membership in the aristocracy of nuclear states that set the standards of international rank. India also perceives the US-led nonproliferation regime as a racist colonial project to deny India the fruits of its own labor and tools of its own security." In the face of its new found national pride and its memories of Western imperial domination, it would be almost impossible for an Indian government to become a convert to the cause of nuclear nonproliferation and abandon its nuclear weaponization program.

The religious and nationalistic overtones carried by India nuclear weapons put them in a different category from the nuclear weapons that have been developed by other countries. That does not mean that they will inevitably be used against India's neighbor, Pakistan. But it does mean that India will go all out to produce a nuclear force superior to that of Pakistan because the prestige of the country as well as its religion will be at stake. Its Hindu fundamentalist leaders and the bulk of its people will be prepared to pay whatever price is necessary to make their country's nuclear weapons dominant. Pakistan's leaders have already said that their countrymen will be prepared to eat grass to make available the resources needed to implement its nuclear weapons program. India's leaders have tried thus far to convince their people that India's "going nuclear' will not cause them that much pain. But if India follows the American example of pursuing a costly nuclear weaponization program for a period of fifty years but, unlike the United States that was able to pay the price out of its bounty, gathers the necessary resources by refraining from implementing desperately needed programs to alleviate poverty, enhance literacy, improve health care, slow down population growth, and repair its environment, its people will not be far behind their Pakistani neighbors in living lives that fall below the level of human decency.

Bibliographical Note

Bibliographically speaking, *India Changes Course* is very much a product of its time. With a time frame that covered developments that occurred in India only a few months before it was written, the sources of the information upon which it is based could not be books produced after extensive periods of research and reflection. The sources would have to be the newspapers and news magazines that reported and analyzed those developments as they were taking place. Given American newspapers' limited and sporadic coverage of Indian affairs and the fact that their reporters and editors viewed these affairs through American eyes, Indian newspapers and news magazines had to be the primary information sources if a picture that was true to India was to emerge. During the pre-computer era, a prospective writer would have had to take up residence in India if he or she were to be able to monitor Indian newspapers and magazines on a continuing basis. With computers and the Internet now available, however, it is possible to be anywhere in the world and glean information on current developments in any other place on the globe.

This is particularly the case if India is the country that one wishes to study. One of India's greatest assets is a free press that includes excellent newspapers and news magazines. Another of its assets is its high level of skill in information technology. These combine to produce a series of web sites, maintained by India's leading English-language newspapers, which provide daily reports and commentary on the important events that are taking place in the country. In addition to their high journalistic standards, these newspapers have the advantage to the researcher of being published in various major cities of India, giving them a variety of regional perspectives that can be integrated into a balanced picture of the country as a whole. Consistent monitoring of the web sites of the following newspapers provided the basic information that went into *India Changes Course*:

Delhi's *Times of India*
Mumbai's *Indian Express*
Calcutta's *Statesman*
Chennai's *Hindu*
Bangalore's *Deccan Herald*

An additional Indian source of information was the weekly news magazine *India Today*. Patterned on *Time* and *Newsweek*, but published in Delhi, it provided invaluable commentary on the events reported in greater detail in the daily newspapers. Using a "no holds barred" approach, it critiqued developments in both the private and public sectors and raised questions with regard to what was happening there. Supplementing *India Today* as an Indian weekly was a newspaper published in New York. *India Abroad*'s readership is the 2 million plus residents of Indian origin living in the United States and Canada. Since its aim is to keep these expatriates abreast of all of the political, economic, and cultural developments occurring in their homeland that they should know about, I found that it included detailed information that was available nowhere else.

While these Indian sources provided the rock bottom information upon which *India Changes Course* is based, it was necessary to balance the picture which they presented with views found in American newspapers. Unfortunately, these were neither comprehensive nor consistently expressed. Only a few newspapers like the *New York Times* and the *Washington Post* maintain correspondents in India. The *Boston Globe* has a correspondent who is based in Hong Kong and whose beat is the whole of Asia. Since she happens to be an Indian woman, she does give India special attention but only if there is something out of the ordinary happening there. The result is that American newspaper reports are sporadic, covering only events which their editors consider to be newsworthy for American readers and often consisting of human interest pieces that have little political or economic significance. Nevertheless, being written from an American perspective, they were an important source for *India Changes Course* because they provided a point of view that balanced any nationalist bias that might have entered into the Indian accounts of the same event. Additional information coming from American sources was provided by the editorials dealing with Indian affairs that appeared in the *New York Times*, the *Washington Post* and the *Boston Globe*. Their editorials voiced American reactions to what was happening in India that would ultimately have an impact on Indo-American political and economic relations.

So much for sources of information. Information became knowledge only when it was prioritized, integrated, and analyzed against a political and cultural background that gave it meaning. If the sources were newspapers and news magazines, that background would ordinarily be provided by books that dealt with the events that were being reported. In the case of *India Changes Course*, which had a time frame covering the months between August 15, 1997, and January 1, 2000, only relatively few books had been published which shed analytical light on the events that had taken place during that thirty month period of recent Indian history. The following were consulted, and they provided the political and cultural background that gave meaning to Indian and American newspaper and news magazine reports:

Barbara Crossette, *India—Facing the 21st Century*, Indian University Press, 1993
Paul Dettman, *Tryst with Destiny—Free India's First Half Century*, Times Books International, 1997
Samuel P. Huntington, *The Clash of Civilizations and the Remaking of World Order*, Simon and Schuster, 1996
Sumil Khilnani, *The Idea of India*, Farrar, Straus, Giroux, 1997
Library of Congress, *India—A Country Study*, 1995
Ved Mehta, *Rajiv Gandhi and Rama's Kingdom*, Yale University Press, 1994
V. S. Naipaul, *India—A Million Mutinies Now*, Viking, 1990
Octavio Paz, *In Light of India*, Harcourt, Brace, & Co., 1995
George Perkovich, *India's Nuclear Bomb, The Impact on Global Proliferation*, University of California Press, 1999
Shashi Tharoor, *India: From Midnight to Millennium*, Arcadia Publishing, 1997
Stanley Wolpert, *India*, University of California Press, 1991

The experience of gathering information for *India Changes Course* left me with an enthusiastic feeling regarding the great potential of the Internet for providing opportunities to pursue cross-cultural learning without having to cross borders. One often sees advertisements pointing out that remunerative work can be done at home using a computer. I commend to anyone who has a computer the possibilities of using the Internet at home to learn about what is happening in India or any other country of the world.

Index

About the Author

PAUL R. DETTMAN began a career as an intelligence analyst at the American Embassy in London and the Pentagon in Washington, D.C., after serving in the Army Air Force. A radical vocational change brought him in 1952 to the American College in Madurai, India, where he spent the next decade as Bursar and English lecturer. His days in India ended with two years of organizing social welfare services in the slums of Madras City. Returning to the United States in 1969, he worked until his retirement in 1987 as an environmental planner engaged in a Clean Water Act project to put out the fires in the Cuyahoga River and bring Lake Erie back to life. In 1996 he began to write about the contemporary Indian scene.